W9-AFD-419

Sasakawa Ryoichi
A Life

Sasakawa Ryoichi
A Life

Sato Seizaburo

Hara Fujiko, translator

EastBridge

EastBridge is a nonprofit publishing corporation
chartered in the State of Connecticut and tax exempt
under section 501(c)(3) of the United States tax code.

Library of Congress Cataloging-in-Publication Data

Sato, Seizaburo, 1932-
  [Sasakawa Ryoichi kenkyu, ijigen kara no shisha.
English]
  Sasakwa Ryoichi : a life / Sato Seizaburo ;
translated by Fujiko Hara.
     p. cm.
  ISBN 1-891936-96-4 (hardcover : alk. paper) 1.
Sasakawa, Ryoichi, 1899- 2. Philanthropists--Japan-
-Biography. I. Hara, Fujiko. II. Title.
  HV28.S228S2713 2006
  361.7'4092--dc22

                                          2006000312

Printed in the United States of America

Contents

An oracular nun, a candid father
An award for good conduct
Two years at a local temple
A curtailed education
Conscription into the Imperial Army
Tsurukichi passes away
Ryoichi the investor
A contrarian in politics
A man of property
Not one to pamper his heirs
Investing for the nation

The PPP and its exceptional leader
The Patriotic People's Party
A classification of right-wing groups
Strong-arm tactics of the PPP
Sasakawa opposed to violence

Science, technology, and aeronautic

Jimmy Carter testifies
How to avoid corruption
Unfortunate conventions
Parasites heaven
Keep them out
Follow the JSIF
Gathering of five thousand barbers
Opting out of politics

Going forward
Giving Carter a hand
A leaning gatepost
Helping the WHO
The memory of a beautiful girl
"I want to shake your hand"
One hundred Chinese students a year
For those with nothing to eat
"We are not Santa Claus"
"Energetically crisscrossing the desert"

The museum with an upper deck
The bridge over the river Kwai
Good investment?
The *Nahimov* (I)
The *Nahimov* (II)
The anchor that cost billions

Transformed by the war
Saving money on an actor
On missing martyrdom
A novelist wonders

Preface to the American Edition

JUDGED BY ANY STANDARDS, Sasakawa Ryoichi was a remarkable man. Born in Kansai in the late years of Japan's great Meiji Era, his long life — he died in 1995 at the age of ninety-six — spanned almost an entire century of tumultuous change. Any appraisal of his career must take into account the drastic, almost seismic transformations that befell Japan — and the entire world — within that time.

He grew up while his country, self-liberated from two-and-a-half centuries of Tokugawa isolation, was speedily converting itself into a world power. He began his political life as a local legislator in the rough-and-tumble twilight years of Taisho democracy. At seventeen, just before two years of military service, he had learned to fly; he later distinguished himself as one of his country's first private aviators. Early in the Showa Era, he entered national politics. The small but highly vociferous National Peoples Party (NPP), which he founded in 1931, played its part in the expansionist nationalism of Japan's militarist thirties. Already rich from successful business investments, he built his own airport, which he presented to the Army as a patriotic gift in 1934.

Jailed with other NPP members for three years in 1935 for extortion in an action instigated by political enemies, he was released after acquittal by an appeals court — in time to be elected as an independent candidate for the Lower House of the Diet. There he served throughout the war period. A firm if highly critical supporter of Japan's World War Two war effort, he voluntarily entered Sugamo prison in 1945 as a suspected war criminal under the American Occupation; his book *Sugamo Diary,* published after his release, was an impassioned defense of Japan's leaders during World War Two.

After his release in 1949, he stayed in touch with Japanese conservatives and played a significant role in backroom politics. Relieved that postwar Japan was rescued from the Communism that so many had feared, he made his peace with the US Occupation and gave his support to Japan's alliance with the United States. An entrepreneur by instinct and experience, he became fascinated with the idea of motor-boating racing — both as a sport and, he felt, as a stimulus to restoring Japan's maritime reputation. His interest in this sport came to fruition with the establishment of the All Japan Motorboat Racing Association in 1954. With motorboating increasingly popular, he had also been able to secure a rare government permission to allow gambling on the races — an accomplishment that testified to his strong connections with Japan's postwar leadership.

In 1962, with revenues from the races increasing exponentially, he was able to realize his plan to channel proceeds from motoboat racing into a new nonprofit foundation for supporting Japan's recovering maritime industry: the Japan Shipbuilding Industry Foundation (Nihon Senpaku Shinko-Kai). The Foundation quite quickly grew into a sponsor of international philanthropy, supporting a wide variety of public affairs and scholarly activities. In 1984 he established the United States/Japan Foundation, designed to support a variety of US educational and research projects. Not long afterward came the Sasakawa Peace Foundation, to do work in Eastern Europe, the United States, and in various Asian and African nations. By 1996 the parent nonprofit's name was formally changed to the Nippon Foundation, as it remains today. All these Sasakawa foundations, taken together, add up to a major player in the world of nongovernmental organizations, ranking with US foundations like Ford, MacArthur, and Rockefeller. Like their counterparts in the United States and Europe, Sasakawa and Nippon have a global reach, supporting and engaged in a huge variety of philanthropic activities throughout the world.

Looking back from a foreigner's perspective at the biography of Sasakawa Ryoichi, his lifetime transition from a right-wing prewar nationalist to a world-class philanthropist seems like an extraordinary achievement in human chemistry. But for Sasakawa, a man who lived with his times, it seemed very natural. Gifted with a strong will and an independent social conscience all his own, he followed his instincts to make the best of situations as they changed. A man of strong convictions, which he was never loath to express, he was a lightning rod of controversy during the leftist-rightist arguments of the postwar period. Yet in a way, his political evolution tells the story of his century — and it highlights the changing and expanding role of his country, from beleaguered, nervous island country to peaceful economic superpower.

Sasakawa was not given to easy compromise; many of the stands he took throughout his life were inescapably controversial. His postwar anticommunism was rigid and doctrinaire. And personally, as an American who spent two long war years in the Pacific, I can only find his blanket defense of his Sugamo colleagues and other Japanese militarists as "heroes" unacceptable and at variance with the facts. Too many bad deeds to ignore took place. Yet in some cases, like that of General Yamashita's all too hasty trial and conviction, he had a point; and one could appreciate the courage with which he argued for better treatment in the prison. By the end of the day, he had turned his indignation and sense of justice to good purpose, with his large and generous benefactions as a world citizen.

The foregoing appraisal of Sasakawa Ryoichi is merely a brief introduction to the late Sato Seizaburo's full-length biography. For the benefit of American readers, I might add a few words about the author. Sato, long a professor at Tokyo University, was one of Japan's leading political scientists. As a member of Japan's rather tight society of academic intelligentsia, he was well aware of the bad image of Sasakawa that his colleagues perpetuated. "The epithets flew," he wrote in his Introduction to this book, "he was a 'Class A war criminal,' 'a mogul of the right,' 'Japan's last Don,' and so on, without cease."

Once Sato read Sasakawa's published diary and his letters, however, his view of the man changed. "I was startled when I read them," he continued. "I found a huge gap between the person who wrote this diary and the prevailing stereotype of him in Japan.... I wanted to know how a human being with such a gift for leadership, as conveyed by *Sugamo Diary*, suffered such a dreadful reputation in our media."

Carrying on his researches further, Sato discovered that the heavy criticism of Sasakawa in Japan contrasted with the generally good reputation that Sasakawa enjoyed abroad. Foreigners who had dealings with him and his foundation reacted favorably. He quotes former president Jimmy Carter, who had worked with Sasakawa on African food relief projects: "From my own experience, I believe in Sasakawa's integrity and that of his foundation."

Summing up his appraisal, Sato concluded: "To analyze why he was held in disrepute by Japanese 'intellectuals,' while he was esteemed elsewhere, should provide, I felt, a vital key to understanding why leaders — men or women who chart a new course and contend with the mass of difficulties that arise — are in short supply in Japan.... I wanted to look further at his performance and at the issues that concerned him, as a means of understanding why leadership is so conspicuous by its absence in Japanese political, economic, bureaucratic and intellectual circles."

I shall leave it to the reader to pass judgment on Professor's Sato's insights. Regrettably, I never had the chance to meet Sasakawa Ryoichi during my years in Japan. But as a longtime student of things Japanese, I find that Sato's biography of this remarkable man makes a valuable post-script to the history of Japan in the twentieth century.

Frank Gibney
Claremont, California
March 2005

Translator's Note

INITIALLY, THE IDEA WAS TO MAKE A DIRECT TRANSLATION and to use footnotes to clarify passages that might be unclear to Western readers. It quickly became obvious, however, that the original text needed amplifying and supporting with additional research. Sasakawa Yohei fully agreed. Iriyama Noriko gave many valuable suggestions. My husband, Martin Blakeway, helped me to pull it all together.

I am especially grateful to Frank Gibney, who read the entire manuscript and gave invaluable editorial guidance based on his deep personal experience and knowledge of Japan and East Asia and his long contributions to East-West understanding.

Professor Sato's original work in Japanese began with a first chapter full of pithy observations about Sasakawa Ryoichi and many of his characteristic witticisms. All of this was fine for Japanese readers. A Western reader, we felt, needed a chronological narrative and more conventional structure. Chapter 2 of the original text began with Sasakawa's birth. That seemed to us the right point of departure. We reached this decision after consultation with Sasakawa Yohei and a small circle of advisers.

We placed the emphasis on producing a readily understandable translation for foreign readers. With that in mind the original Chapter 1 was first moved to the end as an Appendix and later dropped as being redundant. Otherwise, the translation includes the whole of Sato's text, except for a few other deletions to avoid repetition. We have taken the liberty, too, always with acknowledgment in footnotes, of borrowing occasional nuggets from a biography of Sasakawa by Kurose Shojiro published in 2001, the year after Professor Sato's death. We also take responsibility for adding bridging sentences at the start of paragraphs where the continuity was unclear. The author's explanations of a word or phrase are in parentheses. Qualifying remarks by the translator are enclosed in square brackets.

Our Chapter 1 opens with the birth of Sasakawa, describes his up-bringing, recounts his activities as a right-wing leader in the 1930s, and details his outspoken conduct as a wartime member of parliament from 1942 to 1945. This provides a point of departure for Chapter 2, which relates his experiences in prison in Sugamo as a Class A "war criminal suspect." The final chapter features Sasakawa's later years following his release from prison in 1948. The focus is on his motorboat-racing business and global philanthropic work, beginning after he reached the age of fifty and carrying on until his death in 1995.

The formal name of the organization founded by Sasakawa Ryoichi in 1962 to channel funds derived from motorboat racing proceeds into shipbuilding-related causes and later increasingly into worldwide philanthropy is Nihon Senpaku Shinko-Kai (The Japan Shipbuilding Industry Foundation). For some years, since around 1996, it has been popularly known as "The Nippon Foundation."

Hara Fujiko

Acknowledgments

WE WISH TO THANK KUROSE ICHIRO and his publisher, ChiChi Shuppan, for permission to cite material from his 2001 biography of *Sasakawa Ryoichi: Kurose Shojiro, Sasakawa Ryoichi Den Yonotame Hitonotameni* [Sasakawa Ryoichi, a biography: For the world, for mankind] (Tokyo: Chichishuppansha, 2001).]

We are very much indebted to Doug Merwin and his publishing company, EastBridge, which is also dedicated to bridging the cultures of East and West, for his patient counsel and for seeing this work through all its vicissitudes to publication.

List of Frequently Used Abbreviations

CIS	Civil Intelligence Section
GJAA	Great Japan Aviation Association
IRAA	Imperial Rule Assistance Association (Taisei Yokusan-Kai)
IRAPA	Imperial Rule Assistance Political Association
IMFTE	International Military Tribunal for the Far East
IPS	International Prosecution Section
JSIF	Japan Shipbuilding Industry Foundation
MOA	Ministry of Agriculture and Forestry
MOT	Ministry of Transport
NVFS	National Volunteer Flying Squad
PPP	Patriotic People's Party (Kokusui Taishu-to)

Chapter 1

From Childhood in Meiji Japan...
To Patriotism in the 1930s...
To Wartime Membership in Parliament

I

1899-1930

SASAKAWA RYOICHI (1899-1995) was a man of many parts, whose career spanned the twentieth century. No stranger to controversy (he was twice held in prison for periods of years, while never convicted of a crime), this exuberant and irrepressible man went on to establish a name as a philanthropist who gave away fortunes and embraced lepers to comfort and console them. Ryoichi was born on 4 May 1899 as the eldest child of a local brewer of *sake* in a quiet rural community called Toyokawa, some twenty kilometers from Osaka.

The town, today called Minoo City, is strategically located between Osaka and Kyoto, two important and historic cities. Flying into Itami, the older of Osaka's two airports, the whole area is visible from the air. You see a great splash of dark green below, a national park established at Minoo in the late nineteenth century, and then rows and rows of apartment blocks known in Japanese as *danchi*.

At the time Ryoichi was born, however, the landscape was entirely rural. Osaka had yet to send out its tentacles that far. There were wooden farmhouses dotted here and there and paddy fields in between. The main crop was rice. The boy's father, Tsurukichi, used some of the rice to brew his sake, following in the tradition of his ancestors as the head of a family business established 150 years earlier. The seasons decided everything. The rice seedlings were planted in early summer and the rice was harvested in late September. Larks sang overhead in summer and tawny-winged kites floated over the forests and hills.[1]

The Sasakawas had long owned considerable plots of land and served as village headmen or *shoya*. Local records indicate that the family line was established in the middle of the Edo Era (1603-1868). They also show that the authorities let the earlier generations of Sasakawas use their surname and permitted them to carry swords until the great social reforms of the ensuing Meiji Era (1868-1912). These were privileges normally reserved for samurai in the premodern Edo times, and were granted only to non-samurai of exceptional standing. Tracing the origins of their family line to 1747, the Sasakawas were a force in the community.

Tsurukichi, in fact, was the tenth-generation head of the small but stable family enterprise. Photos taken of Ryoichi's parents in the early twentieth century show his father looking wiry and determined in a western suit, and his mother, Teru, in a kimono. The settled look of the couple suggests that they were rooted in their neighborhood and comfortable with their place in the community. Toyokawa consisted of a number of villages, including one called Onohara. That was where the Sasakawa family lived a quiet existence centered on the local primary school, a Buddhist temple or two, and Shinto shrines, where the locals celebrated their festivals and weddings.[2]

Thus, Ryoichi was born into a family with deep provincial roots. Yet we do not know a great deal about his childhood. He himself was not a delver into his family past, although he was the eldest son and was devoted to his parents. He was one who always looked forward, and rarely back. He was busy with his projects, especially once he started up in business in Osaka in his mid twenties as an investor. Ryoichi was restless and he dreamed of distant lands. He was excited by the future. He kept remarkably few records of his early or middle years. Marriages and births hardly figure in Ryoichi's records. At most, Ryoichi described one or two episodes from his boyhood to others. Not that he lacked the time to write his memoirs had he wished to do so. He lived to the great age of ninety-six, rare for one born in the Meiji Era.

Never one to set modest goals, Sasakawa imagined himself, whether in jest or not, living to be two hundred. He had several heart attacks late in life, but he mostly enjoyed good health until very close to the end. Vigorous as he was, rarely missing a day at work, he outlived his contemporaries. Thus, there was no one I could talk to who had witnessed his childhood. Obtaining information about him was not easy. Then again, there was no full biography available at the time when I commenced research following his death in 1995. One explanation of the lack of a scholarly work was that intellectuals in Japan held negative views about Sasakawa. The media treated him as suspect — not that he was discouraged by this, as we shall see.

An oracular nun, a candid father

Ryoichi's birth just before the turn of the century was treated as an occasion for great joy by all in the neighborhood. His parents received many visitors about the time that Teru gave birth, and one of these was a Buddhist nun (*bhikkuni* in Sanscrit), who came visiting from a nearby temple called Kumano Gongen. She informed the surprised parents that their firstborn child was in her words "a gift to the world," and was destined to do good works.

The family should accept that he was "not theirs," said the nun. Ryoichi's parents were devout believers and they no doubt took these oracular words to heart. The gods had enjoined upon them the task of bringing up an unusual child. So be it. The parents considered themselves doubly blessed. But being no-nonsense Japanese country folk they must also have considered that in a practical sense Ryoichi was theirs to bring up and give a start to in life. Apart from anything else, he was the eleventh head of the Sasakawa family line.

Tsurukichi, a candid father, in due course came up with a piece of advice of his own that may have had resonance for a rambunctious son who was destined to spend two three-year spells in prison, even if never convicted of a crime of any kind. The paternal wisdom was that "more important than respecting the law...[is] to follow your conscience." Thus, he urged the twenty-two-year-old Ryoichi to decide for himself for the rest of his life what was right. (Tsurukichi repeated these words on his deathbed, it is said.)[3]

An award for good conduct

I found two books written during Ryoichi's lifetime that contain a little information about his childhood. One was a light work by Yamaoka Sohachi; the other was a short study published in Britain.[4] The former reads well but is overly dramatic; the latter is lively but contains errors. I discovered additional materials in the family archives.[5]

I was able to interview three people who had known Ryoichi early in life: Uoshima Kosaku, who attended Toyokawa primary school with Ryoichi, though Uoshima was five years his junior and they overlapped for only a year; Sasakawa's sister Yoshiko, also much younger than he; and Nagata Shina, a woman who was related to him by marriage and had known him in his twenties. These three portrayed him in colorful terms, though their memories were no doubt swayed by the sheer fact of his fame in later years. Probably they did not intentionally dramatize and romanticize his life, but most likely they saw his childhood through a golden prism. These three, judging by their ages, did not know Ryoichi when he entered school in 1906, only considerably later.

Nonetheless, they provided vivid descriptions of the ebullient young boy, as he was growing up. Nagata Shina portrayed the young Ryoichi as "an eccentric" and again as "a brave little fellow who feared nothing." She stated:

> He had no time for anyone admonishing him for using careless words. He was good at fights, and often took on older boys. He hated to lose or to be criticized. For example, he did not take to his female teacher. On days when she scolded him, he lay in wait for her after school with a baseball bat.[6]

He surely did not attack that teacher — the anecdote is told clearly in jest — but he did get up to tricks. Uoshima Kosaku said that he was constantly making trouble. However, there is conflicting evidence in this regard. At the end of his second year at his primary school he was given a prize for good conduct. We may conclude that he was a stout-hearted and daring young boy, and perhaps a sore loser — he even described himself as "the school bully" in a recollection of these times. But Ryoichi was not an unredeemable rebel and he conducted himself well after his first year at school.

Ryoichi in hot water

His first year at Toyokawa primary school was difficult:

> I was born terribly tone deaf.... I believe I was in my first year at the primary school. The music class was about to start, and I dreaded being pointed at to sing solo I thought of a strategy. I invited a couple of older boys to join me and we had a fine time in the hills behind the school and missed the music class. I got away with it the first time. The second and third times went well, too.
>
> But my luck did not last. I had become overconfident. We were having great games when it started to rain, so we sheltered in the local Shinto shrine close by the main street and waited for the rest of our friends who, unlike us, had obediently attended class.
>
> Carefully calculating the time, I rushed home, innocently announcing my arrival as if I had just come from a hard day at school.
>
> My father greeted me with a stern face. Without a word, he took hold of my kimono collar, lifted me like a kitten, dumped me in the storehouse and locked the door from the outside. I felt a little guilty, of course, but at the same time I was sure my

secret was safe. In the light from a small window I opened on the second floor I found a box of cakes mother had set aside, and ate from it to my heart's content and soon fell asleep. I was awakened by my mother's voice calling me.

"Ryoichi, Ryoichi, apologize to your father."

I had done nothing wrong, I told myself, why should I apologize?

I did not even answer her.

Soon Father came into the storehouse. He twisted my arms, tied them behind me and attached the rope to a beam overhead. Still I could not bring myself to apologize and kept silent.

Father seemed taken aback but he wasn't finished. He told me to walk to the graveyard on the edge of the village and bring back something that he had put by the corner of the crematorium. To go there alone was supposed to be a test of my resolve, but I did as I was told.[7]

From the following recollection we can grasp the dynamics of the Sasakawa home, a shop where family life and business activity were closely linked. On grave matters such as his son's misconduct Ryoichi's father consulted his head clerk. Tsurukichi employed this person to share responsibility for managing both the home and the sake business. The clerk was therefore a third adult of consequence, along with Ryoichi's parents, to whom the boy was answerable when he had been disobedient:

Father spoke in a low voice with my mother and the head clerk of the shop, then turned to me and instructed me to fetch something he had left at the local Shinto shrine.

As a child I had never been afraid of dark streets and ghost stories. So off I set on this new adventure with a certain pride. But when I got to the shrine I suddenly felt as if I had had cold water poured all over me. I felt cold and scared. As I reached for the item that my father had left at the shrine I thought of the naughty things I had done earlier in the day. My knees began to shake.

I ran home and found Mother waiting for me.

"Ryoichi," she said, hugging me tightly.

"You must think that no one knows about the wicked thing you did today. The bad things you do behind the backs of others do get noticed. Go and apologize to your father."

I looked up at my mother and saw her eyes were welling with tears. I decided to change. I went to my father, knelt down formally before him, and apologized for skipping classes.

"Ryoichi, do not ever tell a lie. Never do anything that you know is wrong," my father told me.

Since then I have not once done anything against my conscience. I am full of thankfulness even today to my mother. She was the one who told me through her tears that "while you think no one has seen you do wrong, remember that heaven knows it and you know it, so never again tell a lie as you did today."[8]

Classmate of Kawabata

Ryoichi was full of life. He was strong-willed and inclined to be mischievous, as we have seen. No doubt this made him popular. Early on, he showed an aptitude for making friends at school. One of these was Kawabata Yasunari, a classmate at Toyokawa primary school, who was to achieve national celebrity as a novelist.[9] Sasakawa recalled:

[Kawabata] lived about three kilometers away from our home. We used to sit next to each other in primary school, but our academic performance was not on a par. My parents often told me to "do like the Kawabata boy," meaning to study harder. He stood out a mile as the most excellent pupil and was considered a genius even then. By contrast, I was just the school bully and so I was often compared to him unfavorably.

Kawabata had lost his parents when he was very young and lived alone with his grandfather. Our two grandfathers liked to play *go* — [Japanese draughts], and I was often taken to the Kawabata home. While our grandfathers enjoyed a game of *go*, Yasunari would sit in the wooden corridor running round the house quietly reading a book. That was his way.

Once, after attending an autumn festival, I was walking with Kawabata back to his home. When the house came in sight, I was about to leave him to find my own way home when he burst out sobbing and begged me to stay with him. He was afraid of dark streets. I walked him all the way back. The literary master of the future was a sensitive child.

After finishing primary school, he continued his studies at Ibaragi Junior High in Osaka, now called Osaka Prefectural Ibaragi High School. From there he went to the First High School in Tokyo, and then to Tokyo University. After enrolling he lived very frugally in a rented house at Ueno Ikenohata until he had made a name for himself. When that happened, always short of time, he could hardly ever return to his home town. Of my own accord, I looked after the Kawabata family grave for him.

After he became famous, he was too busy to return home at all. Eventually, he moved his family grave to Kamakura where he lived. By that time I had been paying respects to his ancestors for some fifty years — not that he ever asked me to.[10]

Ryoichi did not hesitate, if need be, to come to his friend's help in other senses, for example with money:

He needed help at times. At one point, when he had taken on the responsibility of chairing the Japan PEN Club and was having a difficult time raising money needed by the club I gave him what he needed.

My belief is that those who have money should contribute it to society; those who have brains should share their intelligence for the benefit of the rest of us; and those who are brawny should do the logical thing and lend us their strength.

Sad to say, Kawabata took his life in May 1972, gassing himself in a room of an apartment building at Hayama where he used to write. The rumor had it that the reason he did this was his failure to collect enough funds to organize a PEN international convention. Others said it was due to a failed romantic affair. As a friend of his from childhood, I think he was just fed up with life — he was too pure a soul.[11]

Two years at a local temple

But to return to Sasakawa's educational career. He attended six years altogether at Toyokawa Primary School. Clearly, he was a success there and at the end of each year he received a certificate from the school, commending him for carrying out his responsibilities as head of the class.

His younger sister Yoshiko remembered: "Ryoichi was fond of small children. He took a lot of them to school every day. He liked the kids." She must have referred to the years he spent in the higher grades. It was now apparent that he was not just headstrong, but a born leader who looked after his juniors naturally.

After graduating from primary school Sasakawa studied for one year at a local agricultural institute that was affiliated with the higher grades of the primary school. At the same time, in a move we may assume his parents arranged, he undertook a course of strict training under a noted Buddhist teacher, Harada Osho, the chief priest of the nearby Shonenji temple.[12]

According to Yamaoka, he served for two years at Shonenji after graduating from the primary school in 1912 at the age of thirteen. Yamaoka relates that his daily duties at the Buddhist temple consisted of waking up very early every morning when it was still dark and mopping the long corridors of the temple with ice-cold water. Then it was time for prayer. We may imagine the young boy seated *zazen*-style on the wooden floor for long hours to nurture such good qualities as patience and perseverance through the practice of these austerities.[13] His knowledge of the Chinese language and of Chinese studies, which enabled him to do calligraphy, must have been the fruit of his training in this period.

A curtailed education

Why was Sasakawa, who was born into a well-to-do family, not sent to a higher academic institution after his six years at primary school? There are two very different explanations given. One of these runs as follows. Tsurukichi, Ryoichi's father, is supposed to have consulted Sawada Nagataro, Ryoichi's headmaster at the Toyokawa Primary School, about his son's future. Such a step would have been very normal. Sawada is said to have responded:

> The child has a strong sense of justice and if he pursues his studies much further there is a danger of him turning into a "red" [a communist]. He has too good a mind. It is better to send him out into the world and let him learn about life [rather than carry on with his formal schooling].[14]

Sasakawa confirmed this record of events. He stated:

> I was due to sit for an entrance exam for the middle school, but the school head, who was afraid of my recklessness, advised my father that if I learned more there was no knowing how I would turn out. Better to keep me at home and to lead me in the ways of benevolence. As a result I had to forego further learning. After completing primary school, I was put in the care of a Buddhist temple in our village.[15]

The other theory as to why he did not go to a middle school has it that Sasakawa himself, against the passionate advice of his father, chose "life" over higher education. Ryoichi is supposed to have felt that he could resume his studies later but wanted to find out what the wide world had to offer rather than stay in school.[16] He is on record as saying when talking to a group of children one day, "You don't have to cram knowledge into your heads. I will teach you all you need to know about life."[17] Yamaoka maintained that this view is true to his character and is therefore credible. He also pointed out that the view that Sasakawa might turn "red" was nonsensical, as the Russian Revolution did not take place until 1917 and the decision for Ryoichi not to go on to a middle school was taken when he graduated from primary school in 1912.[18]

Whatever the reasons for the curtailment of his formal education, one may note that in general fewer years were devoted to education in Ryoichi's time than today. Compulsory free education in the late Meiji years was limited to six years at primary school. Even then, after the basic four-year course not all pupils did the next two years. A far more limited number went on to middle school and beyond. Shunji, Ryoichi's younger brother by two years, also did not go beyond the two senior years of the primary school. However, times changed. Their younger sister, Yoshiko, born twelve years after Ryoichi in 1911, went to Showa Girls High School, a private school in Sonezaki, Osaka, graduating in the early 1920s. By then, following his father's death on 18 January 1922, Ryoichi had become the head of the family. Ryohei, the youngest brother, sixteen years Ryoichi's junior, graduated from primary school in 1928 and went on to Kansai University. Surely, Ryoichi was not averse to higher learning, seeing that he paid to give Ryohei the chance (though he dropped out) at a time when higher education was on the rise in Japan. One other factor may have been relevant in Ryoichi's case. In those days, there was a powerful tradition that the eldest sons of families succeeded their fathers, notably in sake brewing. The business was handed on from one generation to another with great formality, precisely as it had been in the case of the Sasakawas for 150 years. Lack of management continuity could destroy a going concern. Eldest sons might therefore leave school in order to go into the family business early in life.

Ryoichi runs away to fly

Not that Ryoichi allowed such considerations to stand in the way of a dream he had. While still a child, he developed a passion for flying. The Wright brothers had made their historic first flight in the United States on 17 December 1903. That was a little too early for Ryoichi to react to, as he was just four years old. But a few years later, at the age of — eight, according to Kurose, he made his own first attempted "flight." He strapped a pair of *shoji* screens to his shoulders, went up onto the roof of his house, and jumped off. No doubt he crashed to the earth. But his passionate interest in flying remained, and in due course, totally disregarding his parents, he ran away from home to realize his heart's desire.

It all started with a newspaper article. Ryoichi read in the paper about a Japanese pioneer pilot called Nishide Kiyoshi. The article said that he was returning to Japan from America with a plane, but he had one problem. He lacked the money to bring the aircraft through customs. Ryoichi leaped into action. He wrote to Nishide, offering help. He then brought the pilot to meet his parents and persuaded them to put up the money to get the aircraft through customs in Kobe. Ryoichi was just seventeen.

Not long after, without saying a word to his parents, Ryoichi packed his things in a box, and left home to join forces with Nishide. His mother, Teru, was philosophical: "Since he was born to serve the world and to serve people, gods won't take his life."

She was right. Ryoichi spent two years with Nishide and learned aeronautical engineering from him and also stunt flying. He thus became one of the first Japanese to do so, in days when planes had open cockpits, only the most crude navigation systems, and practically no support on the ground, and airstrips were few and far between. Those were pioneering days. God did in fact take the life of Nishide — who died when his plane crashed several years later.[19]

Conscription into the Imperial Army

As a fledgling pilot working with Nishide, Ryoichi kept in contact with his parents, and was responsive to their wishes as their source of finance. However, that was for only two years. Japan, while not a combatant in World War One (1914-1918), had a system of conscription, and Ryoichi was duly called up. In 1918 he passed his army medical and was inducted at the age of nineteen. The next year, his dream came true and he was assigned as a private *(nitohei)* to the Second Air Battalion, an Imperial Army unit based at Kagamigahara in Gifu Prefecture. His aircraft skills, it is said, had earned him his place; once there he studied with a will.

Some sixty-four notebooks and textbooks of Ryohei's survive from those days, and are to be found among the Sasakawa family papers. These books bear witness to his studiousness. One may find his copious written comments in the margins of the textbooks as well as in his notebooks, from which we learn that he was most impressed by Samuelson's aero-engine and also a powerful 150-horsepower engine. He took meticulous notes and made diagrams of parts of the aircraft, as well as working on meteorological maps used by pilots.

We know that he studied well, judging by the certificates that piled up with his name on them. A year after he joined the army — 1920, the year of his twenty-first birthday — he was presented with a graduation certificate in aeronautical engineering. Half a year later, he received a second certificate, for completing a course in the manufacture and handling of aircraft engines. Then in November 1921, he was commended for having the qualifications for higher rank and received a citation praising his conduct, diligence, and achievements in theoretical and practical engineering skills.

Officially, Sasakawa was now a lance corporal (*jotohei*), but as noted he was recognized as being qualified for higher rank. His star was rising. However, he was not destined for a military career. Late in 1921 he had a bad accident. In those days it was standard practice to start an aircraft engine by spinning the propeller by hand. The pilot sat in the cockpit and a mechanic spun the prop. For some reason, everything went wrong one day when Ryoichi was acting as the mechanic. The propeller hit him and smashed his right arm. Accounts say that the jealousy of a superior who was irked by Sasakawa's mastery of aircraft technology was a factor in the accident, but another factor and perhaps a more likely explanation, from what we read, may have been Ryoichi's overconfidence.[20]

Tsurukichi passes away

Whatever the precise circumstances, this was a pivotal moment in his life. Ryoichi quit the army — setting aside, perforce, any plans he may have had for a career in the armed forces, and returned home. His broken arm required an operation. The surgery was successful but he ended up with his right arm shorter than the left, and for the rest of his life when the weather turned cold he suffered pain in that shoulder.

His return home came at a suddenly crucial juncture for the Sasakawa family. Very shortly after Ryohei's homecoming his father, Tsurukichi, died while still in his fifties. His death in January 1922 meant that the twenty-two-year-old Ryoichi became head of the family with full responsibility for the sake business and assorted assets. It was also up to him to find the resources to put his younger sister and youngest brother through school. He made a good show at it, from what we know. For a couple of years he devoted himself to family duties.

There is no doubt that he was a caring big brother. Locally, meanwhile, one thing led to another. Like his ancestors in Toyokawa he was drawn into politics. In April 1925, just before his twenty-sixth birthday, he was elected to the Toyokawa village assembly for a single four-year term. These duties did not detain him for very long, however. Later in life he was to remark that he had done everything in his first two years in the post that a village assemblyman has to do. He did not seek reelection. Village politics was not for this young man.[21]

Ryoichi the investor

Ryoichi certainly had other options in mind. His father had left him considerable assets. There was the family home; there were farmlands; and there were financial assets — national bonds, securities, and deposits. Having inherited them all as the eldest son, he took the plunge in the mid 1920s and invested in the highly speculative rice exchange at Dojima in Osaka. In a short time he made a fortune. This success augured well. Thereafter he traded in stocks. The secret of his success in high-risk financial products was this:

> To watch others and do the opposite of what they do. Most investors buy when shares rise. I do the opposite — I sell. I buy when prices are lowest and people shun them. I sell when others want my shares.[22]

A contrarian in politics

In other words he was born a contrarian. He did not conform to prevailing trends. As in business, so in public life — and politics. Here, we may jump ahead fifteen years to Sasakawa's entry into national politics. He made this move at an extraordinary juncture for himself and for Japan. War had begun in December 1941 with the Japanese attack on Pearl Harbor. Four months later, with the nation by this time embroiled in a conflict spread over a huge part of East Asia and the Pacific, the Tojo government held general elections. These were timed for April 1942, when the war was still going well from a Japanese viewpoint. However, the authorities wanted to ensure that the legislature was docile.

Eager to boost the war effort, the military-led government decided on a policy of recommending and supporting candidates sympathetic to themselves. By contrast, those who were critical would not only not be "recommended candidates," they would have their election campaigns interfered with by the authorities through the disruption of their meetings, tearing down of their posters, and so on. By various strategies, the authorities filled parliament with yes-men. Out of 466 members elected to the Diet in April 1942, some 381 were "recommended" and only 85 were independent — one of them being Sasakawa Ryoichi.

He stood in the election, we should understand, because at that time the elected representatives of the nation were held in the lowest possible esteem. Parliamentary democracy was at a low ebb indeed. Sasakawa's instinct told him that here was an opportunity to be seized and a job to be done. However, he stated at the time that he planned to resign if a golden age of parliamentary life ever returned.[23]

This in fact was typical of him. Following the end of the war, the prestige of members of parliament shot up. Once again the Diet enjoyed supreme national status. True to his contrarian's instincts, Sasakawa bowed out of parliamentary life. Moreover, he declined to seek political office following his release from Sugamo Prison in December 1948, even though he could well have been reelected to the legislature had he wished. He went his own way.

Doing the opposite of what others did was, of course, no guarantee of success in itself, either in investment or in politics. But Sasakawa had an uncanny ability to see ahead. This was his own view of himself, whether as an investor or a politician, while at the same time he was given to great wariness and systematic caution. He said: "My projects are always realized, because I do not ignore reality and can see ten years down the road."[24]

He was in fact cautious as a player in stock and commodity markets. He never used his capital for speculative investments. He had learned since his youth, he said, to "let one eye see through a telescope, and the other through a microscope."

His metaphorical way of speaking had a certain ring of literal truth in Ryoichi's case. His eyes were large and slightly protruding. It was his single most conspicuous feature, something that everyone who met him was bound to notice. Those eyes of his, we shall see, were to be remarked on in years to come — for example, during his time in Sugamo Prison after the war in 1946.

A man of property

Reverting here to the topic of Ryoichi's skills as an investor, his contrarian's strategy worked, as other investors in the market must have become rapidly aware. He became enormously rich at an early age and, wishing to spread his risks, quickly spread his investments far and wide. He put money into mining ventures, piling up his business appointments and job titles. He served as president or director of the following companies:

Kokusai Kogyo KK (International Mining Co.)
Aikoku Sangyo KK (Patriotic Industry Co.)
Sasakawa Kogyo-sho (Sasakawa Mine Works)
Morikawa Boring Keisen KK (Morikawa Boring Co.)

He made and kept fortunes, but Sasakawa was by no means satisfied by mere mundane success. Making money, he said, was only important to him because it gave him the means to offer his services to society. "*Sensei*," he was asked one day, many years later, "how is it that you are

always successful in every venture you embark upon? What is your secret?" He responded:

> Most people who suffer losses do so because they are greedy. I
> have no greed. I only want funds to pay for my public activities.
> All the money I make I use for my compatriots and for society in
> general. The nature of my greed is quite different from that of
> others.

He added:

> I watch my money to the last yen. I refrain from luxury. But I
> have spent lavishly for the country's sake. I have no qualms
> about suffering poverty for this good cause.[25]

Not one to pamper his heirs

He was frank and direct as regards money, even at the risk of sounding
brutal toward his three sons and heirs. When someone asked him in his
later years about making a will, he responded:

> A fortune is of no use to me once I die. I cannot take it with me
> or use it in any way. So what do I do? My offspring may misuse
> the fortune. If I give it to them they could be a nuisance to others
> and sully the family name. If they turn out to be complete block-
> heads they could be robbed of everything I leave them.
>
> So, those cannot be true riches. Don't we all arrive in this
> world naked and leave it the same way? I plan to use all my
> money for society. Donations I make to others cannot be seized
> by stupid sons or even in progressive taxation by the govern-
> ment. My wealth shall be put to perpetual use for good causes.
> ... It makes no sense for me to leave behind worldly goods that
> will be cleansed from me just as my body is being prepared for
> the coffin.[26]

As we shall see, his entire life was testimony to the truth of these
words. He was in no sense hypocritical. Sasakawa's aloof attitude to
money — he saw his life as if it was taking place on a stage on which he
would appear for only one act, led him, paradoxically enough, to be
swamped with worldly success.

Investing for the nation

Not that everything turned to gold in Sasakawa's hands throughout his lifetime — as, for example, during the years when Japan plunged into wars overseas in the 1930s and 1940s. His mining ventures were not as profitable in wartime as they could have been, the family records show. Sasakawa, however, persisted with unprofitable investments and did not pull out when the public interest was at stake.

"It is not in the interest of the nation for me to operate only profitable mines and terminate losing ones," he stated, according to the Sasakawa family papers:

> What is most needed today is metal to make bullets. A hundred yen is a gigantic sum of money, but money cannot be made into bullets. The country is not a loser if I use one hundred yen to excavate ten yen worth of metal. I am the only loser — and that's fine by me. My money will be transferred to the pockets of some of our fellow countrymen, while bullets get sent to the front line....
>
> I wish our entrepreneurs would think as I do, and not always strive for their own selfish interests. They would do well to use some of their great profits in ventures that will be good for the country — even if at their own loss. What is needed most in Japan is a readiness to forego one's own interests for the sake of the country.[27]

These two quotations come from very different periods in his long life — one from his old age; the other from a frenetic time in mid life when Japan was at war. His meaning in both cases is unambiguous, if also unconventional. In the second passage his thoughts run contrary to the free-market principles of the world today, according to which goods move freely across national borders. But the world had set aside free trade long before the advent of World War Two. Leading nations — notably the United States — had raised major tariff and import quota obstacles to trade at their borders after the collapse of Wall Street in 1929 and during the Great Depression of the 1930s. The free flow of goods was impeded as nations were switching to a wartime footing. Sasakawa's thoughts on economics and national strategic priorities then had a stern rationality.

We now turn to the 1930s, an appalling time in world history — and a tormenting decade for Sasakawa, who was to spend three years detained in prison.

II

1930-35

The PPP and its exceptional leader

As Japan entered the 1930s, Sasakawa wanted to do something for the nation. He called this working "in the service of society and the people." What this boiled down to in practice, as a first move, was making himself into a publisher. He took over control of a tiny financially distressed company called National Defence Co. (Kokubo Sha), and made himself president. He also became the publisher of a monthly magazine called *National Defence (Kokubo)*. So far as I am aware, not a single copy of this magazine exists. It is therefore difficult to know its nature or for how long it was published. I assume that it was one of those magazines that advocated right-wing causes.[28]

The Patriotic People's Party

Publishing was a beginning. Sasakawa's first major step into public life was to organize a fledgling political party called the Patriotic People's Party (Kokusui Taishu-to), a group he and others founded on 10 March 1931 at a time of mounting international tension. Elements in the Japanese Kwantung Army stationed in Manchuria were preparing to seize control of all of Manchuria. On 18 September 1931 they provoked an outbreak of hostilities that became known as the "Manchurian Incident" and precipitated the "Fifteen-Year War" with China.[29]

The Patriotic People's Party (hereafter PPP), we know, was one of the many right-wing organizations to be created early on in the Showa Era 1930s to push for "national reform." The platform of the PPP, at least on the surface, did not differ much from that of other right-wing parties founded around that time. Soon after its inauguration, with Sasakawa as its president, the party issued a warning to the Mitsui industrial group (*zaibatsu*) to desist from speculative purchases of the US dollar; next, the party took a position in favor of Japan's forcible entry into Manchuria, the industrial heartland of northeastern China, and designs upon Mongolia; later on it came out in favor of the creation of Manchukuo, as Manchuria became known under Japanese rule. It demanded the "disciplining" of "intractable" China — code words for repression by force; and finally, in 1933, it called for Japan's withdrawal from the League of Nations, while continuing to make criticisms of Japanese business groups — mainly the famous *zaibatsu* or "money cliques" of that era.

On the ideological front the party called for a "clear Japanese identity," an advocacy for a structure of the state built around the emperor and criticized the "heretical" theory propagated by academic moderates that "the emperor is an organ of the state."[30]

On the international front, the party was hostile to Great Britain and positive toward Germany and Italy. Its most carefully considered policy plank concerned China. The party recognized the anticommunist regime of Wang Zhaoming (1883-1944), based in Nanjing, which was sympathetic to Japan and antagonistic toward Generalissimo Chiang Kaishek (1887-1975), the leader of the Republic of China, with its base in Chongjin. The party also favored an aggressive "southward" Japanese advance into Southeast Asia (at the expense of the ensconced Western colonial powers, Britain, France, and the Netherlands).

Today, these positions may smack of the stereotypes of those days, but Sasakawa, a businessman by inclination, appears not to have been greatly interested in the right-wing dogmas. His words and his deeds set him apart from other rightists. In later years, immediately after leaving the prison in Sugamo after World War Two, he drew up a rather elaborate classification of the right-wing groups of the 1930s. The following passage is long, but it may be worth quoting in full, to show how Sasakawa analyzed the Right and distinguished between himself and other nationalists.

A classification of right-wing groups

I classified rightists of the prewar period into four categories. The general public was inclined to lump them all together, but they are quite distinct.

First came the *ronin* — the "masterless samurai," lone wolves for the most part.

Next came the *norito* — the "sacred sprig believers," who leaned toward Shintoism and prayer.

Third, were the *boryoku* — the "violent group" members.

Finally, there were the *taishu* — the "people's rights" believers, the popular right wing.[31]

Sasakawa, it should be clear, placed himself and his party, the PPP, squarely in the fourth class of right-wingers — those who espoused the public interest and who also, a crucial point, believed in parliamentary democracy as a system. This was a major distinction between the first three classes enumerated above, as compared with the fourth category, the *taishu*. The latter flirted with violence, as we shall see, but did not treat it as primary.

To take these classes of rightists, one by one.... The *ronin* dignified themselves with proud names but were one-man outfits.
They bragged; they claimed to take upon their shoulders all the
burdens of the nation, but they had zero political and social impact. Their real objective was to get some pocket money by
knocking on the doors of the military and bureaucrats, politicians and capitalists. They had no ideals and no principles. They
were charlatans, riding on the popular wave in favor of the right
wing.

Next, the Shinto-inclined rightists [*norito*] were different
from the first group. They were ideologues who espoused the
"Record of Ancient Matters" (Kojiki) and the *Chronicles of Japan* (*Nihon Shoki,* the oldest official record of the imperial lin-
eage together with myths and legends, a work dating to the
seventh century Nara period). They considered these two tomes
as the sole guide to proper conduct, whether in politics, the
economy or culture. They believed unquestioningly in the unparalleled uniqueness of the Japanese polity; and they were
quick to denounce traitors in their midst and hostile toward
anyone who questioned on scientific grounds the authority of
their two main books." These people were fanatics who prided
themselves on chanting Shinto prayers, while immersing themselves in freezing cold water in the course of their rituals of puri-
fication. These believers in purifying ablutions behaved as if
they were possessed by the supernatural; they claimed to have
the authority to provide a solid ideological foundation for the
Imperial Rule Assistance Association [Taisei Yokusan-Kai], an
association of members of parliament created in October 1940
by Konoe Fumimaro to buttress public support for the impend-
ing war with the West.[32] These fanatics took the credit for creation of the much-touted "imperial way" [*kodo*] ideology,
placing the emperor at the center of the universe, as the god-
head.

Next, there were those who believed in *boryoku* — in threats
of violence. They belonged, really, in the same category as the
norito, the believers in Shinto ritual. They rejected parliamentary government outright, and also any kind of popular movement such as might take expression in a political party or a trade
union. They wished to bring about what they called the Showa
Ishin (Showa Restoration) — meaning the elevation of the
Showa emperor as a symbol of their highest values, and they
plotted to achieve their goal through violent means. They saw

themselves as spiritual heirs of the young Imperial Army and Imperial Navy officers who attempted to overthrow the government by coups d'état, one staged on 15 May 1932 and the other on 26 February 1936. They ran camps to train young people in the use of violence.

These three groups — the *ronin,* the *norito,* and the *boryoku* — had much in common. In practice, it was difficult to decide into which category to place a given individual. In general, they could all be termed "ultra-nationalist" [*cho-kokkashugisha*], to use a term which was current in the 1930s.[33]

Sasakawa is saying here that the "three groups" identified and analyzed by him were "ultra-nationalists" and would stop at nothing to achieve their goals, i.e., they would commit violence if necessary. He is also affirming that his own category of right-wingers was averse to the ultimate sanctions of violence and murder:

The fourth group — the popular right wing [*taishu*] was totally different from the other three. They were as wide apart as the heavens are from the earth, or black from white. The "people's right wing," as I call it, marched under the banner of humanitarian idealism and believed in progressive political ideas. It embraced political realism and was committed to carrying out political reforms based on the collective will of the people. It respected parliamentary government, a big distinction from the first three groups of right-wingers, and it aimed at achieving its objectives through parliamentary processes. It emphasized the importance of lawful, popular government, and focused on organizing the masses.

It is wrong, from the start, therefore, to treat the party as a right-wing organization. It does not belong, as is generally suggested, with the three former groups or tendencies, as it bears no likeness to them. But if pressed, I would say that we could be called "popular right-wingers" or "law-abiding right-wingers," as contrasted with the others who were not law-abiding. The Patriotic People's Party that I headed as president — later known as the Patriotic Alliance (Kokusui Domei) — belonged, according to my classification, in the fourth category as popular right-wingers.[34]

Strong-arm tactics of the PPP

All this is very intriguing, but Sasakawa's classification and his definition of the PPP are not exactly correct. Some of the party's members, it cannot be denied, had a strong affinity with the *ronin*, the *norito,* and the *boryoku* right-wingers. Take the case of Fuji Yoshio, its senior executive under Sasakawa, who sometimes acted controversially in situations where the party president was not himself physically present to see what was going on. Fuji was a champion fighter of the classic right-wing type, who believed in settling matters by force.

He was known within the small PPP as its eighth *dan* fixer, eighth *dan* being the highest rank in kendo, karate and other martial arts. There are several recorded instances of Fuji openly resorting to physical action. In January 1933, some two years after Sasakawa took over the leadership of the PPP, Fuji led a group of fifteen members — most of the active membership — in a hunger strike; the men took up a position opposite the imperial palace in the center of Tokyo to protest the government's feeble handling of a case against Meiji Sugar Co., in which the company had been accused of tax evasion and had supposedly been let off too lightly. Two months later in March 1933, Fuji burst into the prime minister's official residence and apparently attempted seppuku there.[35] He sent a young member of the PPP to carry out the same action at the residence of the army minister. Buildings such as these two official residences were tightly guarded throughout the 1930s, and any plan to stage ceremonial suicides must have been almost certain to fail.

Nonetheless, these actions did occur. In due course, Fuji followed through with other shows of violence. Thus in 1935 he broke into the home of Ichiki Kitokuro, the president of the Privy Council (suumitsuin) and a constitutional scholar, waving his sword in the air and shouting imprecations.[36]

Eventually, Fuji was arrested, tried, and sentenced to prison with hard labor. It is possible to make excuses or claim extenuating circumstances. Hunger strikes are nonviolent. Moreover, all those PPP members who participated in the hunger strike in front of the palace, it was said, had taken the precaution first of formally withdrawing from the PPP, so as not to embarrass Sasakawa or the party. Moreover, for someone to disembowel himself, though this did not in fact happen, would have been to commit violence against his own person, and not others. As for the forced entry into the home of Professor Ichiki, it might be maintained that to draw a sword was not the same as causing bodily harm — that that was not the intention, but rather "to frighten members of the Ichiki family and thereby to put pressure upon Minobe Tatsukichi, a member of the House of Peers up to 1935, from advocating his "organ of the state" theory and encourage those who opposed it.[37] In the final analysis, however, there is no denying that only a fine line existed between the *boryoku* rightists and Fuji Yoshio, judging by his behavior.[38]

Sasakawa opposed to violence

At the time, the PPP would not refrain from using violence, so it was thought, if the situation called for it. The Justice Ministry classed the PPP then with such groups as Nakano Seigo's East Association (Toho-Kai), Hashimoto Kingoro's Great Japan Youth Party (Dai Nihon Seinen-To), and Akamatsu Katsumaro's Japan New Progressive Party (Dai Nihon Kakushin-To).[39] They were grouped together in the ministry's classification as "national socialism-oriented" *(Kokka Shakai-Shugi Kei)*. The ministry noted that the PPP conducted public meetings in order to double its small membership. The party, it has been recorded, trained a group of its followers for direct physical action *(kyoryoku kodo-tai)* and was considered by the government in 1940 to be "not averse to taking direct action" if called for.[40] Sasakawa himself was, however, consistently negative toward the use of violence. Fuji Yoshio, while disposed to physical force, may well have restrained himself in the light of the strong opposition from the PPP party president, whom he respected.

It all boiled down to who was leader. Sasakawa was not only the party's nominal head, it was he who raised the funds the PPP needed to keep going. As a result, he believed that no party action could be taken without his approval. Individual party members might choose to act on their own account, but that was their affair. When it came to the party he was in charge, he asserted. When he and the other leaders of the PPP were arrested in 1935 and indicted on charges of blackmail, Sasakawa told the lower court: "Nearly every action of the party is taken at my discretion. Resolutions adopted by the general affairs committee are acted on only after I approve them as being consistent with my wishes."[41] He may have intended to take some of the pressure off the party's officials and deflect it to himself, but there is no doubt that he believed what he said. Thus, Sasakawa's opposition to the use of physical force by his followers was a basic tenet of the PPP. In this sense, his classification of the party was correct.

III

1935-41

Science, technology, and aeronautics

Be that as it may, Sasakawa Ryoichi set himself apart from other right-wingers on several counts.[42] First, he never depended on others financially.[43] In this regard, he was decidedly different from the *ronin* rightists, as he referred to them. He was once asked whether a truly patriotic man should engage in business. He responded as follows:

> Whether patriot or *ronin,* everyone has to have food, clothing and shelter. Services to the nation, too, cost money. In the past, patriots and *ronin* alike received money from government and from business concerns. The times have changed. There is no such thing as unconditional money. If we take money from the government we will be reduced to acting as bodyguards; likewise, if we take money from the *zaibatsu* we will become just their watchdogs.
>
> That means death to our principles. It is not good for the country, and no good for the people either. We will be reduced from patriots to paupers. I would not for anything become a government bodyguard or a *zaibatsu* watchdog. But I cannot give up my struggle for patriotic reform because it is my life. I was in business even before I founded the Patriotic Alliance. I believe this is the right choice for a patriotic activist — to conduct business — and I am vain enough to think that I can represent my people in an honorable way.[44]

Declines to join the government

Sasakawa, we know, kept his independence. He never accepted a government position. In fact, he is on record as having declined all such offers. When Koiso Kuniaki took over the reins of government from Tojo Hideki, he or his supporters reinstituted the post of parliamentary secretary *(seimukan)*, at all major ministries.[45] Members of the House of Representatives, the lower chamber in the bicameral system, vied for the post. Foreign Minister Shigemitsu Mamoru, who knew Sasakawa, offered him the post of parliamentary secretary at the Foreign Ministry. He politely turned down the offer, saying that it would be his honor to continue to serve as a back-bencher (an independent). He was too proud, or perhaps one should say too shrewd and independent, to accept a post in government, even working with Shigemitsu whom he respected.

Sasakawa has often been compared with another well-known rightist with business interests of the period, Kodama Yoshio. Kodama belonged to Sasakawa's PPP from early on, but they differed in respect of their operations notably after World War Two and their three-year detention in Sugamo without being charged. Prior to that, during the war, Kodama built an apparatus to amass wealth on a grand scale by making the most of his opportunities in the employ *(shokutaku)* of several ministries.[46]

Sasakawa worked very differently, as contemporary records dating from the 1930s make clear. He was much more in the public eye than Kodama. Kiyosawa Kiyoshi (1890-1945), a liberal essayist and journalist before the war, regarded Sasakawa as a *ronin* rightist, and had this to say in his diary for 1942-45:

Alas, Japan is today full of rightists and hoodlums. The streets of Tokyo are filled with flyers, announcing public speeches by Akao Bin, a rowdy anticommunist and member of parliament. The newspapers report in huge Gothic type headlines the comings and goings between Osaka and Tokyo of Sasakawa Ryoichi, the president of a party calling itself the Patriotic Alliance Party. These are the men who set the tone of the times.[47]

Here is another extract from this diary:

Heard criticisms leveled at Toyama Mitsuru from people in his camp — rightists — that Tojo Hideki (1884-1948), the prime minister, was furnishing him with a considerable amount of money....[48] His third son, Hidezo, escaped conscription into the armed forces, as "a person with special skills." Toyama himself had no grounds for going around presenting himself as a concerned patriot. The truth is he mainly spent his time buttering up the military. Alas, this is a world of ruffians and blackmailers. A man called Sasakawa Ryoichi, the boss of the Patriotic Alliance (Kokusui Domei), apparently is a man of property, worth tens of millions. Every rightist is rolling in money. That is why one cannot but have a war![49]

Is this justified? Kiyosawa was usually extremely sharp and to the point in what he wrote. But the reference here to Sasakawa looks like nothing more than passing on gossip, the talk of the town. The writing style is vulgar and lacks persuasive power. On the other hand, this is an extract from a diary. Kiyosawa may just have let his emotions get the better of him. Sasakawa himself was alert to the fact that he had become a butt of criticism. He noted in a short work he titled "A Commoner's Memoir" (Heimin Shinsho), published in 1942 in typewritten form that he had become a target of volatile praise and criticism. He was prone to be misunderstood, especially by the so-called intellectuals *(interi)* — journalists and academics writing for the press, for example, usually left of center. The latter always chose to depict Sasakawa hand-in-glove with Kodama Yoshio, as the terrible twins of the Right. In fact, this was wrong. As noted, Kodama belonged to Sasakawa's PPP (later the Patriotic Alliance) and he served for some time as the East Asia director of the PPP. The two men continued an uninterrupted friendship until the death of

Kodama in 1984. For these reasons, they were often considered to be as close as two peas in a pod. In fact, as stated, their behavior differed radically even before World War Two, and all the more so after the war.[50]

Business first

For Sasakawa, business came first, and not politics. This can be seen from his behavior, going back to prewar days. He observed a simple principle, staying away from visiting acquaintances once they occupied government positions, and taking up with them again only after their departure from such posts.

This was quite deliberate on his part, as he explained, according to a note found in his papers:

> I look for friends who point out my failings and comfort me when the going is rough, and I return the compliment. Friends who have a huge success in life don't need me; visitors pour in to see them, like ants converging on sweets. Then, when circumstances are reversed and they are in the depths of despair no one wants to see them. That is the time when I want to be a true friend. People who are in their prime are too busy. One cannot sit down with them and have a chat. However, when they have few visitors, that is when one can really talk. My principle, in this as in other matters, is to do the opposite of the norm.[51]

He went against the stream and was consistent in this regard, both before and after the war. He did not try to use people in power to promote his own interests.

Sasakawa built a fortune — several times in his life. He used this money for generous purposes and for causes close to his heart, keeping little or nothing for himself. In fact, he led an austere and frugal life beyond all imagining for a man of such immense wealth. People who lived promiscuously without working drove him to distraction. He was terribly critical of right-wingers who conducted themselves that way, the record shows. One day, a certain rightist of the *ronin* type showed up drunk at Sasakawa's Osaka office, having traveled down from Tokyo to see him, and demanded money.

Sasakawa was enraged, according to a note he left among his papers. He spoke to the visitor, a young man, as follows:

> I do not waste a drop of water. I even stop and calculate when I am not in a hurry which is cheaper, whether to travel somewhere by train or to walk and wear out my shoes. I do not treat myself to extravagant meals. And you, young man, have the

money to buy yourself booze whenever you like it. I am not giving you a cent because it would be wrong for me to do so.[52]

He kept on roaring:

If you have the money to spend on booze during the day, you should be the one making the donations to yours truly, who gives all his money to patriotic causes.[53]

Sasakawa was a believer in self-help and independence of mind. He lived simply, and he expected others to do likewise.

Interest in science and technology

A second characteristic that set him apart from other rightists was his keen interest in science and technology. He was highly critical of those who put their "spirituality" before technology, ignoring the latter. To him that was simple arrogance and stupidity, yet far from uncommon. He was an eager pilot — a stunt flyer in his earliest years, as we have seen. He trained himself in aircraft maintenance. He really knew his stuff. He was also far ahead of his time in that he loved automobiles and drove the classic models or whatever came to hand. One major source on the topic of right-wingers in Japan in the 1930s — the *Grand History of the Rightists* — states that "Sasakawa was the only right-winger in those days who piloted his own plane and flew wherever he chose to go in the world. He left the country speechless."[54] He was a special breed before the war, but there was no one in public life who rivaled him after the war either in respect of his passion for flight.

Naturally, he was not content with just flying himself. He wanted others to share his passion. Early in 1932, he organized a National Volunteer Flying Squad (Kokusui Giyu Hikotai), which he headed. The objective of this flying club was like all such organizations to teach people to fly, in this case civilians. The National Volunteer Flying Squad (hereafter NVFS) was officially a volunteer body. However, it had a serious underlying purpose. The intent was to furnish a supply of trained pilots who could be mobilized for action in a national emergency.

Sasakawa foresaw, in other words, that the age of the airplane had come. He had known this from his teens. This was not a new insight, but one he wished to share. At the time, the civil side of the aviation industry was in a slump in Japan, and he sensed that this was bad, not only for the future of the industry but for Japan's national mission. In keeping with the times, he saw this mission as a duty to peacefully spread the authority of Japan's emperor all over the world. At a time when there was an urgent need to strengthen national defense, especially air power. National defense — or, more exactly, the expansion of the military, led by the nation's strength in the air — had to be mobilized as a top priority; and to promote civilian air services and keep them in top form was obviously desirable. The urgency of the situation may be seen from the wording of a prospectus put out for the NVFS. The prospectus stated:

> In terms of performance, an aircraft is just that — there is no distinction between a civil plane and a military one. In an emergency, air strength needs to be mobilized, just as any other organ of the nation, and deployed as a front line of defense. It follows that if our civil air strength is weak relative to other powers our defense capability as a whole will be inadequate. Can the superior spirit of our people, outstanding as it may be, make up for inferior defense? Recent wars have shown quite clearly that notwithstanding our unparalleled spirituality and the great bravery of our fighting men we still have little chance in modern warfare [unless we are fully prepared in the air, on the ground and at sea].[55]

What Sasakawa is saying here is fundamentally different from the line taken by the *norito* fundamentalists, who were believers in Shinto, pure and simple. The latter spoke of repelling B-29 bombers by using bamboo spears. They put their hopes in another kamikaze, a miraculous divine wind like the typhoon that saved Japan by smashing the fleet of the invading Mongols in the twelfth century. To Sasakawa, that was all nonsense. He was a self-proclaimed pro-German and pro-Italian Anglophobe, but he was reluctant to fight America up to the very last moment when Japan attacked Pearl Harbor on 7 December 1941.

Corresponding with the admiral of the fleet

He knew all too well that in all probability Japan stood no chance against the superior industrial, scientific, and technological strength of a formidable foe like the United States. His certainty on this score brought him into contact with men of like mind, notably Admiral Yamamoto Isoroku, the vice minister of the Imperial Navy and commander-in-chief of the Combined Fleet destined to attack Pearl Harbor. Letters written by Yamamoto to him are kept among the Sasakawa Papers.

Here are some key passages:

> If there is war no amount of bragging will stop a single enemy bullet. That makes the mission of our fleet all the more grave. There is nothing for us to do but to apply ourselves assiduously to training, and do our best. (9 October 1940)

If war breaks out between Japan and the United States, my destination will not be Guam or the Philippines. Nor will it be Hawaii or San Francisco. It has to be the streets of the District of Columbia — Washington, D.C. We will have to seize the White House. Are our statesmen ready for this, I wonder? Do they have the resolve and the confidence? (24 January 1941)

How pitiful! There are these people who say that Chiang Kaishek cannot be defeated, because he is receiving a trickle of supplies from the Anglo-American forces sent overland through Burma. If we cannot put down Chiang Kaishek, how can we hope to defeat the Anglo-American forces in the field and subjugate East Asia under a new order? It is perfectly absurd.[56] We have to be coolheaded and think matters through. Just suppose: should the UK and US forces cross the oceans and mount a direct assault on us, will there be a single brave Sagami Taro (Hojo Tokimune, 1251-1284, a regent of the Kamakura Shogunate at the time of the attempted Mongolian invasions) in the whole of Showa's realm able to stand and resist the increasingly menacing enemy? (12 February 1941)

Primacy of aeronautics

Sasakawa, one may be sure, fully shared the beliefs confided to him by Admiral Yamamoto, probably Japan's most distinguished military officer of that period.[57] Certainly, Sasakawa, whether by design or force of circumstances, distanced himself from almost all other rightists in Japan and conducted himself unlike any of them. Thus, in keeping with his passion for aviation, he constructed an entire airfield, for training purposes, in 1934. The location was Nakakawachi County in Osaka. Sasakawa billed this as an "air defense field." As such, it was the first in the nation. To construct the airstrip and facilities, he raised funds from business people in Osaka and the surrounding Kansai region, and contributed money himself. Sasakawa took the view that the airfield should not be private property and donated it to the Imperial Army, on one condition: that his volunteer flying group, the NVFS, could be based there. That was agreed.

In August 1935 Sasakawa and many of his top lieutenants in the PPP were arrested without warning and charged with the blackmail of some of the most important private sector companies in Osaka. They were held in prison for three years while their trial dragged on, as we shall see later in this chapter. In 1941, when the Great Japan Aviation Association (GJAA) was formed to integrate all civil aviation activities in the country, Sasakawa dissolved the NVFS, thinking that its mission was over, and donated all its facilities and aircraft to the GJAA.

This illustrates how Sasakawa thought as regards property. He gave unstintingly for the benefit of the public. He believed in big gestures.

One final note is in order on the history of the NVFS. Women were welcome to join the unit if they wished to learn to fly or to maintain aircraft. No other male leader in Japan treated women equally in that era. Sasakawa was the sole exception.

IV

1941-1945

On the side of the people

The third point that distinguished Sasakawa from other rightists was his unswerving dedication to the public interest, in the sense of the people's daily lives. Few other right-wingers in Japan ever entered parliament or had any respect for parliamentary institutions. Nor did they demonstrate much interest in the common people, let alone devote themselves to working on their behalf.

Just as Sasakawa was exceptional among rightists in the prewar days in that he had money, and just as he was quite unique when it came to mastering and applying modern technology, notably aviation, in the national interest, he was equally unusual in his curiosity about the basic issue of how to govern a nation. The Sasakawa papers include the following thoughts dating to prewar times:

> The secret of good governance, I believe, is the ability to satisfy as many people as possible. For that, the basic requirement is to know what grudges people hold, and what hopes they entertain. The way to find this out is for politicians and people in public life to go to the people. I make it a point to frequent public baths and barber shops. I ask masseurs to come to me, because those who have lost their sight seem to me to have a healthy sixth sense. I even use fortunetellers, to let me study and understand what moves people twenty-four hours a day. To deal with grievances the people's representatives must not be obsessed with face-saving or with personal honor.[58]

Sasakawa was the last person to care about "face-saving and personal honor." One of his first actions when he was elected to the House of Representatives, the Lower House of Parliament, in 1942 was to dispense with the first-class free travel pass that came with his seat. Instead, he went second class. According to him, riding first class was like being in solitary confinement. One could not communicate with anyone. In the second-class coach, he could hear people's complaints and aspirations. That could be useful. The job of an elected representative of the people, he considered, was to address those complaints and to let people realize their hopes. The Sasakawa papers show that he applied similar principles to his PPP. To mark the tenth anniversary of the PPP in April 1941, he issued a statement to "Our One Hundred Million Brothers and Sisters" (Ichi Oku Kyodai), pledging that: "The Party will keep pushing forward as your representative to resolve all your complaints and grudges."

Sasakawa had the feelings of the people at heart. He showed this not only while he was serving in parliament, but afterwards when the war had ended and he no longer held a seat. In December 1945 he had entered Sugamo Prison in Tokyo as a Class A "war criminal suspect" (hereafter without quotation marks). Shortly after that, he became embroiled in a debate about the treatment of the remains of those killed in action overseas. Writing from prison, he submitted the following statement to an Allied Forces inspector, making a plea against discrimination between officers and lower ranks:

> Our party, the Patriotic People's Party (PPP), makes a point of marking the return of the remains of those killed in action by sending welcome parties to the station. We carry a flag draped in black. However, the remains are treated according to a class system even then. The armed forces division concerned sends a high-ranking officer to be there when the remains are those of officers. But not when they are of members of lower ranks. Once deceased we are all the same as human beings. I was infuriated by the discrimination, which I considered wholly unreasonable. I made it my practice to be at the station when I was in Osaka, together with members of our party who were always there for the homecoming. I sent a protest to one army division responsible for this discriminatory practice. On another occasion, the remains of a certain civilian employee of the army arrived on a freight train. Someone on the station staff, knowing of our party's position on this matter, contacted us in advance.
>
> The party made a solemn protest to the army minister. The media duly covered this protest, whereupon the infuriated army spokesman accused the PPP of being leftist through and through, from the president, that is myself, all the way down.

The army sent their military police to summon me for a repri-
mand. I stood my ground, and told them that I was only making
a legitimate demand, and I had no bad conscience. I refused to
bow.… These are the reasons why I and my party were labeled
as "liberal." I insist to this day that we are neither left nor right,
but a patriotic group on the side of the people.[59]

"On the side of the people"

Sasakawa's notion of being always "on the side of the people" bears further examination, in the context of his wartime duties while serving in
parliament. Here is an extract from a speech he made in the Budget
Committee of the House of Representatives on 10 February 1943, about
the time the war could be seen to have turned decisively against Japan
on almost all fronts, and with mounting military casualties — an unusual time for a member to complain about the privations of working
people. Still, in his animated style, he gave voice to the woes of ordinary
Japanese:

> A few days ago three men visited me from my home town and
> explained why they could not work as hard as they would like
> to. They were a farmer, a laborer and a low-wage earner. Let me
> tell you briefly what the farmer had to say. First, he had not
> enough fertilizer to increase production. Second, the viscose
> rayon clothing everyone was forced to wear instead of the tradi-
> tional cotton was not strong enough for working in the fields.
> Third, the government had on two occasions forced farming
> households to donate rice they had set aside to last them until
> the next harvest, whereas they had been assured that they could
> depend on rations. What incentive is there for farmers to work
> under such conditions?
>
> Fourth, on top of it all, the president of the Osaka Prefecture
> Food Corporation, a former governor of Mie Prefecture, re-
> ceives a salary of fifty thousand yen — ten times what he earned
> as governor — while under the wage control ordinance the
> farmers have to work all night without sleep in the most produc-
> tive rice paddies for three yen and forty sen a day. They are pre-
> pared to do their utmost to serve the country until we are
> victorious. They tell me that if they have to labor to produce
> cheap food to feed more people, they will endure every hard-
> ship — but not to pay fifty thousand yen to a public corporation
> president who comes to his office by car and sits there all day in
> his comfortable chair doing nothing. They don't have the incen-

tive to work to pay such a man. I strongly believe that this has to change. We must think of the farmers and workers who sweat and toil in all weathers.[60]

How to respond to such a cry of pain? Needless to say, the response was lame. Ishiguro Takeshige, the vice minister from the Agriculture and Forestry Ministry, took the floor. He not only failed to respond properly, but made things worse. "Sir, the remuneration of the public corporation president is twenty thousand yen." Sasakawa shot back:

All right, let's say twenty thousand yen, but that is still four times his salary as governor...and it is more than likely that he is receiving substantial secret funds [kimitsu-hi] under the table as well. Still, let us say he is getting twenty thousand yen and, according to what we hear from the vice minister, is suffering gravely in the course of his present duties. It would be scandalous if he received twenty thousand yen for idling away his time. It is only to be expected that he works. I would like you to ponder deeply and to have empathy for a farmer who toils in the paddy, with sweat on his brow in all kinds of weather.[61]

Sasakawa did not mince his words, so the family papers show, as on the topic of prison conditions, a subject on which Sasakawa had strong personal views. Following his experience of incarceration from 1935-1938 on charges that were eventually dismissed, he made a point of inspecting prisons wherever he went, at home or abroad. Asked one day by a journalist how he was able to see much on just a short visit to a country overseas, he answered:

The usual way would not take me far. I enter by the "front door" when I visit a country — I meet my hosts, usually heads of state or high officials, and observe the niceties — and I leave by the back door that they were not expecting to show me, that is to say, the prisons. This approach gives me a rough picture of a country.[62]

Sasakawa reserved his harshest comments, however, for conditions in his own country. As a member of parliament, he took his opportunity to loose off a few rounds at government and the administration of prisons, based on his own experience of three years in confinement:

The Ministry of Justice handles the most important commodity, the human being. In this matter I can say with confidence that I am a professional with a bitter experience behind me. For this reason, I always check on the prison policy of any country I visit, be it Germany or Italy, Mongolia, China, Korea or even Manchuria.

I make it a point to do so, and I judge a country on this basis.... One day I visited a Korean prison to comfort and encourage the inmates. We talked about the food. The warden explained that he as well as the director general of the Justice Ministry were under pressure for feeding the inmates "too well." Why should unproductive inmates eat better than ordinary Koreans, that was the question.[63]

I met the [Japanese] governor general of Korea on behalf of the warden of that prison. Inmates suffer from psychological stress, I said. They are dropouts from society, really. Today's prisoners are not "unproductive," though. They work more than those outside, actually. I have visited prisons in Kyoto, Osaka and Kobe, and I found that those serving their sentences are contributing enormously to the war efforts.... I have seen them working for the country with my own eyes. People do not know this, and complain that those who are "not productive" should not be fed so much. This is wrong.

I make it a point to visit prisons all over the country, to encourage the inmates.... It is not that they are bad people. Their minds have been damaged. All that is needed is for them to change their mindsets. I go in and I talk to them. I say that at this time of grave national crisis they have to change their attitudes. Second, they should atone for their sins with full sincerity. The best way to do that is by their actions. I remind them that they should not degrade themselves by thinking that as ex-convicts they will always be criminals.

I urge them to change their souls and be models to those outside. I call them "dear citizens" to their faces. I let them know that I do not look down on them. I am convinced that they have increased their production by 20 to 30 percent compared to the prewar period. As they are contributing so much to the country I would like someone to calculate the number of hours they work as overtime or the amount of work they actually perform, so that their time in prison can be shortened by that amount.[64]

So much for his attitude to "the most important commodity." Who can doubt his sincerity, in view of his actual words spoken in parliament in the middle of a war? No other member of parliament, it is safe to say, could have taken up the issue of prisons. He rose naturally to the challenge, and he learned to have empathy for those at the bottom of society from his own experience of prison.

Not without reason he called his party the Patriotic People's Party. He liked the name. It was perfectly natural for him to address his message to society on the tenth anniversary of the party to the "Dear hundred million brothers and sisters" of his country.

One day, on being thanked by someone he had helped out, he responded:

> All the one hundred million children of the emperor are brothers and sisters, and it is only natural for a brother to help out another in need.... It is a human obligation and one's right to do so. I enjoy being on the helping side. When you succeed later, keep this in mind and help others...and serve society. You need not write me a long letter of appreciation at a time when goods and energy are wanting. Now, you are in the rut of misery. Put yourself to trouble on behalf of others once good fortune has come your way, and you will be the richer for it.[65]

"No reason to oppose democracy"

The political changes propelled by the United States after the war left many in Japanese politics floundering. He "found no reason to oppose the democratization of Japan, which had come about as a result of accepting the Potsdam Declaration."[66] As stated earlier, he "had gone into politics fired by democratic principles to represent the interests of the people." Nonetheless, it was a crucial moment for Sasakawa, as for all Japanese. Many of the myriad right-wing groups in the country dissolved and disappeared. Sasakawa pressed on. His party — originally the Patriotic People's Party before the war, then the Patriotic Alliance (Kokusui Domei) during the war — changed its name again to the Japan Workers' Alliance (Nihon Kinrosha Domei). Sasakawa, however, did not participate in the Japan Workers' Alliance (JWA). He had made up his mind to be sent to prison, and there was a high possibility that he would be executed as a Class A war criminal suspect, or so he believed, going so far as to prepare a tomb for himself in the Kansai. However, he actively supported his old PPP comrades Fuji Yoshio and Yoshimatsu Masakatsu in leadership roles within the renamed party.

Professor Maruyama's criticism

In due course — years after the end of World War Two — Japanese historians analyzed the fate of the nation's many right-wing groups. Foremost among these scholars was Maruyama Masao of Tokyo University. His studies of postwar nationalism in Japan included essays gathered together in his *Collected Works*.[67]

In one such essay he noted how Sasakawa and his colleagues re-named their wartime Patriotic Alliance as the Japan Workers' Alliance. Maruyama pointed to the JWA as an example of a right-wing organiza-tion that ostensibly changed its colors, but in fact simply took down one set of signboards and repainted them in democratic hues, while in fact retaining the same people and all the characteristics of the old party. Maruyama's point might have applied to many right-wing groups and to some members of the old PPP, who professed new democratic faith while clinging fast to their rightist ideals, though not to their former leader. Sasakawa had no need for repainting the signboard.

Back in the 1930s, when right-wing groups had sprung up like bamboo shoots after a shower, the PPP stood out due to its brilliant cam-paigns.[68] This had much to do with Sasakawa's able leadership, his power of action, his gift of self-expression, and his commitment to his people. He was a born leader who faced the post-1945 era head on.

V

His tenets

We now turn to Sasakawa's beliefs. They were the core of what defined the PPP. His basic tenet was his concept of "brothers and sisters" — the universality of humankind. He applied this not just to his countrymen and women but to all peoples of the world, regardless of ethnicity and across national borders.[69] In his vocabulary the word *kokusui* or "patri-otic," as found in the name of his political group Kokusui Taishu-To (Pa-triotic People's Party), alluded to the beautiful old traditions of Japan and absolutely not to a chauvinistic ultra-nationalism of the type found in the 1930s.

For Sasakawa, the reign — the existence, not the rule — of the em-peror was the foremost feature that constituted the "enviable tradition" of his country. Along with this went the values of filial piety and the love of parents for their children. Parents and children were all children of the emperor and formed "an inseparable unity." He liked to say that "the love between a mother and her child" created an inseparable bond, as was the case between Ryoichi and his own mother. The parents' protec-tion of their children and the children's devotion were "the spirit of Ja-pan." "Anyone who does not understand this is not worthy of being Japanese, nor a child of the emperor."[70]

Today, his slogan "The World Is One Family. Human Beings Are All Brothers and Sisters" comes to mind. From his point of view this was a continuation of his prewar thinking, and not an abandonment of his prewar position. So to nurture universalism, total freedom from racial prejudice, was the fourth characteristic of his PPP group.

Taiwan and Korea

Sasakawa applied his notion of universalism first to those neighbors in Asia whom Japan had colonized a century earlier. He saw the concept of "brotherhood" working in the cases of Taiwan, colonized in 1895, and Korea, annexed in 1910. Their peoples, according to him, had "thereby become Japanese — the children of the emperor."[71] He applied the same notion of "brotherhood" to those other neighbors in Asia whom white imperialists had colonized. His thinking was expressed in a manifesto that Sasakawa issued on behalf of the PPP on its tenth anniversary in early 1941. The party's "avowed objective," he said, was "to save our one billion brothers in Asia from untold suffering and misery."[72] He developed his thinking on this subject in remarks he made in the Imperial Diet in the thick of World War Two in 1943:

> I speak as a frequent visitor to Korea and Manchuria. Friends from the Korean peninsula say that they want to become "true Japanese," especially now. However, certain obstacles hamper them. They say that, while "true unity" is encouraged between Japanese and Koreans, still they are aware that their treatment is not equal. If we call them "children of the emperor," they say, they want to be treated just like real Japanese. To begin with, there is no equal treatment even in such a simple matter as crossing the Korea Strait by boat between Pusan and Shimonoseki. Koreans, including those of high rank, are required to show their identity cards. But no Japanese, even a jobless tramp, is required to present a document of any kind.
>
> Second, Koreans who finish school and pass the high-level civil service examination equivalent to the Class 1 examination for elite bureaucrats in Japan are not offered promotions to compare with those accorded their Japanese counterparts with inferior exam results to theirs. Third, let me mention a matter that applies to all Koreans living over there on the peninsula. A good Korean friend of mine who uses a Japanese name and speaks Japanese as well as any native, says that Koreans are not allowed to enter Japanese schools. My friend had expected his child to be treated as a Japanese, but when the time came for him to be enrolled the child was rejected. The child now realizes that he is different and begs his parents to explain to him why he cannot go to school with his friends.[73]

In these remarks in parliament, made in wartime, Sasakawa stops short of showing sympathy for Korean nationalism or for Korea's wish for independence from Japan. His remarks reflect the times, and for that one has to make allowances. It was a time when full Korean independence from Japan still seemed out of the question. To become a Japanese national was the only way for Koreans to achieve equal treatment. However, it does not require great perspicacity to detect a vein of thinking — of sympathy for Koreans in the street — that few other members of parliament would have considered, let alone voiced in the Diet.

Once Korea obtained its independence, on 15 August 1945, Sasakawa turned sympathetic to the cause of Korean nationalism and became respectful of their independence as his homage to the tomb of An Dhung-gun (1879-1910, a Korean independence activist shows. He had been executed for murdering Ito Hirobumi, the Japanese prime minister and former governor-general of Korea). A cynic could say that he cut his cloth to the times. But it might be closer to the truth to say that he showed his universal respect for humanity when the time came in 1945. When Korea was Japan's colony he pushed for Koreans to be treated on the same footing as Japanese. Once the nation regained its independence it was only natural for him to show respect for Korean patriotism.

Lessons for a Chinese visitor

This attitude was clear even before the war as regards China, which was never a colony of Japan. Sasakawa tended to take an unambiguous stand when faced with something he did not like. When a visitor from China asked Sasakawa for an introduction to the Japanese military authorities, saying that he would like to work for Japan. Sasakawa brusquely turned him down, saying:

> I expect any Japanese or Chinese — it makes no difference which — to be true to his country. As a Japanese I will work for Japan, and I would like to be of benefit to China.
>
> You are Chinese, so you must first work for China, and then think of ways to be of use to Japan as well. That is the way to create goodwill and unity between the two peoples. You tell me that you want to work for Japan rather than for your own country. Japan does not need any Chinese who forgets his country like that. Therefore, I decline your request for an introduction."[74]

Asked by the Chinese visitor for advice — the man was seemingly hard-pressed — Sasakawa responded that:

It is unreasonable to ask any Japanese to forget Japan and work for China. By the same token, it would not be right for a true Japanese to ask a Chinese person to forget his country and work for Japan. Nothing comes of such unreasonableness. If you want my friendship in the future, please observe the following six rules. One, be so kind as to point out what I and my country lack. Two, tell no lies. Three, be strict in your use of time. Four, dispense with formalities. Five, keep your promises. Six, please do not treat me to dinner.[75]

Wang Zhaoming

Sasakawa spoke his mind. Materials found in *Sasakawa Papers* show that he made numerous trips to China during the war years, times of tremendous tension between the two countries, and in turn received visitors from China in his capacity as a Japanese member of parliament.

He was on friendly terms with Wang Zhaoming (1883-1944), a senior Chinese politician who had studied at Hosei University in Tokyo. Wang had worked with Sun Yatsen (1866-1925), the first president of the Republic of China, and later in life, when China was riven with conflict, served as a pro-Japanese leader based in Nanking.[76] A first meeting between Sasakawa and Wang took place in Shanghai — we do not know exactly when. The family papers show that Sasakawa spoke out bluntly in a manner indicating that he played a certain role in Sino-Japanese affairs although not in the government.

He told Wang:

I have pioneered to have your government recognized in Japan, so I am accountable to my people for whatever happens to your government. Let me tell you about myself. I always seek as friends those who are ready to point out my shortcomings and who stand by me in hard times. Therefore, I am kind to others. Up to now Japanese people who have visited Your Excellency must have brought you fine presents. I have brought you the gift of my soul, which I am now glad to bare. If you do not like it, still please accept what I say in the spirit of what I have just said.

The key to good government is to satisfy as many people as possible. For this, one must listen widely to the people's grievances as well as their hopes, and do all in one's power to help them realize their dreams.

I have visited your country a dozen times, and have asked those I have met in every walk of life for their candid views as to why Chinese people continue to support Chiang Kaishek, even though he is responsible for repeated defeat in battle. I have inquired how popular support can be turned away from the Chiang regime in Chungking to the Wang government in Nanjing. I shall now report to you my findings.[77]

What Sasakawa said then, we do not know. There is no official report. But he must have spoken sharply, to judge from his own notes. He recorded that "members of the [Wang] traveling party all turned pale with astonishment."[78] A staunch nationalist himself, Sasakawa did not trust foreigners who had no love of their own country or government leaders who did not have the support of their citizens, even if they were well disposed toward Japan.

The issue was evidently one of trust.[79]

The eight corners

Sasakawa's transborder doctrine of brotherhood and sisterhood, it is clear, had something in common with the doctrine of "Hakko Ichi'u" (Eight Corners of the World under One Roof), which served as a slogan for Japan's overseas adventurism in the 1930s.[80] Furthermore, Sasakawa's postwar saying, "The World Is One Family. Human Beings Are All Brothers and Sisters" was derived from "Hakko Ichi'u," according to Awaya Kentaro, a critic.[81] Another noted slogan of the prewar era," our one billion brothers in Asia," has its foundation in the Pan-Asianism of the era and served as a powerful ideology used to legitimize Japan's advance overseas. For Sasakawa, these slogans meant realizing world peace and liberating Asian peoples suffering under the yokes of the Western colonial powers, Britain, France, and the Netherlands. One could criticize him for hypocrisy for not arguing the case for the independence of Korea and Taiwan, if he was serious about liberating Asia. This is logically possible, but it was just too unrealistic a proposition at the time.

What is important in all this is that there was no essential difference between the Sasakawa who led the PPP before the Pacific War, and the one who touted the high-sounding cause of "The World Is One Family. Human Beings Are All Brothers and Sisters" after the war. This does not mean that he covertly remained a nationalist after 1945, but that his version of nationalism did not conflict with open internationalism from the beginning.

Watching the world

Sasakawa's internationalism far transcended "Pan Asianism" long before war broke out in the Pacific in 1941. When Italy invaded Ethiopia in

1935 some members of his NVFS wanted to join an Ethiopian Air Force. "They felt righteous indignation that Italy, which regarded itself as one of the world's civilized powers, should bully a small, less-developed state, and were determined to back up Ethiopia without fear in the face of Mussolini's black shirt [brigades]."[82] While he was sympathetic to the feelings of his men, Sasakawa could not agree to them joining the Ethiopian forces to fight Italy under the prevailing conditions.

However, on 3 August 1935, he organized and chaired an Ethiopian evening in Osaka, and he invited those connected with Ethiopia and living in the Kansai region to attend. The meeting passed a resolution to establish a Japan-Ethiopia Association, in order "to crush the despotic ways of the white race and to fully assist Ethiopia."[83]

But some years after that Sasakawa, in common with Japanese officialdom, became a supporter of the Japan-Germany-Italy axis. He underlined his position in no uncertain way in late 1939 and early 1940 by flying to Europe in his plane, the *Yamato,* and paying a courtesy call on Benito Mussolini in Rome.[84] This was far from being consistent. But by then Italy's control of Ethiopia was a fait accompli. The Japanese were in a dilemma: whether to build an anti-white alliance to oppose white colonialism, or tie up with Germany and Italy, the "late modernizers," and fight against the vested interests of the "early modernizers," meaning Britain, the United States, and France; or to succumb to the whims of the United States and other leading powers. This was a dilemma broadly shared among the Japanses at the time. And Sasakawa too was unable to solve this paradox. Given the international milieu, the nonwhite alliance was the worst option, as an "alliance of the weak," and as such it ran counter to Japan's national interests. To collaborate with the Anglo-Saxon powers was the safest choice, but this meant vindicating world domination by the whites and the vested interests of the advanced nations. The Axis Alliance provided a middle alternative not as weak as a nonwhite alliance, but it was nonetheless a weak alliance among the late modernizers, and represented a risk. The middle course provided a choice that could gain considerable support within the nation.

How had this come about? The Great Depression of the 1930s had triggered a rift between the advanced countries and the late modernizers, including Japan. As Japanese products became the targets of boycotts in the home and colonial markets of the major industrial nations, it became progressively harder to align with the Anglo-American side. This became a non-choice. It did not help that Asian countries were colonies under the domination of the Western powers — with the exception of the two Japanese possessions, Korea and Taiwan. In fact "solidarity" with these colonies ("Asian solidarity" was the slogan) had strong support in Japan. The Second World War had already begun in Europe and it seems not altogether unreasonable, in order to advance the cause of Asian solidarity, for Sasakawa to have judged that it was good to establish ties with Germany. It did not escape him, of course, that Germany appeared to be faring well in the early stages of World War Two.[85]

A constant traveler

Sasakawa was an inveterate traveler. He paid frequent visits to foreign countries long before the Pacific War. This was hardly strange for one who was curious about conditions outside Japan and who loved to fly. This may be seen as a fifth point that set Sasakawa apart from other rightists back in Japan.

As far as I know, his first trip overseas was in March 1932, immediately following the establishment of the Japan-sponsored republic of Manchukuo and half a year after the Manchurian Incident of 18 September 1931, when the Japanese military blew up a major railroad, triggering the start of fifteen years of conflict with China. With the permission of the military, Sasakawa led a group from his PPP to Manchukuo, taking with him as gifts some five hundred barrels of pickled vegetables and three hundred bottles of top quality sake from Nada. This was to "comfort" Japanese army officers on duty there, and to congratulate Pu Yi, the newly designated titular monarch of Manchukuo and the twelfth and last emperor of the Manchu Dynasty — the "last emperor" of China.

Sasakawa continued his journeys overseas. Just going by published newspaper articles, he made fifteen visits overseas between 1932 and the end of World War Two in 1945. This is an astounding record, considering that he spent three years in Osaka prison (1935-1938) during that span of time, and always had a hectic schedule. This was all the more impressive in view of the poor standard of civil aviation and the risks involved in flying during the last part of the Pacific War when the United States had command of the air.

Whenever possible, Sasakawa liked to pilot his own plane, *Yamato*. Perhaps the most remarkable of his flights was the one to Rome. He was now flying constantly despite the fact that Japanese civil aviation was still at an early stage of development and fraught with danger. In 1938 a Japanese plane had made the country's first round-the-world flight. His flight to Rome the next year was the second longest ever made by a Japanese pilot. Today, one flies to Europe nonstop in eleven to twelve hours, but at that time Europe was several days away and a risky and expensive undertaking. To accomplish this, Sasakawa started out from Haneda in Tokyo, with overnight stops in Taipei, Hanoi, Bangkok, Rangoon, Calcutta, Karachi, Baghdad and Rhodes, and additional fuelling stops in Fukuoka, Guangzhou, Akyab, Jodpur, and Aleppo, before finally reaching Rome.

Flying to serve

Sasakawa liked to talk about his aviation thrills. In a 1942 interview, following his election to the House of Representatives in Tokyo, he is reported as saying:

> I make it a point to travel abroad whenever time permits. The reason is indeed simple. If one aims to be a patriot, one cannot afford being a frog in the well, knowing nothing of the great ocean. In every way, I seek as much as possible to expand my stock of information. Armchair theories, half-baked ideas and secondhand knowledge from newspapers and magazines can be very harmful, and do no good at all. I feel that I must share with the people what I have seen abroad with my own eyes and what I have heard with my own ears. Since I flew my *Yamato* to Germany and Italy during the New Year holidays of 1939-40, I have continued to fly.
>
> Last year I covered 150,000 kilometers in 380 hours, which translates as flying on average of at least an hour every day. I travel to bring news of Japan and what Japanese people are thinking, and to monitor international developments affecting our compatriots working abroad. I do my best to bring comfort to our brave fighting men, and at the same time to listen to their true voices, which I then communicate back to policy makers in Japan. In other words, I try to serve my one hundred million compatriots by listening to their grievances and by representing them.[86]

Some of those close to him were alarmed by his practices. His brother Ryohei asked him not to fly, because planes crashed all the time. Sasakawa admonished his younger brother, saying that it was too late to make a fuss after an accident. It was like fetching a doctor after a funeral. It was vital, he said, to take precautions to avoid accidents. Because of crashes, people are careful, therefore one can feel quite safe, he maintained. One has to be most careful when there are no accidents.

Materials found in *Sasakawa Papers* show that he knew the excitement and the danger of flying when air travel was at an early stage, having trained as a pilot. He knew that performance improved day by day, but he also knew the dangers inherent in flying. As a result, he was bold, but he was careful.

One day he was flying back from Shanghai to Fukuoka when the weather turned foul. The plane dropped until it was barely clearing the angry waves. The passengers were beside themselves with fear. A solemn-looking man with the air of a government official sitting next to Sasakawa asked him what he thought would become of them. Sasakawa replied that there was nothing to be done but to leave it to fate. Pilots want to live too and they do the very best they can. The passengers should trust their pilot to do everything possible. If the plane went down they would all share the same fate. There would be

> a big splash, and that would be the end of us.
> This is a time to cultivate your mind...it doesn't help to worry. In an hour we'll be in Fukuoka so use the time well for mental training. When one has learned to overcome the fear of death in a perilous situation like this, one can say he has achieved manhood. I used to be terrified of flying in the beginning, but not now. In the end, there is nothing more important than disciplining your mind.[87]

VI

Jail and trials

Sasakawa experienced tremendous ups and downs throughout his life. Thus it was in the 1930s. Prior to the Pacific War his greatest ordeal came in August 1935 when he was arrested, together with a dozen executives and members of the PPP, and summarily confined in Osaka Prison for three years, pending trial and without bail. The charges were extremely grave for one in the public eye. He was alleged to have ordered party members to blackmail outstanding companies — Takashimaya, a leading department store, Osaka Railway and Hankyu Railway, two rail companies in the region, Iridismin Mining, Tokyo Life Insurance, and Godo Electric.

The case dragged on and on while the prosecutors took their time. Finally in December 1938 the court of first instance handed down a verdict: seven out of a total of seventeen defendants were found not guilty on the grounds of insufficient evidence. One of these was Sasakawa. Ten of the defendants were found guilty and were sentenced to penal servitude of eighteen months to one year.

Still, this was not an end of it. The prosecution appealed, and the Osaka appellate court reversed the verdict on Sasakawa as the leader of the PPP. He was sentenced to two and a half years in prison (altogether six hundred days on remand). Two PPP executives were given sixteen months of hard labor in prison, but were given credit for pretrial detention. Two others were found not guilty. Sasakawa and the PPP appealed on the day the verdict was handed down. The highest court (Daishin-in) under the Meiji Constitution then reversed the original decision and sent the case back to the lower court.

These tangled and time-consuming legal proceedings finally came to an end on 9 August 1941 when the reconvened Osaka appeals court found all seventeen defendants not guilty.

A legal process that dragged on forever

It was a marathon case for Sasakawa who had never until then been in trouble with the law. Altogether, the legal process consumed a total of six years, from the day of the arrest to the final verdict excusing all the defendants. Not that the case was without its nonlegal side effects. The PPP suffered a massive setback as a result of its president and executives being held in custody for over three years, and then tied up for another three years of legal proceedings with no means of redress. It is no wonder that the party celebrated its tenth anniversary under the slogan, "The Tenth Anniversary of Adversity."

At that time, in the spring of 1941, the PPP executives had yet to be cleared of wrongdoing. It was a time of great uncertainty for the party and a period when party leader Sasakawa suffered, both physically and financially. An excerpt from the concluding statement by the prosecutor, of which a stenographic record is preserved in the Sasakawa family papers, attests to this. The prosecutor said: "It has taken a full two years (in fact, Sasakawa had served more than three years) to conclude the criminal investigation, so this turned into an unexpectedly long trial. I can imagine that it was an extremely trying time for the defendants."[88]

Sasakawa was severely restricted in his freedom to raise funds for the party. This was at a time when he had to look after not only his own family, but the legal and household expenses of all the men arrested and held in prison. There are indications, judging from the way in which events unfolded, that the police, the pretrial investigators and the prosecutors deliberately prolonged the trial. If this is true, the prosecutor who sympathized with the accused in his summing up could have been a hypocrite.

To top it all, the prosecutors and the media deliberately spread negative information about Sasakawa. On 18 August 1935 the Osaka edition of the *Asahi Shimbun* splashed a headline that read: "President Sasakawa Decides on PPP Dissolution: Tells Prosecutors He Reflects on Past Conduct." The prosecutors were very likely the source of this groundless report that upset rank-and-file members.

In fact, a lot was going on behind the scenes, as indicated by Sasakawa in remarks he made to the presiding appellate judge some years later:

At the very beginning, when I was confined in prison, the prosecutor incited my co-defendants and witnesses to take sides against me, claiming that I had used my men to amass bank deposits in the amount of hundreds of thousands of yen as well as property worth tens of millions, and that I had not, even then, sent anything to support and encourage them.

[He continued, still addressing the judge:] Two of the members of the party believed this to be true, having been so informed, and they resolved to kill me in revenge, and that was not all. Certain witnesses, incensed with righteous indignation decided to denounce me.

The prosecutors had invented a total fiction. Sasakawa completed his statement to the appeals court, saying: From the day of my incarceration in August 1935 to the day of my release from prison in 1938 I have not only had things sent to the men directly under my orders, but I have taken care of their families to the best of my ability. I beg you to question them.[89]

Acquittal after six years

The prosecutors in the lower court called originally for Sasakawa to be sentenced to six years of hard labor, and for sentences ranging from three years to ten months for the other sixteen defendants. At the end of it all, as we have seen, all seventeen executives of the party were acquitted. How is one to account for the wide gap between the prosecutors' initial demand for heavy sentences and the final complete acquittal? To judge by the statement made by the prosecutor to the appeals court, what counted most was a difference in perception of the real nature of the PPP as a party. According to the prosecutor's statement,

In the final analysis, I believe there was a drastic difference of perception regarding the PPP held on the one hand by the court of first instance, meaning the judges of this lowest court where the judicial process began, and on the other by the police, the prosecutors and the preliminary examiners. This is to say, while the original judgment had not clearly stated this, it could be deduced from reading the records and the decision that the court had deemed the PPP to be a patriotic organization professing nationalism. And it had seen the party conducting itself since its inception in numerous patriotic activities. It saw no grounds for criticism in that.

In fact, to see the PPP instead as an organized group of gangsters or to interpret individual actions as self-seeking publicity is wrong. In contrast to the court it appears to me that the police, the prosecutors, and the preliminary investigators, while not entirely ignoring particular actions — acts done for the state — come across as going out of their way to find any peccadillo, even a small amount of self-advertisement. These differences, I believe, have resulted in a large discrepancy in the decisions, amounting to two-faced or conflicting perceptions of the PPP, as stated above.[90]

The statement of the prosecution to the appellate court is an arbitrary one, signifying that judgment was made based not on evidence of concrete criminal actions but on a perception of the essential nature of the organization that is alleged to have created the incidents. This is almost confessing that the true purpose of the wholesale arrest of the PPP executives was to suppress the "dangerous" group.

According to the statement, the "essence" of the party was determined first by its principles and platform and second by actions taken by the party and its members. It raised an argument based on the dubiousness of the past records of the main members of the PPP. As to this second point, they were close to pressing mostly trumped-up charges.

To begin with, the prosecution avoided reference to Sasakawa's personal records, saying that he was not president but just an advisor and not a central figure at the time of the founding of the party. This implied that the police and the prosecution could not find any fact that could resemble a criminal act on his part.

Hatakeyama Yoshio, who was the head of the executive council of the party (*hitto somu*) and a central figure at the time of the founding, was picked on as having a past record of blackmail, and having been found guilty by the Osaka District Court in August 1930 and sentenced to prison with hard labor. Likewise in November 1934, he was sentenced by the Osaka Ward Court to three years of hard labor, also for blackmail.

However, Hatakeyama was not a defendant in the case that involved Sasakawa. The 1930 judgment predated the founding of the PPP. The case that was concluded in 1934 had nothing to do with the PPP, as the prosecutor of the appeals court himself stated: "Needless to say, the PPP probably had no knowledge of this." It was a strained interpretation to have used these episodes as grounds for arguing that the essential nature of the party was dangerous.

The prosecutor, in his statement, then proceeded to take up the case of Fuji Yoshio, another PPP leader who, again, was not a defendant in the case before the court. The prosecutor noted that Fuji had been sentenced by the Osaka District Court to prison with hard labor, having been indicted for inflicting grievous bodily harm, interfering with official business, violence, and blackmail.

As in the case of Hatakeyama, Fuji's indictment had nothing to do with the entirely separate case of alleged blackmail before the court. But still the prosecutor claimed that these cases illuminated the essential characteristics of the PPP. That was far-fetched reasoning. The prosecutor cited two other members of the party, Takada Takashi and Itakura Yazaburo, noting that they had been indicted by the Osaka District Court in 1929 and sent to prison with hard labor for committing acts of violence, for blackmail, and for interfering in official business.

These cases too, like those of Fuji and Hatakeyama, arose prior to the creation of the PPP in 1931.

The prosecutor of the appeals courts also introduced into his statement a selective polling of twenty adults by the police, asking for their reactions to the not-guilty judgment handed down by the court of first instance. The prosecutors claimed in their statement that only three out of the twenty adults approved of the decision, while the other seventeen were critical of it. "You judges and prosecutors really don't know how society works, do you? Don't think that we are that stupid!" was cited as one reaction. In exchange, the counsel for the defense asked for the names of those who had been polled. The prosecutor rejected the request, however, saying that he did not wish to cause inconvenience to the people who were polled.

It is wrong, in the first place, to take public opinion into account in a judicial matter. Needless to say, the opinions of twenty unidentified people have no value as a popular opinion poll, either. As to this matter, Sasakawa himself noted, as found in a document stored among the family papers, that:

> The police aimed to make us into social outcasts. They collected the views of those opposed to Sasakawa, and neatly presented them to the court. The prosecutor was embarrassed when asked to produce the names of those who had been questioned.[91]

Tough conditions in jail

The conditions inside Japanese prisons at that time were extremely severe. On this point Sasakawa noted:

> We were sent to prison at the height of the summer. The first winter, lacking any heating in the cells, was indescribable in its severity…we could have frozen to death. In the hot weather, the little draught that came through a crack in the wall could hardly be felt, but in winter it turned into a biting wind.[92]

In summer, the prisoners came under attack from lice, fleas, mosquitoes, and bedbugs. However, Sasakawa, the incurable optimist, used the experience to good effect, turning the hardships into mental training.

His friends asked him later how he had coped with the conditions. Kodama Yoshio, for example, who had himself had direct experience of living in prison, asked Sasakawa what he had learned from being inside. The latter responded positively as always:

> Human beings can change, depending on their level of maturity. There are, of course, different ways to cultivate the mind. Zen meditation is one. Coming through a grave illness is another. Or surviving under fire in battle. Or being confined in prison. I was lucky, in fact. I was sick when I was sent to prison. I had the opportunity of a lifetime. No visitors were allowed, no alcohol, no smoking, and no sex. In my case, three years of life in prison proved to be more effective than hundreds of years of Zen. Cohabiting with fleas and bedbugs was no hardship, always assuming that I had no guilty conscience. Living under a strict prison regime, I was able to conquer all my illnesses.[93]

He had suffered, he said, from scrofula, liver ailments, pleurisy, diabetic conditions, and gastro-intestinal ailments. On top of that, prior to prison, he had hankered after money, position, women, and alcohol, and he was overly sensitive to criticism by others. In prison he lost these disabilities. Once he could accept reality philosophically, the thunder on a stormy day sounded to him like heavenly music and earthquakes lost their power to frighten him. They just meant the earth was enjoying itself. After that, he thought of all his trials and tribulations as his sworn friends. Nothing, he found, no amount of thunder and lightning or severe earthquakes could shake his determination.

"Is there any better reward than this?" he asked. "Three years of imprisonment have made me what I am today," he told Kodama. "In that sense, I am forever grateful to the police and the prosecutors."[94]

> Whether one is in or out of jail, paradise is a place where one has perfect bliss. You must think that prisons are filthy, but it is not so. Prison is a pure and clean place where one's freedom is restricted, and where one practices austerities, nonsmoking, and abstention from alcohol. Your bed and board are free, and so is your health care. You are served your meals on time, and you have people patroling every five minutes to check if everything is all right. In conclusion, there is no better place than the cells to train your mind. If you have committed a crime, on the other

hand, it is hell, wherever you are. Only if one commits no evil, then one is in paradise, even in prison.[95]

The praying mantis

Sasakawa may be assumed to have been speaking the literal truth to Kodama, as found in his papers. The most memorable experience from his time in prison was the friendship he developed with an unexpected partner, a praying mantis.

> I bought some flowers while I was in prison. Along with the bouquet, as it happened, came a huge praying mantis. To while away my time while in solitary, and to study whether human love can be communicated, I decided to share my cell with him, as a partner in life. First I tried peeling a grape in the middle of a meal, offering it to him. But he just looked annoyed.
>
> He was too cross to eat it. At every meal, I tried again to share a grape with him, but he rejected my gesture every time. One day, however, whether out of sheer hunger or because he at last accepted my gestures of affection, the time came when he consented to nibble at a whole grape I had peeled for him. In the end, he would come to me for a grape at every meal.
>
> The cell was poorly ventilated, and it was boiling hot. So in the evening, he cooled himself by clutching onto the wire netting. At dawn, he would land on my head to say hello, and tease me with his whiskers to wake me up. He became a treasured member of my family. Thus, I confirmed the fact that human affection can be communicated to an insect. One day, it seemed to me that his time had come. Gradually, as I watched, his color changed and he took on the hue of dead grass. He seemed not to be able to see any more. He stopped moving about, and he even took no more water. I stroked the feelers at the tip of his tail and touched his leg, and he gently twitched.
>
> It was close to the end. He continued to breathe quietly, and he took a whole day and a whole night to fade away. He died as a drop of dew falls from off a leaf. I carefully observed his way of dying, and I came to see that nature keeps a peaceful death in store for the humblest of creatures. By contrast, we human beings pride ourselves as the lords of creation, but our end is worse than that of a praying mantis. We die such unnatural, artificial deaths. I felt that we must put aside the notion that people live, basically, to fifty. That way, I became convinced that we can die as nature intended. This conviction cured me of all illness. I

never used medicine again, and the color returned to my white hair.

This story illustrates Sasakawa's eternal optimism, as well as his warm-heartedness and his scientific mind.[96]

Learning the law in jail

Thanks to the prolonged trial, Sasakawa mastered ways in which to present himself in court. He learned the skills needed to fight a legal battle. One of his party members asked him about this, it seems. He wanted to know how Sasakawa came away from it without any conviction.[97] Sasakawa replied:

> It may happen that a doctor will make a mistaken diagnosis. In the same way, a good man can be mistakenly perceived as a villain. I spent three years in prison on remand. I experienced two trials during the next three years when I was out on bail. And after six years I was finally found not guilty.
>
> The secret is simple: one, I had in fact done no wrong; two, throughout the questioning and examination process by the prosecutors, in the preliminary hearings and in the first and second courts of instance, then the high court and finally the Osaka Court of Appeals, I stated nothing but the truth. Finally, I convinced them. I never pandered to the prosecutors or the preliminary investigators. I made no false presentations just to get out of prison, even if I wanted to. Three, I never played mean tricks or sought to get my fellow defendants indicted, nor did I try to conspire with them so that we did not contradict each other in giving evidence. As a result, the guiltless person that I am received a verdict of not guilty.[98]

Another of his associates asked Sasakawa what one should do if one came under suspicion. Sasakawa responded:

> Everyone wants to be released from prison as soon as possible. That is understandable. But the police and the prosecutors will not let you out until they have completed their investigation. And, just imagine you want to stay longer inside, they will not let you do so, once their investigation is over. So be composed and be patient. Always tell the truth under interrogation, and even if you are tortured or beaten.
>
> Never seek to appease them. It is your right to speak truthfully. It is not an obligation. Look at it that way. Work with the

person who is examining you, to establish the truth. Heed what
I say and the truth will come out. This remains the basic principle — to defend your rights and illuminate the truth.[99]

Years later when World War Two had ended, Sasakawa volunteered
to go to prison in Sugamo, as we shall see in the following chapter. He
was motivated by a desire to speak out in defense of the emperor and in
the interests of Japan at the Tokyo Trials. His successful experience in
winning his earlier legal battle gave him confidence that he alone could
do what he had in mind.

VII

1941-

After the outbreak of the Pacific War, following Japan's attack on Pearl
Harbor on 8 December 1941, Japanese politics evolved in a manner dictated by the government. The first elections held during wartime were
the twenty-first elections for the House of Representatives, the Lower
House of Parliament under the bicameral Japanese system, held in April
1942. These were extraordinary elections in that they were dominated
by the ad hoc creation of an entity the government called the Imperial
Rule Assistance Association (IRAA) (Taisei Yokusankai).[100]

The IRAA was headed by the prime minister. It was set up basically
to enhance support for the government through the election of a massive majority of members, all "recommended" by the IRAA, to support
the war effort. The way it worked was that the IRAA designated "desirable candidates," and provided them with various means of support, including money.

On the other hand, the "non-recommended candidates," as they
became known, meaning all those outside the scope of the IRAA, were
officially regarded as undesirables from the government's point of view,
which was to give utmost priority to the war. The campaign activities of
"non-recommended candidates" were markedly restricted. All public
meetings and election rallies were observed by the police, who could
suspend such meetings at will. Posters were torn down as soon as they
were put up.

Not that the system was totally foolproof. There were still eighty-
five successful nonofficial candidates for the 466 seats that were open to
contest, who had dared to campaign without backing from the government. This number is impressive on the high side in that the Japanese
military were brilliantly successful in the early phases of the Pacific War,
and to stand aloof from them invited violent repercussions.

Sasakawa, entering national politics for the first time, stood as a non-recommended candidate for the fifth electoral district in Osaka, the core constituency in the Kansai region that returned four members to the Lower House. He was elected with the second largest number of votes, attracting just one thousand votes fewer then the top candidate in the district, and fully ten thousand votes ahead of the next candidate.

Wartime member of parliament

Sasakawa decided to stand "because the prestige of an elected member of parliament was at its lowest" at the time, and he wanted to do something to bolster the legislature. Indeed, members were extremely restricted as to their actions. Once elected, in order to speak, everyone in parliament had to become a member of the Imperial Rule Assistance Political Association (IRAPA) whether they had stood as "recommended" candidates or not in the elections.

This IRAPA was the parliamentary arm of the umbrella organization. Sasakawa became a member of the group, having no choice in the matter, but for good measure he kept his PPP going. It was his way of expressing his resistance to total conformism. However, as the war went on and the situation deteriorated, he came under pressure and was obliged to change the party name to "Patriotic Alliance" (Kokusui Domei). "*To*" or "party" signified in Japanese a degree of independence — a special interest group, and not a general interest one — and "*taishu*" or "People's" had a populist tinge that made the wartime authorities uncomfortable.

Sasakawa was far from content. He felt himself put in an awkward position. Asked by a magazine reporter at the time "what do you consider the hardest thing in recent times?" he responded:

> I had intended to serve my country as a spokesman for my one hundred million brothers, as long as I live. But in a period of centralized control when the government decides everything, even the elected representatives of the people are controlled by the IRAPA. It pains me terribly that I cannot be useful, even one hundredth part of what I would like.[101]

He made his dissatisfaction known. Using his authority as a member of parliament Sasakawa called for the abolition of the system under which certain candidates were "recommended" by the authorities and others not. He called for the deletion of Article 7, Sections 2-4, of the Wartime Special Penal Code (Senji Keiji Tokubetsu Ho), a draconian law that greatly limited freedom of speech; and he urged especially strongly the abolition of an infamous "provisional law" (Genron Shuppan Shukai

Kessya nado…Rinji Tori Shimariho) giving the authorities powers to control the rights of speech, publication, assembly, and association. His chosen forum was the Diet and there he gave his views regarding the system of "recommended" candidates in his blunt way, as he did, for example on 6 February 1943 when he addressed the Budget Committee of the House of Representatives. The war was starting to go very badly it had become much more difficult to criticize the government:

> At present, the people are all rallying in support of the Tojo government. We do not receive stipends from the State, but we are resigned to living under strict government control, and prepared to sacrifice ourselves, if need be, at a time of national crisis. Every single one of us goes along with this. In the last election, however, the government constantly talked of the need to resolve strife within the country and the need to enhance a law-abiding spirit. Our people are law-abiding. What good reason do you have to divide the emperor's children into foes and friends by making such rigid distinctions between those members of parliament who were recommended and those of us who were not?
>
> I am not raising the issue just because I was not recommended by the government. A kind word from the prime minister to me — I received such assurances from his secretary, Mr. Akamatsu — is all that it takes for me to forget the matter. But let me say this. Elected members of parliament are elected. There is no difference between those who are "recommended" by the government and those who are not. I happen to know one member of parliament who is much embarrassed because he was recommended and people in his constituency now label him as the representative of the police — indeed, as a man who was recommended by the police, would you believe it. I beg you to ponder this.[102]

Not an MP to keep quiet

Sasakawa did not let matters rest there. He was outspoken on other crucial subjects of that era in parliament, notably on the whole question of freedom of speech. He criticized the Wartime Special Penal Code and he attacked the provisional law just mentioned, that controlled speech, publication, assembly, and association — in roughly that order. He did so on the original grounds that suppression of the freedom of speech would impede the war effort.

Furthermore, he supported a formal proposal for deletion or abolition of the two laws in question; this was jointly submitted by a handful of members of parliament including Sasakawa. The proposal stated in part:

> It is the essence of the national polity [*kokutai*] to allow free expression of opinion and uphold high public morale. In this spirit, to place trust in the loyalty of the people, respecting the basic principles of the constitution, and to be open-hearted and respectful and encourage honest discourse is of utmost importance.[103]

In other words, the proposal argued that recognizing freedom of speech in its various forms was far more effective than disallowing open exchanges of opinion between people when it came to carrying on a war. That was because it heightened loyalty and the will to fight. Needless to say, such assertions were unacceptable to the government of the day.

Sasakawa found himself at an impasse. Discouraged by the lack of scope for action in parliament, he shifted his focus to extra-parliamentary activities. He organized local town meetings, and he went on trips overseas. These were important activities for a man who considered that the role of a parliamentarian was to represent the will of the people. He made public what he thought, as best he could. Soon after his election in 1942 he wrote an article for the Osaka edition of the *Asahi Shimbun* about his aspirations as a member of parliament and criticizing the new system of "election by recommendation."

> An elected representative of the people must know more of the world than just the two cities of Tokyo and Osaka along with his home and the parliament building.... Mito Mitsukuni[104] was a great leader, because he had a profound knowledge of society. Government must make as many people happy as possible. Elected parliamentarians must go forth from the Diet building in Tokyo and see the world. This holds particularly true when our world as Japanese has expanded greatly to include Manchuria, Mongolia, China, French Indochina (Vietnam, Cambodia, and Laos), Thailand, Malaya, Burma, and the Dutch East Indies. As soon as this parliamentary session is over, I intend to fly to Manchuria.[105]

An itinerant parliamentarian

True to his word, Sasakawa embarked on his foreign travels, though Japan was at war. Indeed, according to the minutes of the House of Representatives, Sasakawa did not speak in parliament after its eighty-first session closed in 1942. He stuck to his independent line. When asked by the IRAPA to serve on its board and to oversee the lives of the people, he declined, saying that he was unable to discharge such duties as he would be kept busy on the mainland in China, and in Southeast Asia.[106]

The press of the time gives some hints as to his movements. From what I could glean from the newspapers, Sasakawa toured Manchuria's strategic border areas with the Soviet Union in October 1943. He visited northern and central China in November that year. In the following year he again went to China. While there, he kept an appointment with Wang Zhaoming, the head of the provisional government in Nanjing. In April 1944, he made yet another trip to China. In July, he was in Korea. With the war approaching its end, he still went on foreign trips. He was in China in April and May 1945. This was at a time when Japan had lost its supremacy in the air and overseas travel had become ever more dangerous as each month passed.

Visiting the jails

Sasakawa left almost no records about this dramatic period in his life, and the papers yield little. As for his activities within Japan, we know that he made frequent public speeches and that he was particularly interested in visiting prisons.

A single notebook exists dating to 1945. This is kept by his eldest son, Katsumasa. It is a small official notebook issued by the House of Representatives. Based on the entries in this notebook, we know that Sasakawa made visits to several prisons around the time of New Year's Day 1945. He was at Osaka Prison on 2 January, then at Kyoto on the following day, then at Nara on the fourth, at Himeji the next day, back in Osaka the seventh and Wakayama the day after that. He took presents and spoke with the inmates in the prisons in each city.

He was extraordinarily thorough in preparing his visits. Due to lack of communication, a planned call on the prison in Kobe on 6 January could not be arranged. On 8 March he spoke at Shizuoka Prison. His empathy for people in jail was very real, and to judge by these records Sasakawa put his heart into every visit. He did more. To cheer up those on the home front he gathered professional entertainers, who were at a loose ends at this low ebb in the nation's fortunes, and he established and headed the Japan Entertainment Company (Nihon Geino-Sha). He was not always present but someone close to him usually was. Sasakawa's faithful "companion for life," Shizue, was a member of the company and played the *biwa*, a four-stringed Japanese lute, and recited Chinese poetry.

A losing war

By early 1945, it was clear to informed parties, if not to the general public, that Japan was fighting a losing war. Early in this last year of the war Sasakawa was in frequent contact with Shigemitsu Mamoru, a distinguished diplomat and statesman, who served as foreign minister in the Koiso cabinet.

Shigemitsu resigned along with the rest of the cabinet in April 1945 and was succeeded by Togo Shigenori. However, with the installation of the Higashikuni government after the war ended, Shigemitsu was back in his old job as foreign minister. By this time Sasakawa was among his confidants.

According to entries in his 1945 diary, he and Shigemitsu met on forty-three occasions between January and September. Allowing for the fact that Sasakawa spent half a month in China between April and May 1945, he and Shigemitsu met frequently. In March they met fourteen times. They must have met on average every other day. On the night before the emperor broadcast Japan's surrender to the Allies on 15 August, the two were in the coastal city of Atami.

They also had a base in the capital. According to Shizue's recollection, Sasakawa had secured a Western-style home in Iikura, Tokyo, so that Shigemitsu, who had lost a leg, would have a comfortable place of his own in the event that his house was destroyed in the Allied bombing, which had by that time flattened 90 percent of the city. Sasakawa preferred a Japanese-style house, but he made this effort on behalf of Shigemitsu.[107]

Sasakawa had a bird's-eye view of the evolution of Japanese affairs at this time, but he was also a participant in events. As one who was close to Shigemitsu he must have had advance warning of the historic defeat that Japan was about to suffer. It is almost certain that Sasakawa knew ahead of time of the decision that the emperor should accept the Potsdam Declaration made by the Allies in late July 1945 calling for Japan's unconditional surrender. Yasuoka Masahiro, who was asked to go over the emperor's statement, did so apparently at Sasakawa's office in Ginza.

15 August 1945

Sasakawa has left a record of his state of mind at the astounding time of the surrender:

Although I expected the war to end in our defeat I put in my best efforts up to the very end as a fighting citizen. I can comfort myself at least on this score. I knew that there was nothing more that I could do now that the situation had come to this pass. I took heart, however, in reckoning to myself that I should foresee, as clearly as possible, all the events that would follow and do the best I could. The fifteenth of August duly came, and I found myself carrying out my plan.[108]

Sasakawa's calm is impressive. It is unlikely that Sasakawa is dissembling in his words above or just being wise after the event. He had decided, by that time, to make himself a defendant in the forthcoming war trial, and to do his best to put Japan's case before the court and defend the emperor from any suggestion of responsibility for the war.

Once it was clear that the Japanese government was about to accept the Potsdam Declaration, Sasakawa immediately began putting his affairs in order. On 14 August, on the eve of Japan's surrender, he decided to dissolve the Patriotic Alliance. He also dissolved his Japan Entertainment Company in the same year.

His main decision was to withdraw from parliament. On 7 September 1945, immediately after the end of the eighty-eighth extraordinary session of parliament, he tendered his resignation to Shimada Toshio, the Speaker of the House of Representatives, saying that this was "to assume my responsibility for approving the military expenditure [budget] and numerous wartime laws." The Speaker declined to accept his resignation and told Sasakawa that the resignation of a member required a resolution of the whole House. This did not satisfy Sasakawa. On 5 October he appealed to his parliamentary colleagues to resign en masse.

A call for resignation

A copy of his letter of appeal to his fellow parliamentarians is among the Sasakawa family papers. It reads as follows:

Gentlemen, fifty days have already passed since 15 August. Whereas the prospects for our defeated land are terribly severe, nothing has been done to prepare for the future as regards state policy. The bureaucrats among us have reorganized the National Youth Corporation (Zenkoku Seishonen-dan) and the Workers' Association for National Service (Romu Hokoku-Kai) but this looks like window-dressing and little more.[109]

In coping with the many issues that must inevitably be addressed at this point, and while taking into account the whole matter of relations between our country and the victorious powers, nothing less than a bloodless revolution can save our country from further decline. I fear that if we do nothing the situation will evolve contrary to our hopes. There can be a gradual hardening against us of public opinion among the Allied Powers. We would miss our opportunity to arouse the courage of the people, overcome all the hardships ahead, and build a new nation. Japan needs to start anew, as a peaceful state, and to earn the trust of the world. To do that the first consideration must be to replace our wartime leaders. The military no longer exists.[110]

Sasakawa then came to his proposal. Those responsible for Japan's first defeat and surrender in history must draw the obvious conclusion. They must pack up their bags and go.

In his words (*Ed:* underlined in the original text):

At this point our senior statesmen, the heads of our *zaibatsu* business groups and our bureaucrats must take responsibility. In other words, it is indispensable that our elder statesmen all return their honors and ranks and withdraw to their homes; the *zaibatsu* chiefs must resign from their position, and sever all ties with public life; as to the top-ranking bureaucrats, all those who rank above section chief [*kacho*] in the central government ministries, and all those above the rank of department chief [*bucho*] in prefectural governments should tender their resignations without delay.[111]

He continued with these sharp words, scolding his parliamentary colleagues by implication and probably aware that they might not take any notice:

Sad to say, it is a deplorable fact that these people have not the slightest remorse, however. I conclude that if we, the elected representatives of the people resign en mass first, then the others will surely follow our example. As you gentlemen will be aware, I have spoken up as a non-recommended representative in the House on a number of issues, drawing a line between right and wrong. I have studied ways to tender my resignation at the end of this extraordinary session, and I have learned that this requires the approval of the House. It seemed ungentlemanly to steal a march on my colleagues and to resign, and so I have reluctantly remained where I am.

My view is that the only way is for all of us, regardless of background, to resign together. If the House of Representatives acts thus, then the House of Peers will do likewise. Hopefully, this will pave the way for a nationwide "Showa Revolution" (Showa Ishin). With this short letter, I respectfully urge my wise colleagues to support my humble proposal.[112]

Sasakawa's appeal did not fall totally on deaf ears. Eighteen members of the House of Representatives responded to his call for a mass resignation, but the rest sat on their hands.[113]

The party changes its name again

At this crucial time, from Sasakawa's point of view, the question of war responsibility, the process of democratization, and the realization of a Showa Revolution were all one and the same. "Showa Revolution" had been chanted as a slogan all the time by the right wing in the early part of the Showa Era when there was a great deal of state control and a stifling atmosphere. To Sasakawa, "Revolution" *(Ishin)* meant "reform" — democratization and abolition of class distinctions.

Actually, Sasakawa felt the same way before and after the war. In that respect, he had not changed his views.

> As I have all along stood for the principles of democratic government, I see no reason to oppose a complete democratization of Japan, to be carried out by accepting the Potsdam Declaration in good faith.[114]

Here, a brief word is in order on the PPP and what became of it and its members at the end of the war. As already noted, they reorganized themselves as the Japan Workers' Alliance. Sasakawa supported what they were doing, but he refrained from joining them, as he had made up his mind to be incarcerated in Sugamo Prison along with General Tojo Hideki and other war leaders, as also mentioned earlier.[115] In fact, the Occupation authorities put pressure on the newly renamed group; its two main leaders, Fuji Yoshio and Yoshimatsu Masakatsu, were purged along with thousands of other figures from many walks of life. Under the new rules, they could hold no official post of any kind. All political activities were suspended. These moves came as a great shock, as may well be imagined. Yoshimatsu wrote to Sasakawa in prison, to sum up the situation outside:

> It's all over. Running for political office is banned, and all political activities have been prohibited. We are just so many living corpses. We say to each other, first things first, we should be in some kind of business, whether this is out of character for us or not, and make some money.[116]

Three months later Yoshimatsu wrote: "We are feeling gloomy over the future prospects of Japan. But perhaps those of us who were purged are no longer qualified to have views on the country or our people."[117]

By midsummer the situation was no better. Yoshimatsu wrote a pathetic note: "The Communist Party is destroying the country. Having been purged, however, all we can do is to watch with our arms folded. I am sorry."[118]

A prisoner in high spirits

Sasakawa, by contrast, was cheerful, for all that he was in prison facing a possible death sentence. He was in high spirits, day after day. He wrote to his downhearted friends outside, offering them constant encouragement, as we shall see in the next chapter. Just when Yoshimatsu was writing to him about "living corpses" in January 1946, Sasakawa was noting hopefully and positively in his prison diary: "Citizens of a defeated country, such as ours today, have the grave responsibility of doing their utmost to establish peace."[119]

These were no idle words. In fact, while in Sugamo, he drew up a "Permanent Peace Plan," intended to save humankind, and mailed a copy of this proposal to President Harry Truman in Washington.[120]

Meanwhile, Sasakawa wrote back to Yoshimatsu chiding him for his pessimism:

> There is no law or regulation that says a defeated country must unquestioningly obey its conqueror. We should resolutely put forward what is reasonable and just. Whether the victors will listen to us or not is their problem. Silence on the part of the defeated will stimulate arrogance and disdain on the side of the victors, and justice will perish. Defense of justice is the first obligation of every man. Anyone who fails in this duty is without worth or honor.[121]

How to run a business

Sasakawa encouraged his comrades, who had now been prohibited from engaging in politics, to go on the offensive. Knowing how impractical and unqualified they were for the world of business he wrote them offering guidance on the basics of trade.

> In business, success or failure depends on the seller, the buyer, and the employees. Therefore, make your customers happy and be sure to satisfy your employees. You are sure to fail if you forget that this calls for three-way coexistence.

Total cooperation is what counts. Business has its ups and downs, so take care not to spend wastefully when you are making a profit, because if you fail to control spending at that time, you will instantly go under when you suffer a setback.

Engrave it on your mind to save. Suppose you sold some item and gained a profit of 50 percent, but the price doubled the next day. You would have lost for selling a day early. A company only survives because it saves when the going is good and is prepared for bad times.

Do not forget this. Nothing can succeed if you do things absent-mindedly. Business has to be done at the risk of your life. I earnestly wish that you put your lives on the line and work together.[122]

He summed up: "Start by saving on expenses, then share your profit with your client, and then, and then only, make money. I ask you to practice what I preach."[123]

The leaders of the former PPP applied themselves to doing business as best they might. However, they lacked Sasakawa's touch, his knowledge, and his nerve. They operated on *samurai* lines — putting honor and personal relations before profit — and they were not successful. Years of painful endeavor followed during which they whittled away Sasakawa's remaining Tokyo real estate assets.

Fuji Yoshio wrote to Sasakawa on 15 October 1948, just before the latter was released, to report on the lackluster results of the group. Fuji mentioned that one of their comrades, lacking funds, "was barely able to pay the salaries of his staff." Another colleague was "getting into trouble for failure to pay his tax bill last year." A third person was "in great distress, along with his family and his friends and everyone in his circle." Sasakawa was the businessman. His men were lost without him.[124]

The PPP colleagues stay together

But still the old members of the party stuck together, struggling under the tough conditions of postwar Japan. Food was lacking and famine threatened at every turn. Much of the population was homeless, as the cities had been burned to the ground by Allied bombing. Employment opportunities were few or nonexistent, as most offices and factories throughout Tokyo had been destroyed. The black markets prevailed on many a sidestreet. All the prominent right-wing groups had collapsed and fallen apart under the combined pressure of the purges and the economic distress, as Fuji Yoshio reported to Sasakawa on 18 May 1946, naming several well-known leaders from the 1930s:

Yoshida Masuzo from Osaka, an orthodox rightist from the Great Japan Production Party (Dai-Nihon Seisan-To) and the Black Dragon Society (Kokuryukai); Akao Bin of Tokyo, president of the Great Japan Imperial Way Association (Dai Nihon Kodokai); Sasai Kazuaki of the New Japan Patriotic Alliance (Shin Nihon Kokumin Domei); the Japan Progressive Party (Nihon Kakushin To), among others, have all failed, and are no longer in sight.

Our party is the only one that remains in place, while others have transformed themselves. I am all the more in awe of your personal qualities and your love of humankind.[125]

Yoshimatsu wrote to Sasakawa on 25 August 1946: "We are struggling to do business, unfamiliar as it is." Sasakawa could do little for his men from inside Sugamo. There, momentous issues faced him — matters that had nothing to do with business, but a great deal to do with the future of his country as he saw it.

Notes

1. See Kurose Shojiro, *Sasakawa Ryoichi Den Yonotame Hitonotameni* [Sasakawa Ryoichi, a Biography: For the World, For Mankind] (Tokyo: Chichishuppansha, 2001), 17. This work ranks as a full biography, researched and written by a veteran businessman in Kyushu.

2. Ibid., 17, 19.

3. Ibid., 20.

4. Yamaoka Sohachi, *Hatenko Ningen Ryoichi Sasakawa* [Sasakawa Ryoichi: One of a kind] (Tokyo: Yuhosha, 1978), and Paula Daventry, ed., *Sasakawa: The Warrior for Peace, the Global Philanthropist*, 2d ed. (New York: Pergamon Press, 1987).

5. Known as *Sasakawa Papers* (Sasakawa Ryoichi Kankei Bunsho), they are now kept at the Nippon Foundation. There are no page references. Date unknown. Hereafter cited as Sasakawa, *Kankei Bunsho.*

6. Ibid.

7. Sasakawa Ryoichi, "Watashi no Teigen: Nikutai Nenrei 77 sai, Seishin Nenrei Jiyu Jizai" [My proposal: Biological age 77; Spiritual age, free], *Zenkoku Motaboto Kyosokai Rengokai Kaiho* [Bulletin of the Federation of All-Japan Motorboat Racing Associations], Fukuoka, 1 September 1976. (Hereafter "The Bulletin.")

8. Ibid.

9. Kawabata Yasunari (1899-1972) achieved prominence after World War Two, in 1968, as the author of the novels *Yukiguni* [Snow country] and *Izu no Odoriko* [The Izu dancer], and other works. He was the first Japanese to be awarded the Nobel Prize for Literature. The Stockholm judges preferred Kawabata, the older candidate, over Mishima Yukio.

10.   Sasakawa Ryoichi, *Jinrui Mina Kyodai* [Human beings are all brothers and sisters] (Tokyo: Kodansha, 1985), 162-63.

11.   Ibid. Sasakawa, never one to deliberately spread word of his private acts of generosity, was not known by the Japanese public to be close to Kawabata, a revered figure.

12.   Priest Harada was famous locally because he had been called on to recite Chinese poetry to the Emperor Meiji at the age of eight and was considered a child prodigy. See Kurose, *Sasakawa Ryoichi*.

13.   Yamaoka, *Hatenko Ningen*, 48.

14.   Ibid., 76.

15.   Nihon Gin Ken Shibu Shinkokai [The Japan Recitation, Dancing, and Fencing Association], *Sasakawa Ryoichi Kaicho to Zaidan 25 Nen no Eiko no Kiseki* [Chairman Sasakawa Ryoichi and twenty-five years of the glorious history of our association] (Tokyo: Nihon Gin Ken Shibu Shinkokai, 1993), 5.

16.   Yamaoka, *Hatenko Ningen*, 76.

17.   Sasakawa Yohei, *Chie Aru Mono wa Chie de Tsumazuku: Doro wo Kabutte koso* [A little knowledge can ruin a man: Be prepared to take the blame] (Tokyo: Crest, 1996), 17.

18.   This refutation by Yamaoka itself appears doubtful. Socialist ideas appeared in Japan long before 1914 and were treated by the authorities with horror. Japan's first Social Democratic Party, announced in 1900, was banned the day it was born. Socialism met fierce opposition, as seen in the case of Kotoku Shusui (1871-1911), who was executed for treason.

19.   Kurose, *Sasakawa Ryoichi*, 91. All of the above passage relating how Ryoichi ran away comes from Kurose.

20.   Ibid. See also Daventry, *Sasakawa*.

21.   Kurose, *Sasakawa Ryoichi*, 100.

22.   Sasakawa, *Kankei Bunsho*.

23.   Ibid.

24.   Ibid.

25.   Ibid.

26.   Ibid.

27.   Ibid.

28.   Not much has been published in the West on the subject of the many small right-wing nationalist groups that appeared in Japan in the 1930s — as international relations deteriorated around the world and Japan's "Fifteen-Year War" with China commenced. The late Professor Ivan Morris's seminal work *Nationalism and the Right Wing in Japan* ranks as a rare scholarly attempt to explore the ramifications of the Right as it evolved during the 1930s and Japan veered toward a collision with the United States and Britain. Morris, a professor of Japanese studies at Columbia University, found that Japan's right wing was divided into scores of small — often very small — groups, sometimes with surprising names, such as the Japan Hobgoblin Party. Sasakawa's Patriotic People's Party (PPP) was one of these small groups. He distinguished himself as its leader by his specialty in aero engineering and aviation.

29.   Historians consider that the "Manchurian Incident" began in 1931 and culminated in 1933 in the conquest by Japanese forces of the entire region of Manchuria. The intention of this lunge for control of the northern Chinese province was to enhance Japanese military security in the region, parts of which had been ceded to Japan by treaty, and to secure economic self-sufficiency for Japan. But in the words of historian Mark R. Peattie — (see the *Kodansha Encyclopaedia of Japan*) this action "instead propelled the nation along a perilous new path of foreign confrontation" with China and the United States, and led to Japan's withdrawal from the League of Nations in March 1933.

The Japanese conquest of Manchuria was seen as a major act of aggression. In a surge of criticism, US public opinion mobilized rapidly in support of China and hostility toward Japan. From this point, relations with the Anglo-Saxon powers in particular deteriorated at a rapid pace, leading to war in 1941. The "Manchurian Incident" — a Japanese euphemism that has entered the English language — was a turning point in modern history and helped to poison Japan's international relations. The generally accepted view is that the "Incident" was driven by middle-ranking officers in the Japanese Kwantung Army stationed in Manchuria, and in particular by Col. Ishiwara Kanji (1889-1949) and Col. Itagaki Seishiro (1885-1946); they and others who sympathized with their cause were able to bring about a shift in the initially very reluctant high command in Tokyo and thereby influence the whole direction of the nation still at that time under civilian control. Much that these army officers did was originally concealed from their superiors in Tokyo, and was entirely unknown to the public in Japan until very much later, by which time it was too late to turn the clock back. How much Sasakawa Ryoichi knew of these events at the time is open to question. Like most ordinary Japanese, he must initially have been kept in the dark.

Nonetheless, he and his party supported the creation of Manchukuo, a puppet state that replaced Manchuria in 1932, and in general adopted the right-wing Japanese positions.

30.   This theory was formulated by Minobe Tatsukichi, a professor of Tokyo University, and denied implicitly the right-wing nationalist claim that the emperor was divine.

31.   Sasakawa Ryoichi, *Sasakawa Ryoichi no Mita Sugamo no Hyojo* [Expressions of Sugamo, as seen by Sasakawa Ryoichi: Secret records of a "war criminal suspect"] (Osaka: Bunkajinshobo, 1947), 20-23.

32.   Prince Konoe was twice prime minister in the run-up to the Pacific War. He served in that post until the autumn of 1941; he handed over the reins of power that autumn of 1941, giving way to General Tojo Hideki, who thereby became Japan's leader in the Pacific War.

33.   Sasakawa Ryoichi, *Sasakawa Ryoichi no Mita Sugamo no Hyojo*, 20-23.

34.   Ibid.

35.   The colloquial term in English is "hara-kiri."

36.   Ichiki Kitokuro (1867-1944) was a professor of great distinction who served at the end of his career as chairman of the Privy Council. Earlier,

while a professor at Tokyo Imperial University, he was responsible for promoting the theory of 'the emperor as an organ of the state," the implication being that the emperor was not a deity. As a young man, he worked under Yamagata Aritomo (1838-1922), a further mark of distinction, given the latter's eminence as a war leader and shaper of early twentieth-century Japan.

37.   Ichiki and Minobe were both professors at Tokyo Imperial University. Neither was harmed by right-wingers, although both were singled out for criticism by the extremists and for many years must have felt their lives were in danger. The above direct quotation dates to 7 July 1935, and is found in the judgment handed down by the Tokyo District Criminal Court, Section 9. See Arahara Bokusui, *Dai Uyoku Shi* [Great history of the right wing] (Tokyo: Dai Nihon Kokumin To [Great Japan National Party], 1966), 218. The date of publication of this rare document is sometime after 1961.

38.   Sasakawa associated with some rough characters, some with criminal records, as was to emerge in court — see later in this chapter for an account of his three-year detention, (1935-38).

39.   Shihosho Keijikyoku [Justice Ministry Criminal Bureau], *Showa 15 Nen ni Okeru "Kokkashugi" Undojosei no Gaiyo* [1940 Outline of Nationalist Movements] (Tokyo: Government Publication, December 1940).

40.   Yui Masaomi, ed., *Kokkashugi Undo* [Nationalistic movements], vol. 6 of *Shiryo Nihon Gendai Shi* [Documentary material, contemporary history of Japan] (Tokyo: Otsuki Shoten, 1981).

41.   Sasakawa, *Kankei Bunsho*. See the Prosecutor's Conclusion at an Appeal Hearing (*Koso Shin ni Okeru Kenji Ronkoku*).

42.   The PPP, which may have had no more than a few score active members, was one of hundreds of ultra-nationalist organizations called into existence by the exigencies of a terrible age.

43.   We may note, however, the accusation made by Kodama Yoshio, while testifying secretly to the US prosecutors in Sugamo Prison in 1947, that Sasakawa had confided to a lawyer that he had received one hundred thousand yen from the Japanese military, a huge sum. Note also Sasakawa's indignant rebuttal of a charge by a Japanese general, also detained inside Sugamo, that he had taken a bribe from the army.

44.   Sasakawa, *Kankei Bunsho*. The PPP had changed its name to Patriotic Alliance (Kokusui Domei) by the time these remarks were made. This dates the comments to the wartime period. The party changed its name at the outset of the war under pressure from the authorities, who disliked its use of the words "people" and "party," seeing them as connoting communism.

45.   Koiso Kuniaki (1880-1950) was an army general who entered politics, served as minister of the colonies and governor of Korea, and took over as prime minister from Tojo Hideki in 1944. He was sentenced to life imprisonment at the Tokyo War Crimes Tribunal as a Class A war criminal.

46.   Kodama Yoshio (1911-1984) represented the Imperial Navy in Shanghai during the Pacific War. He made his reputation behind the scenes as a "fixer" par excellence, with ties to the underworld and with friends in high places in the Japanese war machine. After his release from Sugamo Prison in 1948, the US au-

thorities used him in a last vain struggle to halt the advance of communism in China.

47.   Kiyosawa Kiyoshi, *Ankoku Nikki: 1942-1945* [The dark diary: 1942-1945], ed. Yamamoto Yoshihiko (Tokyo: Iwanamishoten, 1990), 11.

48.   Toyama Mitsuru (1855-1944), a white-bearded, patriarchal figure, head of the legendary Kokuryukai (known in the West as the Black Dragon Society), was considered the grand old man of right-wing ideologists. Older than Sasakawa by forty-four years, Toyama was credited with having played a pivotal intellectual role in swinging Japan to the Right in the early twentieth century. His prestige at the time this diary was written placed him far above younger activists and fixers, such as Sasakawa and Kodama.

49.   Kiyosawa, *Ankoku Nikki*, 19. The implication here is that Sasakawa amassed his fortune by acting as a "ruffian and blackmailer." Kiyosawa does not mention here the fact that Sasakawa and his people had just been acquitted at the end of a six-year judicial process, which began with their arrest in 1935 and detention for three years on charges of blackmail.

50.   Sasakawa stayed away from politics when both men were freed from Sugamo Prison in 1948, while Kodama — a bullet-headed man with a shaven scalp, and by repute the big boss of the underworld — plunged into backroom politics, as seen in his fraught relationship with Tanaka Kakuei, prime minister from 1972-74, a principal figure in the 1970s Lockheed scandal.

51.   Sasakawa, *Kankei Bunsho.*

52.   Ibid.

53.   Ibid.

54.   Arahara, *Dai Uyoku Shi,* 345.

55.   Sasakawa Ryoichi, ed., "Kokusui Giyu Hikotai: Enkaku to Taiki" [National Volunteer Flying Squad: Its history and regulations], in Sasakawa, *Kankei Bunsho,* 10.

56.   Chiang Kaishek (1887-1976), Chinese leader and statesman, who took refuge eventually in Taiwan in 1948 to escape the communist revolution on the mainland. At the time referred to in this letter, he based himself in southern China as the nation's main military leader, allied with the United States and Britain as his strong supporters. The latter were sending him urgently needed supplies across the Burma-China border.

57.   It is not known how the two men came into contact and developed trust, apart from their common interest in technology and in aeronautics.

58.   Sasakawa, *Kankei Bunsho.*

59.   Sasakawa Ryoichi, "Bunsho Bango 6 Kokusui Taishu-to no Ryakureki" [Brief history of the Patriotic People's Party, document number 6], in Sasakawa, *Kankei Bunsho.*

60.   Shugiin [House of Representatives], *Shugiin Yosan Iinkai Dai-ichi Bunka Kai Giroku* [First Subcommittee of the Budget Committee] (Tokyo: Government Publication, 9 February 1943).

61.   Sasakawa, *Kankei Bunsho.* See Zenkoku Motaboto Kyososekosha Kyogikai [Japan Motorboat Racing Operators' Council], ed., *Motaboto Kyosoho*

Kokkai Gijiroku [Motor-boat racing law Parliamentary minutes] (Zenkoku Mo-taboto Kyososekosha Kyogikai, 1979).

62.   Ibid.

63.   Shugiin, *Shugiin Yosan Iinkai Dai-ichi Bunka Kai Giroku*. The force of this Diet interpellation lies in the fact that Sasakawa spoke up in behalf of Koreans. Here was Sasakawa taking an openly sympathetic position in the middle of the war when Korea was still under Japanese rule.

64.   Ibid.

65.   Sasakawa, *Kankei Bunsho*.

66.   Sasakawa, *Ryoichi Sasakawa no Mita Sugamo no Hyojo*. The declaration, formulated by the Allied Powers — chiefly the United States and the Soviet Union — in Potsdam, Germany, in late July 1945, called for an *unconditional* surrender. Japan's acceptance of the declaration was announced by the emperor in a radio speech on 15 August 1945, and led to the Occupation of Japan, which lasted from later that year until 1952.

67.   Maruyama Masao, *Sengo Nihon no Nashonarizumu no Ippanteki Kosatsu* [Nationalism and the right wing in Japan: A study of postwar trends], vol. 6 of *Maruyama Masao Shu* [The collected works of Maruyama Masao] (Tokyo: Iwanamishoten, 1995), 100.

68.   Arahara, *Dai Uyoku Shi*, 345.

69.   Compare his TV commercial slogan of the 1970s: "The World Is One Family. Human Beings Are All Brothers and Sisters."

70.   Sasakawa, *Kankei Bunsho*. Sasakawa believed that a mother's love for her child is universal, which it probably is. So apart from the emperor, things Japanese (*Nihon shugi*) had a common thread throughout the world.

71.   Military force was in fact used to impose Japanese rule.

72.   Meaning the yoke imposed by white colonialists — Britain, France, and the Netherlands — in colonizing much of China and most of Southeast Asia — Indochina, Burma, Malaya, Indonesia — and India.

73.   Shugiin [House of Representatives], *Shugiin Yosan Iinkai Dai-yon Bunka Kai Giroku* [Second Subcommittee of the Budget Committee] (Tokyo: Government Publication, 10 February 1943).

74.   Sasakawa, *Kankei Bunsho*.

75.   Ibid.

76.   From about 1940, during the latter part of Japan's fifteen-year war with China (1931-45), Wang ruled a region around Nanking with Japanese civilian and military backing. Meanwhile General Chiang Kaishek, basing himself in Chungking, firmed up his ties with the United States, rallying support for his cause in a struggle for power with Japan and also with Chinese communist forces under Mao Zedong, who was, however, still then not a strong military position.

77.   Sasakawa, *Kankei Bunsho*.

78.   Ibid.

79.   Wang died while receiving medical treatment in Nagoya in 1944.

80.   The saying "Hakko Ichi'u" is often supposed by non-Japanese to have been conjured up by the Japanese military of the modern period. In fact it

has a long history, dating back to the eight-century *Nihonshoki*, one of six Japanese national histories, published in thirty volumes, which date to CE 720.

81. Awaya Kentaro, "Tokyo Saiban eno Michi" [The road to the Tokyo trials], *Asahi Journal*, 5 April 1985.
82. Sasakawa, *Kankei Bunsho*.
83. Ibid.
84. Sasakawa was photographed wearing a formal kimono, standing with Mussolini.
85. Sasakawa abandoned a plan he had made for a call on Hitler to follow on his January 1940 call on Mussolini.
86. Eigasekaisha, *Eiga no Tomo* [Friends of the film] (Tokyo: Eigasekaisha, 1942).
87. Sasakawa, *Kankei Bunsho*.
88. Ibid.
89. Ibid.
90. Ibid.
91. Ibid.
92. Ibid.
93. Ibid.
94. Ibid.
95. Ibid.
96. Ibid.
97. Under Japanese procedures, it is rare for prosecutors to fail to secure a conviction once a person has been indicted.
98. Sasakawa, *Kankei Bunsho*.
99. Ibid.
100. This body was created by Prime Minister Konoe Fumimaro (1891-1945) in October 1940. In effect all political parties were disbanded and the newly created IRAA was in charge.
101. Sasakawa, *Kankei Bunsho*.
102. Shugiin (House of Representatives), *Shugiin Yosan Iinkai Giroku* (The Budget Committee) (Tokyo: Government Publication, 6 February 1943).
103. Sasakawa, *Kankei Bunsho*.
104. Mito (Tokugawa) Mitsukuni (1628-1700), was a promoter of Confucianism and its precepts in the Edo Era, best known for his compilation of *The Great History of Japan*.
105. *Asahi Shimbun*, 14 May 1943.
106. This was as reported in the *Asahi Shimbun* on 14 May 1943.
107. Shigemitsu had lost his right leg in a bomb attack by a Korean patriot in Shanghai in 1932, and he could not sit on a tatami floor.
108. Sasakawa, *Sasakawa Ryoichi no Mita Sugamo no Hyojo*, 18-19.
109. These were nationwide organizations.
110. Sasakawa, *Kankei Bunsho*.
111. Ibid.
112. Ibid.
113. Sasakawa, *Sasakawa Ryoichi no Mita Sugamo no Hyojo*, 62.

114. Ibid., 23.
115. Not that things went smoothly for his colleagues of the old PPP.
116. Yoshimatsu Masakatsu, letter to Sasakawa Ryoichi, 18 January 1946.
117. Yoshimatsu Masakatsu, letter to Sasakawa Ryoichi, 28 April 1946.
118. Yoshimatsu Masakatsu, letter to Sasakawa Ryoichi, 12 June 1946.
119. Sasakawa Ryoichi, *Sugamo Nikki* [Sugamo diary] (Tokyo: Chuoko-ronsha, 1997), 84.
120. Ibid., 117.
121. Ibid., 439.
122. Ibid., 434.
123. Ibid., 445.
124. Sasakawa, *Kankei Bunsho*.
125. Ibid.

Chapter 2

The Hero of Sugamo Prison

I

WHEN THE ALLIED POWERS — led by the United States — occupied Japan in 1945, they decided to purge the defeated nation's wartime leaders from public office as part of the sweeping postwar reform they imposed. In addition, the Allies arrested those whom they held responsible for the Pacific War and for committing atrocities.

On 11 September 1945, less than a month after Japan's surrender, arrest warrants were issued for thirty-nine notables, including Tojo Hideki (1884-1948), the wartime prime minister from 1941 to 1944, and the main members of his cabinets and also those who had been in charge of prisoner-of-war (POW) camps. On 19 November there were eleven more arrests, among them was General Araki Sadao (1877-1966), who served in key ministerial posts in successive 1930s cabinets, including minister of education.

The greatest number was arrested on 2 December, when fifty-nine people were detained. Among those taken into custody on that day was Field Marshal Prince Nashinomoto Morimasa (1874-1961), the fourth son of Prince Kuni; another was Hiranuma Kiichiro (1867-1952), a former prime minister and future Class A "war criminal" who was given a life sentence. Also arrested was Hirota Koki (1878-1948), a former foreign minister and a Class A offender, who was hanged in December 1948.

Finally, nine more warrants were issued on 6 December 1945. Among the personalities named on that day were Konoe Fumimaro (1891-1945), a former prime minister, and Kido Koichi (1889-1977), once a minister of the Imperial Household. Many arrests were made [but Japan's three-time premier, Prince Konoe, avoided detention by taking a fatal dose of poison].

An elaborate classification

The Allies devised an elaborate classification system to specify those whom they wished to hold responsible for the war. They grouped war criminal suspects in three categories, A, B, and C. The Class A prisoners were those considered responsible for the planning, preparation, commencement, and waging of "a war of aggression." Class B detainees were those alleged to have committed "war crimes" as violators of international law and conventions. Class C detainees were those held to have engaged in inhuman acts such as killing, enslaving, and persecution of civilians.

In addition, and quite separately from what was going on in Japan, several thousand Japanese military men and soldiers serving in other countries were taken as prisoners of war, arrested, imprisoned, and tried as Class B and C offenders by the judicial authorities of the Soviet Union, China, the Philippines, the United Kingdom, Holland, Australia and other countries.[1]

Sasakawa was one of the group of fifty-nine ordered to be detained on 2 December 1945 by the Supreme Commander for the Allied Powers (SCAP), General Douglas MacArthur of the United States. As noted, Sasakawa's group included Prince Nashinomoto, Hiranuma Kiichiro, and Hirota Koki. He was unusual among Class A war criminal suspects in regard to (a) the circumstances leading to his arrest; (b) his conduct while in prison; and (c) his dedication, following his release in 1948, in helping the families of convicted prisoners. He was never indicted, and that too made his case unusual [though others were similarly spared, for example Kishi Nobusuke (1896-1987), a future postwar prime minister, who had served in Manchukuo before the war as an economic overlord. Another person who was released after three years, without ever being indicted, was Kodama Yoshio.]

Formally, Sasakawa did not fall into any of the special categories devised to classify the accused war criminals. He had not served in any government organization or in any quasi-governmental institution such as the Manchurian Railway. The only very slight exception was his obligatory membership in IRAPA, a duty that had been forced upon him and all other parliamentarians when serving as a single-term "non-government-sponsored" member of the House of Representatives in 1942-45.

Long before that, going back to his youth, he had done three years of compulsory military service from 1918 to 1921, rising from private to lance corporal. Other than that service, which was in peacetime, he never wore a uniform. Class A suspects were military men — top-ranking generals and admirals — cabinet ministers, businessmen, and right-wing leaders. These included Ishihara Hiroichiro, a businessman, Kodama Yoshio, and Sasakawa, all of whom were were strong characters who had troubles with the Japanese authorities but rose to prominence nevertheless. Ishihara had served on the central council of the IRAA, and Kodama had acted as an outside or "part-time" agent of the Navy and other ministries in procuring war matériel overseas. He served briefly as a councilor of the short-lived postwar Higashikuni cabinet in 1945.

It takes two to fight

Sasakawa was unique in that he offered himself for arrest, imprisonment, and indictment as a Class A war criminal. He was open about his reasons for doing so; he wished to defend the honor of the nation against international criticism, he said. He believed that the way to keep up national pride and to maintain social order was to give testimony before the Allies-appointed International Military Tribunal for the Far East (IMFTE) and to speak out on the basic issues. [The IMFTE, it may be noted, was an ad hoc court dominated by the United States, which tried the accused war criminals from 1945 to 1948. It moved much more slowly than the trials of Nazi leaders held at Nuremburg in Germany and concluded in 1946.]

In short Sasakawa believed that responsibility for the war in East Asia and the Pacific could not be laid on Japan alone. Western powers had colonized the region for centuries and had dominated Asia to their great material advantage, and they had to share responsibility for events. He was especially critical of the Soviet Union for attacking Japanese forces in the last days of World War Two on 8 August 1945, one week before Japan's unconditional surrender, in violation of a prewar Soviet-Japanese neutrality pact.

To sum up, he asserted that it takes two to fight. Japan had not waged a "war of aggression," according to him. To think in such a way was hopelessly one-sided from his point of view. Human beings must struggle to survive once they are born, he maintained. To survive they must eat. To do that, given Japan's lack of resources and its large population relative to arable land, meant either to import food, or to acquire territory overseas to produce foodstuffs and raw materials, or for people to emigrate. However, the United States had suddenly erected tariff barriers in the 1930s to keep out Japanese exports, and had thereby dammed up and blocked the main source of revenue to pay for essential imports, notably oil. In addition, the US government had prohibited immigration from Japan. Thus America had "threatened our right to live. This compelled us to take the easy way out — to go into the continent [of Asia]" according to Sasakawa.[2]

All so much "spineless *konnyaku*"

Sasakawa's was an unusual voice of protest at the time. Hardly anyone else stood up to the Allies after World War Two to tell them Japan had a just cause. "The souls of the fallen soldiers can only rest in peace if others will play fair and square," said Sasakawa, citing his grievances in his diary.

> Some writers and political leaders have done great disservice to our people by sucking up to the US and by accepting their contention that we waged a war of aggression. They are the immortal enemies of the Japanese. Nosaka Sanzo is a case in point.[3] As for myself I have not once accepted the charge that Japan waged a war of aggression, I always argued otherwise. Although mine is a logically sound argument it may not be accepted at this time. When calm returns, however, the soundness of my position will become clear to all.... A couple of days ago the *Yomiuri Shimbun* carried an article by one Ishikawa Tatsuzo exaggerating the Nanjing incident.[4] By writing a piece such as that he may have curried favor but at a huge cost to all other Japanese.... Traitor Nosaka who fled the country at a critical time enjoys the limelight as a hero of the century.... Our people who treat him thus are insane. What a paltry lot we are! Before long the United States will begin to consider us unworthy of their attention. I had thought us to be a spirited lot, but no we are spineless *konnyaku*![5]

"Let Japan turn to the United States"

Sasakawa was incensed by the duplicity of those intellectuals who served as puppets of the Japanese military during the war, and turned around completely after the war to criticize Japan's "aggression."

> I have no words to sum up my feelings about those opportunistic writers who played up to the military clique in command when they held sway and flattered their bravery, and who now compromise Japan's position as the shameless turncoats unwilling to use their pens to rebut the victor's claims. Instead they have gone as far as to say that it was a war of aggression even without being invited to do so by the US Army.
>
> It is too pathetic for words. These are the real instigators of war. And yet they have the nerve to denounce us. This is what is meant by the audacity of the thief. It is wrong to think that the

wise American military would trust those dangerous and un-
trustworthy characters that pay lip service to whomever is in
power, but betray us in their hearts. In the near future thoughtful people will most certainly dismiss them, I am sure. Without
that it is impossible to make Japan into a truly peace-loving
country. It is these sorts of things that make me grieve for the future of our two countries.[6]

Such views as he expressed here might suggest that Sasakawa
leaned toward exonerating the Japanese military for its conduct during
the era of militarism (1931-45). However, he was a constant critic of the
arrogance of the Japanese Army and the poorly managed military administration on the battlefield long before the defeat. While in prison he
noted down his wish that the US Occupation not repeat the mistakes of
the Japanese military and thereby damage Japan-US relations in the long
run:

Because the Japanese military clique took into their confidence
only the sort of people who pleased them with flattery, they
aroused the antipathy of ordinary people in Japan before long.

"General MacArthur, US officers, and men," he wrote in his diary, "do
not make the same mistakes as the Japanese military. I say this in the interest of world peace."[7]
He continued:

Japan has two options for the future: to depend on the communist Soviet Union or on the democratic United States of America.
It is clear that 90 percent of the Japanese will depend on the
United States and become their good brothers and sisters, if the
United States acts on its promises and governs well. I earnestly
pray for our people that this will be the case. In my wish to know
what really went on, I made it a point every time I visited China
and Manchuria during the war to ask both Japanese and Chinese
with principles to give me their frank views of the Japanese military government. What I learned from them was diametrically
opposed to what I read in the newspapers that toadied up to the
military.

That was proof that the military heard only what they wished
to hear. As a result of avoiding the counsel of those who truly
loved Japan and China, our military only antagonized the Chinese people, for whose good the administrative measures were
intended in the first place. Fearing that we were losing the
hearts of the Chinese people I gave the brass some advice. All

they did was to ridicule me for my "myopic and mistaken views" of the Chinese. It is this sort of self-righteousness that led to our defeat in the war.[8]

"Cowardice!"

At a time when the world was entering the cold war Sasakawa held un-compromising views on the Soviets. He considered the Western powers accountable for war to the extent that they had practiced discriminatory policies against Japan, but he reserved his strongest and most vocal criticism for the Soviet Union as the true aggressor. In a passionate letter dated 6 May 1946 that he wrote from Sugamo and addressed to "Mother and my dear friends," he said:

> It is simply outrageous for the Soviet Union, the paragon of an aggressor state, to sit in judgment at a trial condemning Japan all the time as an "aggressor." Japan lost to the United States but not to the Soviet Union since we did not even fight each other. Our politicians and lawyers should advise the Soviet Union to decline the invitation of the United States to sit on the International Military Tribunal for the Far East. It is shameful that our people cannot even speak up about it.
>
> I have been looking forward to giving a piece of my mind to any Soviet judge or prosecutor who comes to investigate me, but they do not. Cowardice on the part of the Japanese is based on a very real fear that they may be imprisoned as American sympathizers in the event, however unlikely, that the United States and the USSR go to war and the United States suffers a defeat. For the same reason, namely cowardice, they do not criticize the Japan Communist Party for its insolent behavior, whatever it says.[9]

It may be hard to imagine today but not a few Japanese intellectuals believed that revolution was imminent and that a Communist government would be installed in our country. So they refrained from anticommunist remarks of any sort just after the war.

Sasakawa was stung into action. However ineffective this might be given the situation, he endeavored to get a dialog going with US leaders by writing letters to them from his prison cell. Addressing President Harry S. Truman and Secretary of State Dean Acheson on 30 June 1946, Sasakawa denounced the Soviet Union and stated that the participation of its judges and prosecutors in the war crimes tribunal risked undermining the neutrality of the trial:

Japan did not fight a war with the Soviet Union, therefore it has not lost it. The Soviet Union violated the Japan-Soviet Treaty of Neutrality, advanced its troops into Manchuria and Korea, where its men invaded and plundered at will, and carried back with them a vast amount of machinery and materiél. If these acts are to be approved, the Military Tribunal of the Far East will be meaningless and unnecessary. However, as the chief aggressor, plunderer, and violator of its own international treaty, the Soviet Union unabashedly sent in its judges and prosecutors and treats Japan as "an aggressor." The Soviet Union is behaving like a robber accusing a thief, and trying him in a court. This attitude sullies the judicial process and will certainly be denounced by historians of the future....

At the risk of being seized by the revengeful Soviet Union and torn to pieces, I shall continue to cry loudly until I am the last man, to demand the return of the Kurile Islands and Sakhalin to Japan in addition to all the things the Soviets plundered and carried off. Now that the Soviet Union, to whom we owe not a cent of compensation, has seized enormous property from us, I fear that we may lose our honor by failing to pay reparations to your country, the Republic of China, and other nations victimized by us, to which we do have an obligation.[10]

Let's be fair

As his criticisms against the Soviet Union indicate, Sasakawa believed that if the victor countries brought up the charges of "a crime against peace," "war crimes," and "crimes against humanity" they should be fair, and hold responsible not only the Japanese but the Allies as well in the context of history. In order to guarantee the neutrality of the process, the judges to preside over the military trial should be chosen from the neutral countries. Furthermore, Sasakawa was critical of the trial because it was predicated on ex post facto law and unfair procedures. The following are more excerpts from *Sugamo Diary*:

> The spirit of law is to punish the one and to save the many. To penalize crime under existing law is a sound principle the world over. However, if, as is said all over town, a new law is to be established in the trial of individuals to retroactively penalize them for their past deeds, its intention in fact is to bring charges against certain people. If this becomes a reality, it is a serious offense against humanity. Not only the peoples of the defeated countries, but men with a sense of justice around the world will

hold such behavior as inimical to humankind and will forever harbor resentment. I declare that in that very moment the seeds of a Third World War will have been sown. For this reason, the defeated will be skeptical if it is the victors who try them, no matter how open and fair the trial.

I believe the critical requirement for the establishment of world peace is to remove any such suspicion and conduct a trial that the whole world can be convinced of, as to its fairness. It is for the very reason of my commitment to world peace that I entreat the United States, which makes utmost efforts to establish world order, to transfer the jurisdiction to a neutral country and have the trial conducted by personnel from neutral states.[11]

Dancing for joy

Sasakawa was deeply disturbed by what he saw as illustrations of "victors' justice" being dispensed in other countries shortly after the war, for example in the Philippines:

> Trials such as that of Lieutenant General Honma Masaharu (1887-1946) raised this question of victors' justice.[12] If justice is not dispensed in the lofty spirit of the US Constitution then mankind either sets aside a claim to be holding to just principles or we let everything degenerate to a low level where all that matters is a bloody purge for revenge. The death sentence against General Honma was clearly a choice for the latter option. I cannot take part in it. Nor can I acquiesce by keeping silent on this. Both General Yamashita Takebumi and General Honma were executed without due process and as such their treatment will open the way to a series of legalized lynchings.[13]

Sasakawa tried to see Japan in a broad scope and to lift himself above the preoccupations of daily events. He believed, coming down to bedrock, that the existence of Japan's imperial system, as marked by the physical person of the emperor, was essential for good order and the rehabilitation of the shattered nation. Society, he believed, was in danger of breaking up.

To avert disaster, he believed, it was essential that the US Occupation not pursue the topic of the emperor's responsibility for the war and at all costs avoid summoning him to the court. Therefore, "he wept with joy" when he learned through a report in the *Tokyo Shimbun* on 21 June 1946 that Chief Prosecutor Joseph B. Keenan had stated that he would not summon the Emperor to be tried at the IMTFE. Sasakawa recorded in his diary:

> This American policy is the only way to go for the rebirth of Japan.... America in its wisdom has understood the heart of the Japanese people and has allowed us to keep the imperial system and decided against the arrest of the Emperor. What a great happiness for Japan, mind you this is not negative for America. I felt greatly relieved at the Keenan statement so much so that I had nothing more to worry about even if I were to be executed tomorrow.[14]

In a letter dated 29 July that same year, written to an acquaintance in his hometown, Sasakawa shared his state of mind: "My objective has been achieved and I literally danced for joy."[15]

Concern for the Showa emperor

Not that that was an end to the matter. Sasakawa, never fully at ease, was constantly concerned that the emperor might be accused of having responsibility for the war. He feared that not a few among the Class A war criminal suspects, who had lived a life of plenty as elite power-holders or had enjoyed aristocratic status, just might testify unwisely, seeking to ingratiate themselves with the Allied Powers in order to escape execution or heavy prison sentences. These defendants might not be cowardly but they lacked experience in answering questions from prosecutors in court and they might inadvertently offer testimonies that would hurt the emperor. Sasakawa's prewar experience of a successful legal battle fought over six years, of which three years were spent in prison, gave him impregnable confidence and a sense of mission that he alone could prevent the worst from happening.

Getting himself arrested

Sasakawa appears to have had not the slightest doubt about the course of action on which he was embarking. Knowing what he did, and having a feel for the future, he embarked on the extraordinary project of volunteering for arrest as a Class A war criminal suspect. This was indeed a bold decision given his background. How could he demonstrate his culpability? He had not even once occupied a government post and his small PPP, while it had conducted itself in a flamboyant manner under his leadership, had always stayed within the legal limits as a political group.

As a right-wing organization it had little or, better said, zero impact on the government's war strategy. In fact far from having influence on affairs of state the PPP was considered a pesky little undesirable organization by some in the government particularly after war with the United States began in December 1941. In a letter written by Fuji Yoshio, a key PPP member, and addressed to Sasakawa when the latter was in prison in the early summer of 1946, Fuji recalled that "during the war the military hierarchy bore down upon our PPP members starting from *sensei* [meaning Sasakawa] and going on down to all the rest of us."[16]

Up to a short time prior to his arrest late in autumn 1945, so common sense suggests, there was hardly any possibility of him being detained — and made a Class A war criminal suspect along with Japan's war leaders. Fully aware of this Sasakawa set out to provoke the Occupation authorities. In October-November 1945 he organized twenty or so speeches in Osaka and he, then and there, announced on public platforms that he volunteered to be arrested as a Class A war criminal — an action of remarkable audacity.[17]

"Why do I wish to be arrested?"

What did he say? And how exactly did he express himself? There are no exact records of these speeches — military censorship no doubt prevented their publication in the newspapers — but once in prison in December 1945 Sasakawa volunteered the following summary in a document that he submitted to the International Prosecution Section (IPS), an organ of the Occupation working to gather material for the trials to come. He wrote:

> An elected representative of the people has an obligation to give explanations to the voters on important issues. For this reason I spoke to my audiences in Osaka in autumn 1945 about the truth of the defeat in the war and I laid bare the secrets of the political world. The gist of my speeches was as follows: The Japanese Army had not carried out research on new weapons. It had failed to send large aircraft forces to destroy enemy bases overseas and to prevent enemy planes from bombing the homeland of Japan. Our forces failed, likewise to attack the US mainland....
>
> In the postwar era there are only two choices for Japan, either to go the Soviet way of communism or to go the American way of democracy. Now, why do I wish to be arrested?
>
> There is no one more suspicious than the Japanese. If I am not arrested and simply organize a movement of some kind and contact the General Head Quarters (GHQ), Japanese people

will not trust me. They will see me as just another opportunist toadying to the Allies. On the other hand, if I am arrested and then acquitted after having squarely stated my convictions in a public trial I will win their trust. Thereafter I can then be in touch daily with MacArthur Headquarters and escape any suspicion. It is for this reason I wish to be imprisoned at an early stage.[18]

A more audacious communication can hardly be imagined, but Sasakawa was drawn willy-nilly to the center of events. Not that it is easy to picture exactly how events were unfolding at the time. Yamaoka has furnished a very different record of what Sasakawa was saying in his speeches in Osaka in autumn 1945 by way of seizing the attention of the Occupation authorities:

In Japan many people starved to death during famines, even when our population was only about 25 to 26 million as in the early Meiji Era. Our population has nearly tripled today, so it is only natural that we do not have enough food to feed our people. Human beings do have the right to live, however. There are only two choices before us, either to produce more food at home or to build up foreign trade, export a lot, and purchase food with the proceeds. Now who was it who blocked these two paths?...

If the Allies determine us to be aggressors then we would be condemned as accomplices of immorality and those who have given their lives for the country would have died in vain.

This must be prevented at all cost otherwise we would have committed an inexcusable blunder against the souls of the departed war heroes as well as our ancestors. Now, hear me well, the ministers and generals who are being arrested one after the other are all fine people but they lack experience in court. If we leave things to them, we will be condemned as aggressors. Well, I have had the experience of spending three years in prison and of winning acquittal at the end of four trials in four years. That is why, I must be arrested as a war criminal so that I can coach the defendants and unify their thoughts.

Fortunately, we have here in the audience members of the Occupation forces, accompanied by stenographers and interpreters. With such reliable witnesses at hand I can be confident that I shall be taken to prison as a war criminal. Once in prison I will serve my country to the best of my ability by stating why the

Japanese are not aggressors. I ask you my voters, to raise a toast
for Japan if you hear of my arrest.[19]

Amazing! Sasakawa no doubt repeated these remarks in many
speeches he delivered in Osaka. Certainly the Occupation was being
provoked by the speaker. The Occupation authorities, in fact, compiled
a dossier on Sasakawa stating that he made a speech in Minoo City, his
hometown near Osaka, on 21 October 1945. In that address he called on
his audience "not to obey the present Japanese government, which is
collaborating with the Occupation."[20]

Sasakawa gained his objective. A document dated 4 December
1945 bearing the signature of James J. Gain Jr., Captain in charge of Information, summarized the grounds for arrest:

> Sasakawa should be arrested for the following reasons: first, for
> leading campaigns instigating aggression, nationalism, and hos-
> tility against the United States. And second, for his continued
> vigorous activities in an organization that strongly impedes the
> development of democracy in Japan."[21]

Of the reasons given for his arrest, the first refers by implication to his
activities during and up to the end of the war, and the second tells of
Sasakawa's success in provoking the Occupation authorities.

A dangerous person?

In the years that followed he instilled into the US military in Japan a
sense that he was a dangerous person. This is indicated by material dating to July 1947. US Army General Staff Section II, G-2, in charge of intelligence, public peace and censorship referred to Sasakawa Ryoichi in its
"top secret" document and concluded:

> In any case, Sasakawa appears to pose a potential danger to the
> future of Japanese politics.... In consideration of his past words
> and deeds and the danger he poses in the future G-2 should
> thoroughly investigate his case, including the possibility of in-
> dictment.[22]

This report can be seen as further evidence of Sasakawa's success in provoking the Occupation authorities, not that he ever managed to be indicted as we shall see shortly.

His main achievement was his arrest. This event found mention in
the *New York Times* of 4 December 1945 — on the day it took place — in
an article by Burton Crane. He reported: "At least one of the war crimi-

nals on General MacArthur's latest list feels honored that he was to be so accused. Sasakawa Ryoichi, ultra-nationalist, declared: "To be named by the Allied Army as a war criminal is eloquent proof that I devoted my whole self to the prosecution of the war." He added that all those on the list were "first-class Japanese."[23]

These words are powerful testimonies to the way the occupying US forces viewed Sasakawa.

II

On the day he turned himself in Sasakawa spoke first to his supporters in front of his office on Ginza. He then proceeded to Sugamo Prison by car accompanied by a truck displaying a huge, white banner that read "A Farewell Celebration" and bearing a brass band playing naval marches. The truck was filled with members of the Japan Workers Alliance, Sasakawa's party under its new name, and youth from a Student Cultural Confederation. If anything, he entered prison like a victorious general returning from a brilliantly successful campaign — in marked contrast to the rest of the newly charged Class A suspects. Here is how he began his parting speech before setting out to Sugamo from his Ginza office:

> I experienced no sense of alarm or fear when I learned that my name had been added to the list of suspected war criminals and that General MacArthur had given the Japanese government a warrant for my arrest. I simply accepted my fate as a matter of course. I was prepared for this and so I had my formal Japanese wear, my *haori* bearing my family crest and my *hakama*, sent up from Osaka. I shall meet my fate as a proud Japanese. I feel a sense of ease that my imprisonment has come about — even a sensation of joy for having achieved my wish....
>
> My dear comrades, consider yourselves dead as of August 15. Yield to no one and never be defeated. Be resolute in fighting for the reconstruction of Japan.[24]

The cheerful five-mile procession that followed through the bombed-out streets of Tokyo to Sugamo — with the brass band playing all the way — must have seemed a deliberate act of provocation to the Occupation authorities. The day after Sasakawa arrived in prison he faced an angry interrogator who struck him in the face and shouted, "Don't you know you belong to a defeated nation?... How come you deliberately make fun of the authorities?" The interrogator accused him of making light of the Occupation in three ways. "First, you made an aggressive farewell speech to your followers full of challenging remarks.... Second, you squared your shoulders and bragged to journalists in the Diet when the names of the Class A war criminals were announced saying "I passed the test! Congratulate me. I shall enter prison in formal attire." Third, "you had the nerve to bring a band and cheering supporters with you."[25]

Professor Royama's evidence

Another reason for Sasakawa's arrest, his provocative behavior apart, was that many informers had volunteered information against him, and these reports gained credibility among Occupation officials. Anonymous denunciations were frequent in those days. People had scores to settle. Sasakawa was certainly not the only target and the stories about him were often misleading and vague but some had their roots in the prewar years and were harshly critical.

An Occupation era memo exists dated 10 December 1945 and addressed to an officer from the Counter Intelligence Corps (CIC) 90th Capital Corps, Army Post Office (APO-660). The memo to the officer, who questioned Sasakawa in prison, summed up what various sources said: "A number of informants alleged that the Patriotic People's Party (PPP) was one of the most active groups that advocated military rule and Sasakawa Ryoichi was its leader."[26]

Some informants made themselves known to the authorities by name. A file of the International Prosecution Section (IPS), a key unit under the Occupation, notes that one Kakehi Mitsuaki, the deputy editor of a publication called by its English title *Contemporary Japan*, reported to the Occupation that Sasakawa was the leader of a political group called the PPP and was the only member of parliament from the party. Kakehi alleged that the party received financial assistance from the Kokuryukai (familiarly known to foreign scholars as the Black Dragon Society) and was its offshoot.

The group, he added, had also received financial aid and support from the Police and Security Bureau of the Interior Ministry as well as from the Military Services Bureau of the Army Ministry. In addition Sasakawa was said to be the mastermind of the National Workers' Alliance (Zenkoku Kinrosha Domei). The union ran large-scale public relations campaigns, put up posters, distributed leaflets and organized public gatherings based on neighborhood associations. Orators appealed for support for the imperial system, anticommunism, and liberal democracy. However, the slogan "liberal democracy" was generally considered to be a smoke screen to hide the true objectives of the union, according to Kakehi.[27]

Another of those who chimed in was Professor Royama Masamichi, formerly professor at Tokyo University and then editor-in-chief of *Chuo Koron*, a prominent intellectual monthly magazine. He offered the following information on 8 November 1945 ahead of Sasakawa's arrest, claiming that the PPP, Sasakawa's group, was an extremely reactionary political party that gathered workers not organized by labor unions. It had acted in collusion with Kokuryukai. Though the party was dissolved after the war, the entire organization was taken over by the National Workers' Alliance.

The Alliance's formal leaders, Fuji Yoshio and Yoshimatsu Masakatsu, were henchmen of Sasakawa. The funds of the National Workers' Alliance appeared to have been rapidly amassing thanks to earnings by Sasakawa on the mainland of China.... Further, it was rumored that Sasakawa and the National Allied Workers' Alliance were closely tied to Kodama Yoshio's Japan National Party (Nihon Kokumin-to). During the war Sasakawa had colluded, Royama maintained, with the Japanese Army and conducted business on its behalf, while remaining a civilian. The Army had given him an aircraft, which Sasakawa flew to China frequently. With the permission of the Army, he had rigged a deal for good quality coal from Taiwan and had sold it to the mainland at exorbitant prices.

Furthermore, this testimony continued, Sasakawa had collected vast amounts of copper ore through forfeiture — with the collusion of the Army and the military police. These supplies were ostensibly for arms production, but the copper was auctioned off to the highest bidder without establishing what it would be used for. Through these bold speculative ventures, concluded Royama, Sasakawa had amassed a fortune of anything between 200 million and 500 million yen.[28]

Rumors do fly. It is clear today that this information was basically wrong. Sasakawa hardly ever had any contact with the right wing as represented by the Black Dragon Society. A genealogical map of right wing groups, compiled by Takahashi Masahira for an encyclopedia article in 1980, treats Sasakawa's PPP as independent from other right-wing groups.[29]

The two organizations, the PPP and the Black Dragon Society, appear at opposite ends of the genealogical map, showing no existing ties. In fact the Black Dragon Society barely functioned by the start of the Showa era (1926-89). It had become a shadow of its former self.

Sasakawa was largely on his own in the world of right-wing groups. A 1952 reference work titled *Who's Who of Contemporary Japan*, edited by Abe Shinnosuke, has this to say in connection with the right-wing groups of the modern period: "The genealogy of the right wing may be classified into: a group headed by Toyama Mitsuru (1855-1944) and Uchida Ryohei (1874-1937); a group lead by Uesugi Shinkichi (1878-1929) and Takahata Motoyuki (1886-1928); and then a group dominated by Kita Ikki (1883-1937) and Okawa Shumei (1886-1957), but Sasakawa does not belong to any of them."[30]

All in all, it is impossible to see how Sasakawa's PPP could have developed from the Black Dragon Society or have received funds from it. Simply put the chronology does not work.

The Black Dragon Society

Japanese right-wing genealogies intrigue the outside world and none more than this group. The Black Dragon Society was organized prior to the Russo-Japanese War of 1904-5 and is best known for favoring Japan's advance into the continent especially against Russia. It had a direct line of descent from the Genyosha, the first right-wing society in Japan established in 1881.

Headed by two charismatic leaders, Toyama Mitsuru and Uchida Ryohei, it was long considered outside Japan to be a large and powerful organization even when it had in reality already dwindled away to a nominal existence by the Showa Era. Kokuryu-kai (Amur River Society would be a conventional translation of its name) took its name from the Amur River, which flows along the Manchurian and Far East Russian border. The name of the group can be rendered in English as Black Dragon Society, based upon the literal reading of the *kanji* for Amur River. The sensational name helped to give to Westerners an exaggerated idea overseas of its existence as some kind of omniscient, all-powerful Japanese mafia or gang.

Making a gift of an airfield

As noted in the previous chapter Sasakawa was tracked and persecuted by the police and by the much-feared military police — and detained without charges for three years (1935-38). He never received official support. He built up connections, however, with the military leadership. As a patriotic gesture, we have seen, Sasakawa presented the Army with an airfield he set up in the Kansai in the early 1930s and even with aircraft shortly before war broke out. But to my knowledge there is no record that he was offered the use of aircraft by the Army. Sasakawa did visit China and other countries before and during the war flying himself.

There is no evidence that I know of that Sasakawa accumulated wealth in collusion with the armed services — as did Kodama Yoshio, who served as a "part-time" and very effective employee of the Army and Navy and the Ministry of Foreign Affairs, created the Kodama Agency — a one-man trading company in strategic commodities, and amassed vast fortunes in China.

His inclinations seem to have run in precisely the opposite direction. A key episode that came on the very eve of the Pacific War, suggests as much. In November 1941, so the story goes, Sasakawa received a sudden, extremely urgent request from Lieutenant General Yamagata of the Navy Air Command to procure military matériel for the war.

The Imperial Navy was desperate to stock up on key materials in short supply in anticipation of an outbreak of hostilities. It was a war profiteer's dream and it was not for Sasakawa. He turned aside the request, saying that he was not good at such matters, and in his place, he introduced none other than Kodama Yoshio. With this sudden new business as a turning point, Kodama proceeded to build up his celebrated if notorious agency.[31] Sasakawa took care to avoid having any connection with government-related business.

Evidence to indict?

Sasakawa's next objectives, once he had himself arrested, was to get himself indicted as a Class A war criminal suspect, to stand trial and to give testimony in court. However, this was more easily said than done. G-2, one of the key units in the Occupation hierarchy under General MacArthur, recommended that indictment be considered in Sasakawa's case as noted.

But the powerful International Prosecution Section (IPS) within the ruling camp in Tokyo found that there was no clear evidence against Sasakawa to support an indictment. That is to say, all the claims that repeatedly appeared in files on Sasakawa lacked any concrete evidence to back them up. For example, it had been alleged that Sasakawa and the PPP had campaigned to abolish the Washington Naval Disarmament Treaty; that the party had joined in planning Japan's southward military push in 1941; that Sasakawa made a deal with the Wang Zhaoming regime in China. None of these grand geopolitical allegations was provable.

The same applied to frequent allegations such as that Sasakawa's solo visit to Italy and Germany in late 1939-40 was to build up the Axis Alliance: he promoted aggression against China; that he participated in planning the war against the Allied powers; that he was one of the most powerful leaders of the prewar fascist movement in Japan; and that he was a powerful advocate of the Great East Asia War. All these claims and contentions collapsed on inspection or could not be verified by the powerful US legal team in Tokyo, they found.[32]

Then what was to become of Sasakawa's project to get prosecuted and testify to the court? Sasakawa explained to his second son, Takashi, his true intention in volunteering for arrest as a Class A war criminal:

> Those designated as war criminals have had the experience of sending many people to jail, but it will be their very first time to experience anything of the kind themselves. I had misgivings

about the possibility of them making inappropriate remarks that
might have a damaging effect on His Majesty the Emperor. With
my experience of three years in jail, I felt that I could squarely as-
sert Japan's position and I could also give technical guidance to
the war criminal suspects [on how to conduct themselves in
court].[33]

His enormous self-confidence was based on experience. According to Sasakawa some of the Class B and C lesser war offenders pro-
tested to him that,

> if only General Tojo had changed places with Sasakawa *sensei,*
> the latter would have done a good job of explaining how Japa-
> nese military discipline demands absolute obedience. The
> Americans would have understood and would not have con-
> victed them for actions carried out under orders. These B and C
> war criminals need not have been detained in the first place,
> they considered.[34]

Who will speak out?

Godo Takuo, a Class A war criminal suspect who had served in key cabinet posts running the economy in the Hayashi Senjuro and Abe Nobu-
yuki cabinets, confided in Sasakawa, telling him of his doubts about his
fellow defendants and their willingness to speak up.

> The twenty-eight defendants who just came in are reluctant to
> speak their minds. They want to protect themselves as they still
> have plenty of worldly ambitions. This does great harm to Japan.
> The few who have nerves are decisive, but they are poor talkers.
> If you were with the group they would cheer up and the result
> could be good for Japan. Unfortunately they will not put you on
> trial.[35]

Togo Shigenori, the former foreign minister who was criticized
harshly for imputing blame to others during the Tokyo trial, was said to
have told Sasakawa: "If only you had been with us during the trial all of
us defendants would have had the benefit of your leadership and would
have come out more favorably."[36]

All this was deeply vexing to him. Sasakawa had wished not only to
be arrested as a Class A war criminal, but to be indicted as a defendant so
as to have an opportunity to state his case in court. He observed that
other inmates became nervous, when they learned of their possible
indictments:

During our walk [in the prison yard], Ohta Kozo constantly asked me and Aoki Kazuo what we thought he would be charged with or why he ended up in the first group of Class A. I told him to consider himself lucky. It was better to be indicted earlier as a Class A suspect because the minor ones were called later. I told him I would gladly pay 50,000 yen to be indicted with Mr. Tojo and stand trial early on. People think the opposite. Why, if you have not done anything wrong, should you be afraid? We should be glad of the prestige of being tried at the international court.[37]

Sasakawa was profoundly disappointed. Contrary to his wishes, the days and months sped by without him being indicted. There simply was no evidence that he had played a leading role in the conduct of the war. He noted in his diary:

Everyone is looking thin and haggard after being served a bill of indictment. They must be worried. There would be no cause to worry if one lived in such a way that investigation brought out only good acts. That's me. I grieve that I cannot stand trial with Mr. Tojo.[38]

If only they allowed me to stand public trial I would first of all challenge the judge and prosecutor from the Soviet Union, which is guilty of aggression and violation of law. I would then stress that the Allied attack on Japan had inflicted great damage on the Japanese, and demand that Japanese judges be allowed to participate in the trial. But would the defendants ever have the energy to speak up in these terms and voice the absolute essential? This worries me.[39]

As a last resort

Things were not going well for Sasakawa. As a last resort, he wrote a letter to General MacArthur, asking the general to serve a "supplementary indictment" on him personally.[40]

As might be expected this demarche came to nothing. He felt driven to the brink and shared his desperation in a letter dated 3 June 1946 addressed to Fuji Yoshio and colleagues of the old PPP:

I have written to General MacArthur entreating him for a supplementary indictment, but to this day nothing has happened. I have not slept for two whole nights suffering from grave apprehension over this and that. Crying does not get me anywhere. I am going through the most searing agony in forty-eight years of my life. As a result I have twice as much white hair as a month ago. Imagine the pain I am going through.[41]

As a final despairing attempt he wrote letters referred to earlier, addressed to President Harry Truman and Secretary of State Dean Acheson. In the letters Sasakawa explained:

> I am sorry to say General MacArthur has not granted me the indictment I requested for the sole purpose of challenging the tyrannical Soviet Union, to reflect seriously on its conduct, thereby making the trial meaningful and contributing albeit in a small way to world peace.[42]

Working with Tojo

Once it became clear that he was not going to be indicted, Sasakawa took a deep breath and switched tactics. He decided to work on those who faced formal charges, Tojo Hideki in particular. The latter, a full army general, had been the prime minister and effective commander-in-chief at the start of the war in December 1941, i.e., at the time of Pearl Harbor. Sasakawa's idea was to let Tojo state Japan's case in a dignified manner and to confirm the innocence of the emperor as regards the war. His correspondence at that time testifies to his concern. Sasakawa wrote to Yoshimatsu Masakatsu of the PPP:

> I used my seniority, as I considered it, for having done time in prison before, to share my own experience with Tojo from the very beginning of our imprisonment in Sugamo. I urged him repeatedly to first of all make sure that responsibility does not fall on the emperor; and secondly, to stress that ours was a war of self-defense; and thirdly, to make vividly clear that certain nations — the Philippines, Indonesia, India, Burma, and Vietnam — gained their independence. Japan's sacrifice had liberated Asia.
>
> Then, fourthly, he was to speak up against the high-handedness of the victors, prompting their self-reflection. And then finally, with great presence of mind, he was to walk to the gallows, shout *banzai* three times for His Majesty and the people, and go to his death.... Most people are quick to heap abuse on Mr. Tojo, but once in prison he became philosophical and accepted his fate. I offered him all the sympathy and support I could.[43]

According to Sasakawa, Tojo welcomed his advice as the following passage found in *Expressions of Sugamo:*

Whenever there was a chance, I shared my experience and thoughts with Tojo saying: "You stand in the face of national criticism and ridicule. I am sorry to think what your family must be going through. You can save your family from shame by how you conduct yourself in court.

"You will not escape the death penalty. You must know better than to hope to walk free from Sugamo, don't ever dream of it.

"If it is written that you must die, take all responsibility upon you. I expect the United States not to be so foolish as to drag the emperor to the court, but there are some blockheads instigated by the Communist Party demanding that he be hanged.

"Please believe that there is no one but you in Japan today who can defend the emperor. Please fearlessly and squarely state the case of Japan as your conscience dictates. If you are convinced that this war was a war of self-defense then use the microphone in the court to shout your conviction to the whole world. Most people believe that they stand to lose by incurring the hatred of the judge if they speak bluntly without mincing words. My own experience in fighting at a trial tells me the opposite. A defendant has the right to explain himself, even if he is under no obligation to make a statement.

"The last victory to be won is to speak the truth courageously.

"It is most important for you to do this."

I repeated this to him again and again and each time he listened quietly.[44]

Building up mutual trust

At first Sasakawa had not trusted Tojo because of his earlier encounter with the general when he was a "non-government-recommended" member of parliament. He wrote in his diary on 10 April 1946:

General Tojo does not have what it takes to explain Japan's position fairly. If I were present and on trial I would have the confidence to take the floor to explain and convince the world that it was not a war of aggression. Without this the war victims would have died in vain.[45]

Sasakawa sharply criticized Tojo in a document he submitted to the International Prosecution Section, i.e., the US prosecutors:

Having had to face few adversities in life, he tends to be haughty in times of good fortune but (referring to his humiliating deportment on his arrest) is unable to see an inch ahead when things go against him. He has strong likes and dislikes and would not appoint worthy people to high office, if they happened to oppose his views. Instead, he gave important posts to his friends.[46]

By "his humiliating deportment on his arrest" Sasakawa meant Tojo's failed attempt to commit suicide by a pistol. Sasakawa was greatly reassured, therefore, when Tojo more than met his expectations on delivering his statement in court. In a letter to Fuji Yoshio of the PPP in January 1948, Sasakawa wrote:

The interrogation of Mr. Tojo in court was a great success. He made good use of my advice. That is to say, most of my reasons for going to prison in the first place have been achieved. I am glad about that.[47]

Tojo appeared to be grateful for Sasakawa's "guidance" and advice, so he noted in *Expressions of Sugamo:*

Immediately after Tojo completed his statement I met him at Ichigaya [where the trial took place]. He indeed looked cheerful. Usually it was my place to initiate a conversation but he walked up to me and took my hand.

"Sasakawa, fortunately the emperor is spared. I did my very best at the witness stand and said all I had to say. The only regret I have is that I was not allowed to go back in history and talk deeply about it. But that is beyond my responsibility.

"In any case, I am profoundly grateful to you for sharing in full detail your experience in public trials and encouraging me to the very last, because you gave me useful information that served me well. I have nothing but admiration for your resolute attitude.

"I wish, therefore, to thank you and to express my gratitude to your mother for bearing and raising a strong man like you. Since I do not have the freedom to thank her in person in this world, I have written a poem in her honor. Is it all right to present it to her," he asked, "as a gesture of appreciation?"

I could not control my tears when he said, "I do not have the freedom to thank her in person in this world."

"Yes, please send it to her. Mother will be very pleased," I replied. He then showed me the poem:

Moso bamboo teaches us to defend what is right.
Noble, it holds up under spring snow.

As Tojo promised, this verse was delivered to my mother at
her home on the outskirts of Osaka.[48]

On New Year's Day in 1948, as a token of gratitude for his advice
and encouragement Tojo had already presented Sasakawa with a *haiku*
he had written:

> Eternal noble presence
> hath Fuji
> this New Year.

Tojo said: "Sasakawa san, 'Fuji' means you."[49]

III

Later in life Sasakawa was criticized by some for his unconventional behavior in going out of his way to be arrested and then trying to get indicted as a Class A war criminal. He was accused of grandstanding. After
all, he fully expected to be acquitted, it was said. At the time, however,
the common understanding in Japan was that arrest and indictment as a
Class A war criminal suspect carried a high possibility of the death
sentence.

Kishi Nobusuke, who was destined to serve as prime minister of Japan from 1957 to 1960, was another Class A war crime suspect who was
never indicted. His comment on his position inside Sugamo Prison reflects the general uncertainty that the accused must have felt. Kishi
wrote:

> "Pondering on the outcome of the trial and considering death as
> a possible outcome gives a different prospect, even though I am
> prepared for the eventuality.... The trial is being conducted by
> the arbitrary will of the other party.... A wish to live to the last
> causes me extreme anxiety. The topic of death, therefore, grips
> my mind in a different way.[50]

Kodama suffers

Kodama Yoshio, who had been jailed a number of times before the war,
spent hard and uneasy times in Sugamo Prison as a Class A suspected
war criminal. He found the uncertainty very hard to take:

In retrospect the three years at the prison were extremely painful and seemed awfully long. Although it was just a matter of three years, it felt more like ten or even fifteen years. This probably had much to do with not having any prospect of knowing the outcome. I imagined that if the worst case meant the maximum penalty or life imprisonment, then even a light punishment would be thirty years....

Furthermore, we had no guidance even as to when the trial would begin. It was under these conditions of psychological uncertainty that scores of us Class A suspects were thrown into detention over a long period.

While a one-sided trial proceeded [for the Class A defendants] at the Ichigaya court [in Tokyo] in the name of justice and humanity, another [quite separate] military court [25 miles away] in Yokohama tried Class B and C suspects [much more quickly], sentencing them to twenty or thirty years of hard labor for just striking prisoners of war.

As we considered these harsh sentences handed down by the Allied Powers, and as we contemplated the truly miserable state of Japan in its defeat, each day at Sugamo, from beginning to end, was filled with mental anguish and a feeling of dread.

If it were just a personal problem, one might have been able to resign oneself to fate and prepare for death, but we were so powerless, and at our wit's end at the thought of how we came to be labeled as war criminals. Indeed, the whole country was under the heel of an unseen huge power. Under the circumstances, it was only in sleep that I was liberated from all the aches and pains of the real world as seen from Sugamo day after day. Yet the dreams I dreamed from time to time gave me small relief.[51]

A slight contradiction

Sasakawa himself assumed that he would not come out alive. He prepared his own grave next to his father's, in his hometown of Minoo City, and he had a commemorative photograph taken with Shizue. He gave thought to her situation, leaving land in Tokyo and considerable assets to pay for her needs, but Fuji Yoshio and other old PPP colleagues used it all up, because according to Shizue they were certain that Sasakawa would not return alive.[52]

To suggest that it was all grandstanding on Sasakawa's part because he was expecting to be acquitted, is being wise after the event, and ignores the circumstances in a mean and suspicious way. In fact, neither Sasakawa nor those around him expected him to emerge from prison in one piece. "Nobody wants to go to prison," he said, "especially if arrested as a war criminal. One's prospects are uncertain and those with a guilty conscience worry themselves sick over ways to escape indictment.[53]

Judging by the entries in his diary and statements he made before the International Prosecution Section, Sasakawa had a clear conscience and believed in his innocence. "What wrong did Sasakawa Ryoichi do up to this day?" he asked rhetorically in what he supposed was his farewell speech made outside his Ginza office on the day of his arrest.[54]

Sasakawa forcefully asserted his innocence not just in regard to "war crimes," and "crimes against humanity," but also in the matter of a "crime against peace," another choice phrase used by the US prosecutors.

If he were innocent though, then he should not have been arrested. Sasakawa's attitude was contradictory in form and logic. But to lie on these points would have been to go against his essential purpose of pursuing the question of the deceptiveness of the Tokyo trial. Sasakawa was confident that he could argue the case of Japan because he was not guilty of anything.

He was nothing if not confident as a person. We know his caustic characterization of Tojo Hideki. Here are some more of his thumbnail sketches of notables of that era. All these men were war criminal suspects and he did not mince his words in describing them when asked to do so by the US prosecutors. The latter kept their notes on his brief remarks:

- Yuzawa Michio, former minister of interior: "Has a fondness for sake and women, and likes to spend other people's money, and not his own. He is a stingy man...but lacking in courage to do anything very bad."
- Hoshino Naoki, former chief cabinet secretary: "A dwarf of a man. Employed by Tojo till the end, but insignificant not worthy even of mention."
- Arima Yoriyasu, former minister of agriculture and forestry: "Has a fondness for radical action, but no intelligence...and is often taken advantage of...unimportant figure, considered to be weak-willed."
- Shimada Shigetaro, former minister of the Navy: "Appears brilliant, but in fact disappointing. He is a man who obeyed Tojo in everything.... Made appointments in the Navy as Tojo willed."

- Ino Hiroya, former minister of agriculture and forestry: "Has a fondness for women, and toadies up to Tojo like a houseboy. His attitude to Tojo in parliament was painful to watch. He is an opportunist who panders to powerful men."
- Iwamura Michiyo, former minister of justice: "Obeyed all orders given by Tojo. But had a hard time, sandwiched between Tojo and his subordinates, who opposed such opportunism.
- Aoki Kazuo, former minister of state: "An insignificant person. They say Aoki is responsible for the inflationary Chinese economy. When Colonel Tsuji Masanobu threatened to kill him with a sword he fled petrified. This is another cowardly person."
- Goto Fumio, former minister of the interior: "A henchman of Izawa Takio [former superintendent-general of the Metropolitan Police; former governor of Taiwan; and a member of the Privy Council], rumored to be a seeker after distinction, who listens to high officials but not civilians and a doyen of the Interior Ministry who arrested many who opposed his boss."[55]

Of the seventy-three people covered in his statement, Sasakawa had very few to praise without reservation. They were:

- Shigemitsu Mamoru, former foreign minister: "The best person of the present day."
- Kishi Nobusuke, "A wise man and among the best of the Tojo circle...more daring than most."
- Ayukawa Gisuke, entrepreneur: "An important figure among businessmen, and has grand conceptions that take people by surprise."
- Kuhara Fusanosuke: "An "important figure with intelligence and courage."
- Mazaki Jinzaburo: "A true warrior... not expected to change sides and can be trusted."
- Toyoda Fukutake: "A man of spirit."
- Murata Shozo, a former businessman: "A fine man with courage for a businessman."
- Yasuoka Masa'atsu, former scholar: "An upright...courageous scholar who can be trusted."[56]

A cautious witness

These character sketches tell one about Sasakawa. He was a fairly unrelenting observer and he did not pull his punches in describing people, even when addressing the prosecutors. However, while severely criticizing and castigating many of the suspects, he offered no information on specific events that could be used against them in court. Captain Samuel B. Healy, who examined the interrogation records, stated that he "could not find any testimony that had evidential value."[57] Sasakawa knew well how to respond to interrogation without telling a lie and without putting himself or others at a disadvantage, even while seeming to offer juicy information.

He was "a player on the stage." On occasion Sasakawa hurled abuse at fellow suspects, and one senses that he was using tactics he learned in court to give the prosecutor an impression of their insignificance and thereby to win verdicts of not guilty for the accused. For example, Sasakawa showed contempt for Arima Yoriyasu, the former Minister of Agriculture, whom he had disparaged as "insignificant" and "weak-willed."

He remarked of Arima:

> The Allies brought him here [to Sugamo] because he had served
> as Minister of Agriculture and Forestry but it was simply his turn
> to take the post. Why bring that fellow here? He is not worth
> even a Class B or Class C suspect let alone a Class A one. The rest
> of us mock him, calling him "the incompetent Mr. Oh no!"
> [based on a reading of the Chinese characters of his name]. It's
> sickening to have him among us, get him out of here![58]

Using these words Sasakawa may have had some stratagem to spare the luckless Arima further trouble. The inspiration for his contemptuous remarks about Yuzawa Michio ("lacking in courage to do anything very bad") and Hoshino Naoki ("insignificant, not worthy even of mention") may have sprung from similar tactical intentions of deflecting the Allied prosecutors from troubling certain individuals Sasakawa wished to help.

Two badgers in the same burrow?

Here we may consider how Sasakawa and Kodama were seen by Awaya Kentaro, who worked during the Occupation as an editor of the English texts of Class A suspects' responses under interrogation, and had read the prosecution's files on their questioning. He found something that surprised him very much:

There was a large gap between the real and false images. The heroic tales circulated by them and their friends about the gallant pair dauntlessly facing their interrogators had become legendary and intrinsic to their Sugamo experience. The prosecutors' documentary materials expose these two as being submissive and defensive.[59]

This assessment applies in good measure to one of the two, namely, Kodama, as I shall duly explain. Sasakawa, however, is not to be put in the same category or class as his longtime friend Kodama.

To have done so was a mistake on the part of the interrogators resulting from a failure to understand Sasakawa's strategy of pushing for indictment while believing his own innocence — and from his successful court tactics. Basically a misunderstanding came about, I consider, because of Sasakawa's words and deeds. He worked far outside the intellectual frame of reference of Awaya. The latter was trapped by a preconceived idea that Sasakawa and Kodama were "badgers in the same burrow" or belong to the same gang.

A fair trial, please

In fact, Sasakawa spoke out vehemently and persistently on general topics he cared about, while Kodama was the one who kept his mouth shut on political issues. Sasakawa was outspoken, while Kodama was timid. Nothing held Sasakawa back when it came to telling the prosecutors his opinions on two major topics, the injustice of the Tokyo trial and the beastliness of the Soviet Union.

Sasakawa believed that "if the United States of America wishes to make the Japanese into true lovers of peace, then it must first win their trust. And the only way for the US to do so is to keep its word."

Starting from this perspective on the Occupation, Sasakawa made a list of contentious items for the US prosecutors that he titled "Proposed Ways to Dispel the Misgivings of the [Japanese] People."

The list was lengthy:
- "The public had discovered that US censorship of the press was even harsher than under the Tojo government [during the war]."
- "The Japanese wanted to know how America, which claims to respect the will of the people, could justify arresting and interrogating an elected representative of the people [meaning Sasakawa], especially during a session of the Diet."
- "The public wanted to know on what law and on what grounds civilians were being arraigned and tried."

- "The Japanese wondered how the United States, which claims to respect human rights, could imprison people without even reading to them a written indictment beyond asking their name, domicile, and profession.... If such careless handling of arrests is kept up, then people may want to go to prison simply to get free food and lodging."
- "A trial by the victors of the defeated, no matter how fairly it is conducted, will fail to do away with the misgivings of the loser. If the United States wishes to be recognized by the whole world as a truly fair nation that respects due process, then the trial must be conducted strictly and only by citizens of neutral countries and not by the victors."

Thus Sasakawa listed his blunt criticisms of Occupation policies and practices. Most of his statement was not translated into English, no doubt his pronouncements were considered provocative.[60]

General Tojo as the villain

As already stated, Sasakawa did not divulge to the prosecutors any specific facts that could disadvantage others among the accused nor did he offer them any ammunition of a real kind usable in court. The grand exception was his statement on General Tojo, Japan's actual war leader and the principal figure among the accused. Sasakawa stated that:

"During the war Tojo's power and authority can probably be said to have surpassed that of the emperor."[61]

"To describe him in one word, Tojo became a military man seeking his own personal success — he commenced hostilities and deployed the armed forces at his pleasure."[62]

"The leaders who were preparing for war at the time were the military — Tojo."[63]

In other words he pointed at Tojo. Sasakawa had resigned himself to the idea that the general could not escape the death penalty. Tojo had to be made out as a villain in order to save the emperor.

Cash on the move?

In marked contrast to Sasakawa, Kodama made concrete statements. He named people and he specified events and actions with the possibility of placing other suspects at a disadvantage. Notably he gave testimonies voluntarily without waiting to be asked to do so by the prosecution.

Thereby in certain ways that we now know about, he collaborated with the prosecutors. For example, at an interrogation on 20 June 1947 Kodama made an offer of cooperation stating that he would like to convey "something extremely important" — something neither the defense nor the prosecution knew anything about. It had to do with the close collaborative relations between the Army and right-wing organizations in Japan, and it bore on the prewar economic aggression, going southward into Southeast Asia. He asked for "sufficient time to talk in detail about these matters."[64]

As a consequence, Kodama was duly interrogated by one William Edwards a month later on 21 and 23 July 1947. At these sessions, Kodama spoke up about the activities of Showa Trading Co. Ltd. (Showa Tsusho Kaisha), a company that the Imperial Army had established to procure the strategic raw materials necessary for war; and he gave details about the Banwa Agency (Banwa Kikan), an organization that the Imperial Navy set up for the same purpose. In particular regarding Showa Trading, with which he was directly involved, he explained how proceeds obtained from sales of heroin in China were used to purchase tungsten, and he gave the names of the people concerned. On top of that, he stated that all responsibility for these operations rested on the shoulders of a certain Muto Akira, director general of the Military Services Bureau of the Department of War. All Showa Trading's activities were conducted under him. Kodama further stated that he did not know much about Banwa Agency since he was not directly involved. But he told them that he believed Major General Tanaka Ryukichi was informed.

Furthermore, going into another matter, Kodama testified to US interrogator Edwards that Sasakawa had received 100,000 yen [a sum equivalent to $1.5 million today, calculated at 1 yen in 1940 as today's 1,618.19 yen], from the Army between 1941 and 1942. This testimony of Kodama's opened the way, as it happened, for a head-on confrontation between General Tanaka and Sasakawa, in front of the same prosecutor, with that same person hearing both parties. In fact, the ground had already been laid for this clash. Sometime earlier Tanaka Ryukichi had said that he "remembered another defendant named Sato Kenryo handing to Sasakawa a substantial sum of money around May 1942."

An angry denial

Sasakawa refuted this. He said that it was absolutely not the case, and he was very angry indeed, so he remembered:

> I had not vented as much fury during three years in Sugamo as I did against Tanaka Ryukichi's repugnant and unfounded

charge....

When Tanaka saw me in the interrogation room he began awkwardly, as might be expected, "Sasakawa san, I am extremely well disposed to you. This sort of matter will not disadvantage you.

"I do not wish you to have goodwill toward me. Whether it will be advantageous to me or not I will say what I have done and simply say I do not know if I don't know."

Prosecutor William Edwards turned to Tanaka and asked, pointing his finger at me: "You told me you saw a man receive money from Sato. Are you sure it is this man who received the money?" Tanaka very hesitantly mumbled: "If my memory is correct I think it was this person."

What a roundabout form of speech that was!

The prosecutor then turned to me and asked what I had to say to Tanaka.

"I do not even accept a cup of sake let alone money. I will immediately offer my life, if I have received as much as a cent. Tanaka, boastful as he is, would still probably not be able to bet his life on which of us is truthful and who is telling a lie. I swear by heaven and earth that Sasakawa Ryoichi is innocent."

As I spoke, Tanaka Ryukichi, powerfully built as he was, hung his head dwarfishly.

Prosecutor Edwards observed the scene in silence. He let me go, and, as he sent me away, he took my hand and held it, saying: "You are a gentleman."[65]

All about an airfield

There is a second record of this episode. It was made by the same William Edwards, the US prosecutor in the case, and recorded in an official English-language document. This runs as follows:

Sasakawa told Edwards that he would "never embarrass him" by making a false testimony on his own account or anybody else's. To which Edwards responded that he was grateful for the guarantee, but that it seemed to him that "the case is going nowhere." Edwards proposed that the examination end there.[66]

Edward's allusion to Sasakawa being "a gentleman" must have referred to Sasakawa keeping his composure in spite of his rage against Tanaka.

The day after the confrontation Sasakawa wrote a letter to Edwards.

Those who wish to take their grievances out on me may say I resort to use of force. I have not once hit anyone since I was born. I am confident the righteous person will always win so there is no such need at all. I state unequivocally that defense of justice requires nonresistance and readiness to risk one's life.

Well, I enjoyed yesterday's confrontation and I thank you for it.... Until the truth is out I will not make any slanderous remarks about Tanaka. Indeed I will not take out my grievances on him. I pity Tanaka for acquiring a bad disease of unashamedly making slanderous charges.[67]

According to prosecutor Edwards, however, there was a further installment after the face-off. Major General Tanaka told him, so Edwards recorded, that he had "heard from one of the Japanese defense counsels" who had interviewed Kodama in Sugamo that Sasakawa had admitted to him that he had received 100,000 yen from defendant Sato Kenryo of the War Ministry.

Whereupon, to pursue the matter further, Edwards examined Kodama in the presence of Major General Tanaka. At that point Kodama, when questioned, acknowledged that he told the Japanese defense counsel that Sasakawa had told him that he had received 100,000 yen from the War Ministry, but he denied that Sasakawa had received that money from defendant Sato.

However, Kodama went on to say that, if the money had come from the War Ministry, then it had to have come from secret funds, and since Sato was the director general of the Military Services Bureau within the ministry at the time, any substantial payment could only have come from Sato. Kodama further stated that he thought that the money paid to Sasakawa was in return for his donation to the Imperial Airfield, (Teikoku Hikojo), his own private airfield on the outskirts of Osaka. Kodama then pointed out that the airfield was widely believed to have been a donation. So it was extremely wrong of Sasakawa to have received 100,000 yen, because that meant he was deceiving the public.[68]

Kodama vs. Sasakawa

The English-language document gives more or less the same account as the Japanese one. Kodama, on condition of secrecy, told the prosecution that he had heard that Sasakawa had said in answer to questions from the prosecutor that he had not received any money from the Army. So when he met Sasakawa later he asked him why he said such a thing...and he asked if Sasakawa had not received any money for the airfield he had donated to the Army. Kodama said that he understood that

Sasakawa maintained at first that he had donated the airfield, but had later received money from the Army.

Sasakawa, according to Kodama, said that the latter was right. Kodama then repeated this to defense counsel Kawauchi. He also added that the amount was 100,000 yen and was received either in 1941 or 1942 almost certainly in the office of the Military Services director general, in other words, Sato Kenryo.

Kodama went on to say that almost all the right-wing nationalist organizations went to General Tojo or to the Military Services Bureau of the Army, and received money.[69]

He added that he didn't know what relationship Sasakawa had with Sato, in ideological terms "relative to communism and nationalism." But he did know that Sasakawa had met those top figures in the military, such as Sato, Muto, and Tojo.[70]

Who told the truth?

It is impossible to be sure today which of the two, Kodama or Sasakawa, was telling the truth. Having said that, however, Kodama's statement about Sasakawa is at odds with what we know of the latter's movements both before and during the war. On grounds of common sense, and of chronology, Kodama's statements appear to be wrong.

Sasakawa had donated his private airport to the Army in 1934. If Sasakawa received the payment for it either in 1941 or 1942 it is clear, whatever the pretext, the Army would have been offering a bribe. But, as previously noted, Sasakawa was at odds with the authorities, and not in cahoots. He was a fierce, vocal, and open critic and opponent of the way the Imperial Rule Assistance body was used after the 1942 election, to solicit everybody who had been elected, forcibly, as members, regardless of whether they were government sponsored or not, and he was one of the very few members of the legislature who opposed, until the end, both the special law introducing the wartime penal code and the ad hoc control by the authorities of freedom of speech, publication, assembly, and association.

On Sasakawa's own account, on notifying the government of his intention to make a critical statement in the parliament against the handling of the April 1942 IRAA election:

> Sato Kenryo came to see me.... He told me not to question the government on the issue. He said he had been sent by Tojo ...and told me to drop my own inquiry, and instead to ask questions along the lines that the Army had prepared. That would be good for both sides, he said. And, if Sasakawa complied, it would be written up in the Japanese newspapers.... Sasakawa

had responded that was not right, saying: "I did not become a member of parliament to have my name appear in the papers." And he added: "The papers are controlled by the government. So they may not print a word of my own inquiry and that is all right by me.[71]

A thick envelope produced

This vignette illustrates how the heavy hitters of the Japanese military operated in wartime. This may be seen, precisely, in relation to the government's handling of criticism by Sasakawa on the wartime special penal law (Senji Keiji Tokubetsu Ho) and the ad hoc control law on freedom of speech, publication, assembly and association (Genron Shuppan Shukai Kesshya nado...Rinji Torishimari Ho). Initially more than one hundred parliamentarians opposed the highly repressive legislation, but only thirty or so remained after the government got through with its covert campaign of blackmailing and bribery. Sasakawa was the central figure campaigning against the government, according to what we know. The matter went all the way up to Prime Minister Tojo Hideki. Sasakawa received a message that Tojo wanted to see him, according to author Yamaoka. On presenting himself at the prime minister's official residence Sasakawa was ushered in to Tojo's office:

> Tojo began by saying: "It is about those bills...your formidable opposition has been a serious blow to the government. Unless I have them passed in a couple of days I will have to resign over it. So I have asked you over to hear what you have to say." Sasakawa offered a cryptic Zen-like response to which Tojo offered, "Thank you for your counsel. By the way, Hoshino [Naoki, chief cabinet secretary], is expecting you, so please drop in to see him." Sasakawa did as the prime minister suggested and stopped by at Hoshino's office. There, Hoshino offered Sasakawa a thick envelope saying, "Excuse me, Sasakawa san, this is not much but we have prepared this as it must be difficult for you to provide for such a large contingent of men...." By his account, Sasakawa's face changed color. He said: "Nothing of the sort!... I don't ever receive money from others. I give money. Though I say it myself I always have 500,000 or a million yen in my safe. Don't mistake me, I am not such an easy mark, you fool...." He stormed out of the room leaving behind a startled Hoshino.[72]

This was not quite an end to Kodama's squealing behind Sasakawa's back in prison. Kodama was not always entirely truthful in what he said about Sasakawa, claiming, for example, that Sasakawa told him that he "frequently fly to Europe before the war."[73]

This was not the case. [In fact, he made only one such visit, a matter that could easily be checked by the US prosecutors.]

Kodama, for his part, requested that his testimony regarding Sasakawa should be kept secret. What a contrast this made with Sasakawa's unvarying openness. Thus Sasakawa replied in the affirmative, when he was asked by the prosecutors, whether he was willing to testify in court regarding the conversation that took place that day. The prosecutors said that they could summon him to the court, if they chose, naturally, but they wanted to know whether Sasakawa was willing to bring up the subject discussed of his own accord.

"I shall act as I wish," he appears to have said. "It is my desire to go to the witness stand."[74]

Some collateral damage?

As it happens, Kodama's statement appears to have given the IPS prosecutor a bad impression of Sasakawa. Sasakawa was not told of Kodama's statement, as the prosecutor duly respected Kodama's request to keep his statement secret. There was, therefore, no face-off between Kodama and Sasakawa of the kind that took place between Sasakawa and Major General Tanaka Ryukichi.

On this issue the interrogator Edwards, after thoroughly studying the materials, concluded that Kodama's testimony had "an important meaning" in that it "broke the integrity of Sasakawa's claims" not to have received money from the military. However, Sasakawa repeatedly denied doing any such thing and had not changed his stance, even when confronted with Major General Tanaka, the prosecutors recalled in their records. And yet they concluded that "his secret confession to a Japanese lawyer friend that he received 100,000 yen appears to be a fact."[75]

Sasakawa, it seems, never learned of Kodama's disloyalty in Sugamo. But if he had known, he would no doubt have forgiven Kodama reasoning that he acted under extreme duress. Sasakawa, it will be seen, covered up for Kodama right to the end.

IV

It is open to question how many Japanese of his generation thought beyond their own shores, with memories of the defeat fresh in all minds, most of the big cities in ruins, and the population starving. Perhaps Sasakawa was right, being in prison had its merits. In any event he kept up his one-man effort to think ahead. Not one to keep a low profile Sasakawa wrote frequent letters to General MacArthur at his headquarters in Tokyo and to President Harry Truman in Washington, D.C., urging them to consider Japan and its need for help, and to agree with him concerning the Soviet Union.

He expressed himself trenchantly on world politics in much of his, no doubt unanswered, one-way correspondence. For example, in a letter he addressed to President Truman dated 15 April 1946 Sasakawa began:

> In the future a major war will be fought between the United States and the Soviet Union, and the timing will be determined by the speed at which the reconstruction of the Soviet Union is completed and atomic bombs are made ready....
>
> There are but two choices before Japan and the Japanese, either to depend on a communist USSR or on a free United States. I am convinced that we would be happier with the United States. However, the ultimate choice will depend not so much on the Japanese but on the US Occupation policies. I state this frankly with the respect and affection due to a big brother and sister, because I long for Japanese citizens to enjoy continued happiness as good little brothers and sisters of the citizens of the United States of America.[76]

As to Japan, he asked for help on several fronts: food aid, since the population was starving; advice on how to grapple with a vicious inflation that was just taking hold of the shattered economy; a reduction in the levy on Japan introduced by the United States to cover the expenses of the Occupation army; and a fair war trial that should be so conducted as not to nurture anti-American feelings.

Be fair, be impartial

Japan was up against it in many ways, the nation's future was highly uncertain. However, Sasakawa focused his priority on what he thought was the biggest topic long term. This was the need for punishment of war crimes to be handled in a fair and impartial way, without discrimination as to whether those charged were from the winning or the losing side:

> Those who violate the rules of war must be strictly punished. The US Army has arrested and detained over a long period many men including those who have committed minor offenses such as slapping prisoners of war or who have nothing to do with the war. By contrast the United States has indiscriminately bombed

Shinto shrines, Buddhist temples, and hospitals, and shot and killed noncombatant women and children.

In an instant 78,000 lives were lost in Hiroshima where, with the exception of the nearby naval port of Kure, there were few military targets. Its choice as a target of nuclear attack is certainly the greatest violation of the rules of war. However, I have yet to hear of anyone responsible being punished. Application of the laws and norms of war must not depend on a country's wealth or lack of it or its victory or defeat.[77]

Sasakawa sent similar letters again on 30 June that year to President Truman and Secretary of State Dean Acheson.[78] Prior to that he wrote to General MacArthur on 30 April 1946 as well as at the end of the previous year.[79]

It is highly doubtful that the letters addressed to Truman and Mac-Arthur were delivered to them. The letters may not even have made it out of Sugamo. Sasakawa noted on 1 July 1946:

This morning, Fukabori [a Class B and C war crimes suspect and a roommate of mine at the time] saw a guard open and read my letter to President Truman, which I had entrusted to the guards to drop in the mailbox at five p.m. yesterday. I promptly asked interpreter Sasaki to negotiate to have the letter dispatched expeditiously to the United States. It is inexcusable for that guard to open the letter. The guard who was on duty yesterday was also irresponsible. Some Americans do not keep their promises. How would the US military leadership react to this?[80]

The next day Sasakawa wrote:

At three in the afternoon, the letter addressed to President Truman was returned to me with a tag attached saying to mail it through Dean Acheson, the US representative on the Council on Japan. I did as instructed and attached a cover letter to Mr. Acheson and entrusted it to the General's guard at five o'clock through Mr. Asano.[81]

It took courage to send these letters from Sugamo to the US president and to General MacArthur, the de facto ruler of Japan. From a third party perspective Sasakawa's letters were foolhardy and quixotic.

But he was incapable of sitting in his cell all day twiddling his thumbs. Looking back later, he remembered:

I was of course prepared for the worst having volunteered myself, and that helped me to do things fearlessly. I wrote boldly to President Truman and General MacArthur concerning Occupation policies. I also communicated freely and fearlessly with my friends and acquaintances outside. I hurled insults at the communists. As one who has a profound love of Japan I am convinced that the future of the country lies only in developing goodwill toward the United States.

For this reason I ardently wish for a strong solidarity between Japan and America, I want to promote cordial relations between our two countries as much as possible. In this regard I am convinced that I should be frank regarding the Occupation policies and say what I think are good and what are not. My ultimate love of Japan and the United States of America has made me call a spade a spade. Letter writing was the one means I had of taking action from the prison and I used this at every opportunity.

One person who bore most misgivings was the great "Mr. K." (most likely Kuzuo Yoshihisa [1847- ?], who participated in the establishment of Kokuryukai [Black Dragon Society] and served as its editor from 1937.) He asked Abe (believed to be former interior minister Abe Motosune) and Kodama to censor Sasakawa's letters before they were sent out. He feared they might have repercussions. No one took seriously that sort of silly talk. Abe and Kodama laughed it off.[82]

The abode of the blessed

The great enemy in jail is tedium. Sasakawa told jokes and tried in every way to encourage those around him who were depressed over their prospects. The guards opened all the cells at a fixed time of day to allow the inmates to visit and talk with each other. Sasakawa used this time to do what he referred to as "making the rounds." Later, he remembered, "Indeed I looked forward to sharing my philosophy of life especially with those who showed signs of moral and physical injury."[83]

Among all the prisoners, he knew best how to survive in jail, thanks to his three-year prewar detention. It was important for them not to despair and to find something to enable them to make light of their situation. Sasakawa thought up a play on Chinese characters by taking the two characters that denote "prison" and switching them into a pair using similar characters but with different meanings. Thus, prison (or "containment place," *kangoku*) became "comfortable place" *(gokuraku),* and then finally "paradise" *(gokuraku).* So, prison could after all become "the abode of the blessed."

His *Sugamo Diary* contains various reflections and memories of the three years he spent there after the war:

> If a rich man lives in a grand house but commits a crime he goes through hell. If one lives in prison but has done no harm it feels like paradise. Even a scholar cannot turn hell into paradise, but it is easy if one is without guilt to feel one is in paradise even living in hell. All it takes is a determination to make the most of things. (14 December 1945, pp. 35-36)

> An [American] guard came with interpreter Mr. Okada to check my towel. It seems there is a thief even in jail where thieves are locked up. I tell the guard that this is an abode of the blessed and there are no evildoers in paradise. The guard had a hearty laugh over this. I named my own cell the abode of "the blessed in Sugamo." (9 January 1946, pp. 66-67)

> It is already a month since I came here. Happy time flies in paradise, more like a bullet than an arrow." (12 January 1946, p. 71)

> The others all suffer because they want to get out of prison with only some minor offense. Despite all that they eat, they get thin and haggard. It is because they waste their spirits…if one has done no evil, no matter where one is, it is paradise and one's enemy can be one's friend…. If asked about my abode in Sugamo, I tell them it is a university of paradise on earth. (20 January 1946, p. 80)

> The other day a group of those who allegedly mistreated prisoners [Class C war crimes suspects] came over. Each in his different way asked me how I could be so cheerful. I told them it was because I didn't have a bad conscience. In contrast you have done things that make you ashamed and you are frantically looking for ways to escape punishment. No wonder you are gloomy. Accept that the time has come for you to pay for what you have done. That will put you out of your misery. (23 January 1946, p. 83)

> I am protected by the sacred spirits of the tens of millions of war dead and the spirit of my late father. That is why wherever I go gloom is dispelled and the place becomes a cheerful paradise. (18 February 1946, p. 104)

Admiral Takahashi Sankichi told me, he found prison to be what I told him, the best university of life. Alas, he said, he was too late in enrolling in it. I said in my capacity as its president I would be presenting him with a diploma. The admiral laughed heartily and thanked me. (18 April 1946, p. 126)

Pity me that I have not found ways of turning hell into paradise but fortunately I know to enjoy paradise while living in hell. So please have peace of mind with the thought that I am happy and hopeful here. (10 June 1946, a letter addressed to Atake Tsutomu, p. 302)

No one in my room has ever been involved in a brawl. We live harmoniously. After dinner when I practice calligraphy my roommates take turns to read me an interesting novel. I practice my calligraphy and enjoy a novel at the same time. When I play cards with a roommate the other will sit by my side and cheer. In this way although I live in prison I have all the wonderful life of the innocent. It is paradise. (23 November, 1946, a letter addressed to Shizue, pp. 363-64)

Other inmates noted that Sasakawa made merry in Sugamo. Ishihara Hiroichiro, for example, wrote in his diary:

Sasakawa has lived the life of a *ronin,* a master-less samurai of the feudal age and has an odd sort of vitality compared to others.[84]

Sasakawa-san, the president of the PPP, is somewhat of an eccentric who came to the prison escorted by a brass band. He is exceedingly cheerful and keeps our room always merry.[85]

Today (21 January 1948) during our exercise Sasakawa took his walk alone with a blanket over his back, humming a tune. I called out to him, "Hey, you are as high-spirited as usual!" "That goes for both of us!" returned he, with a grin. How he keeps up his jovial spirits!"[86]

By contrast, Kodama Yoshio seemed exhausted, for all that, like Sasakawa, he never took up a high government post and had experienced prison life before the war and was the youngest among the Class A inmates.

According to Ishihara, "He must worry about himself as he is often deep in thought and appears more tired than when he arrived, although he is still in his thirties and should be the most vigorous of us all."[87] Kodama had this to say:

> When I was jailed as a political offender before the war there was an air of passion and enthusiasm as many of us were young, with political persuasions of left or right. Sugamo lacks that. Young men classified as Class C suspects are stunned by the irresponsible attitudes of their senior officers and have become cynical. Most of the Class A people are busy clinging on to what is left of their lives and have no hope for the future of the country. I would rather not see human weakness but there is not much choice in this communal setup.... Sasakawa with his strong spirits drives away the cheerless drudgery of our life.[88]

As a Class A war criminal suspect I was sent to Sugamo where, I must say, I learned a great deal. There were of course wrongdoings and undesirable occurrences, but I would rather not talk about them because I hate to slander others. There were few who left an indelible impression on me for their dauntless attitudes. Among them was Kishi Nobusuke for whom I had an especially high regard. Many of the war criminals were restlessly devouring every piece of news printed in the daily papers wondering what their fates would be. Mr. Kishi was indifferent to the progress of the legal proceedings. "This is a political trial," he would say. "It is up to them whom they choose to hang. We will learn nothing from their arbitrary decisions." In contrast Mr. Sasakawa stood firm. "Go ahead and try us. I will tell them straight at the risk of my own life." Abe Mototsune kept his silence and was above it all. Matsui Ishine took the whole thing coolly. Only about six people among the sixty or so war criminals were great men.

There we all wore the same prisoners' uniform and that's when one gets to know the true value of a person after all decorations and honors are stripped off.[89]

The gratitude of Admiral Takahashi

Admiral Takahashi Sankichi, who received a certificate from the "Sugamo Best University of Life," wrote how much he was encouraged by Sasakawa:

For the first few days after being sent to prison I had no wish to do anything, not even to paint. An hour a day of outdoor exercise was the happiest time of the day when we could talk to each other. Conversation went like this: "I don't have any reason to be here"; "Communists must have given my name to the Occupation authorities"; and "When will we be permitted to leave?"

One day Sasakawa stood behind me and gently touched my shoulder and said; "Well, you are also here Mr. Takahashi. I expect you to leave here soon. I have decided to stay three years." I asked him why and Sasakawa said, "I had spent three years in Osaka Prison earlier. After I left the prison I spent a day with the chief monk of the Tenryuji Zen temple in Kyoto, the Reverend Seki Seisetsu.* My own conclusion was that spending a year in Osaka Prison was equivalent to ten years of Zen training at the Tenryuji Temple. Destiny had led me to Sugamo Prison this time and I want to spend three more years here at what I call a university of life."

These reflections of Sasakawa's made me ashamed. I decided to adopt Sasakawa's attitude and that brightened up my days. I owed my life in prison to him.[90]

As told earlier, I learned a great deal from Sasakawa early on in my stay at the prison. Since then whenever I saw an unfamiliar face or a depressed-looking person during the exercise time we spent outdoors I walked with him and listened to his complaints. I then urged him in Sasakawa-style to consider the time spent in prison an immeasurable opportunity to train his mind and body in preparation for a big job later.

Training in prison has easily twenty times the value of living outside.[91]

Sasakawa's diary records many words of gratitude expressed by inmates and roommates for the encouragement he gave them. For example, Sasakawa had promised his two young roommates, Class B and C war crime suspects, that he would do everything to acquit and get them out as soon as possible so that they could enjoy a happy family life and contribute to society. For his part he was not in a hurry to get out because he could not contribute directly to production increase. The two, somewhat bewildered, thanked him and said it was like meeting a "Buddha in hell." They had told Sasakawa that they had come from a cell where there was no laughter. They were truly merry after joining the happy room. I told them that my cell was the "Paradise of Sugamo," Sasakawa wrote.[92]

One day, one of his roommates was leaving the prison after he was found to have been wrongly detained due to mistaken identity. He wanted a graduation certificate and Sasakawa obligingly complied by writing on a ceremonial Japanese paper that he had graduated from the "Sugamo University" and signed it, "President Sasakawa Ryoichi." With the certificate in hand, the man said he would not complain for the wrong done to him. As the trial neared the men became thin and worn out. "But those in my room were cheerful and looked well fed to the envy of the others."[93]

Sense of humor

Sasakawa understood the inner workings and subtleties of human nature, and was kind to the younger men, especially the Class B and C suspects in his room. He was enormously popular with them. They enjoyed his dirty jokes and their laughter rang through the prison. Among his papers, he kept a number of *tanka* (Japanese poems of thirty-one syllables), Chinese verses, and personal letters. But his *Notes in Prison* (Gokuchu bobiroku) also included lists of dirty jokes. Sasakawa was a professional of a kind in prison service.

Not that all within Sugamo was sweetness and light. There were some grim moments. One time, a Class C suspect by the name of Yokoyama Kanzaburo was sent to Sasakawa's room. He suffered from a lung disease, ran a high fever in the afternoon, and occasionally brought up blood. After vomiting, Yokoyama would turn to Sasakawa and mumble to himself, "It is wrong to smoke, isn't it, *sensei?*" But he could not stop smoking. In Sasakawa's judgment the man would get off rather lightly as a Class C suspect, but he wished the young man would stop smoking for his own sake. Sasakawa proposed that he would keep him company and refrain from smoking if Yokoyama would do the same.

"Yokoyama, you really should stop smoking!"

"Yes I know, I keep telling myself that, but it's really difficult, especially with you puffing away, *sensei*. I absolutely cannot stop."

"Hmm, it may be cruel to tell a nicotine addict to stop smoking, but it can hardly be compared to losing your life. If you say it is harder for you to stop because your cell-mate keeps smoking, all right, I'll have to stop smoking too."

"Let's try it out for three weeks."

Yokoyama and I began a three-week no-smoking campaign. Naturally, it was painful for me as well. At times I wanted to smoke badly, especially after a meal. I missed the indescribable comfort of the smoke and I felt sorry for making such a rash promise. It appeared that Yokoyama was having an even harder time than I.

In a matter of days he became listless. He stared into space and stopped talking. During our outdoor exercise I saw him join another prisoner who was smoking so that he could sniff his exhaled smoke. He obviously craved the drug. I had to control my urge to tell him, "Go ahead. Let's give up!" I was more concerned for his health than anything else. On the fourth or fifth day he cried: "I'd rather die than not smoke."

Outside prison there are things one can do to ease the urge to smoke, such as chewing gum or candy. Even work can help one forget. It is much harder in prison because there is nothing to distract one. I had to admit I was asking too much of him. I simply did not have the heart to insist any more. Our oath to abstain for three weeks lasted less than a week. Yokoyama broke his promise, but I kept it up to the end.[94]

Without other diversions, it was hard to stop smoking to help a young man suffering from tuberculosis. Sasakawa remembered that some of the Class C and B suspects would come and bid him good-bye when they left the prison. They would ask him to write a few lines in memory of their time together. After the defeat the calligraphy of the ministers and generals was worth little, they told him.[95]

Well liked and respected by the young Class B and C suspects, he was often asked by them to write a line with brush and ink, which he never failed to do, attesting that "So-and-so has completed the course at the University with honors," and signed it "Sasakawa Ryoichi, president of Sugamo Best University of Life." They loved this and thought it their best memento.[96]

Another incident may be cited showing Sasakawa's considerateness. It was January 1946 and the inmates were being treated to a ration of *mikan* (tangerines) as a luxury. Realizing that there were not enough to go round for everyone Sasakawa declined his due.

I declined to take one for myself. If it was put in my hand then I would be obliged to accept it. Otherwise I think the young people should have it. It is only decent to be considerate of the young and respectful of the elderly.[97]

Those were times when provisions were short and "even bigwigs begged for more soup and rice in their bowls." Sasakawa was a rarity and his young roommates were duly impressed.[98]

V

Sasakawa distinguished himself from other Class A detainees by taking on unenviable chores. He noted:

> I did two things in the jail. One was to play devil's advocate and the other was to take on jobs others were loath to do.[99]

What did he mean?

> Compared with other Class A residents in Sugamo I am a nonentity with so little to offer. My only claim to seniority is the experience I have of serving time in jail.... Under the circumstances, I will not only be doing myself dishonor but, if I may say so, I will risk lowering the general morale if I complain of our treatment here. I appointed myself "president" of the "Sugamo Best University of Life" and decided to live up to the responsibilities that came with the role. I volunteered, therefore, for the thankless task of playing the bad boy.[100]

In practice this meant bringing grievances to the attention of the US soldiers who had the ungrateful task of serving inside the prison as guards. This was no light undertaking because for an inmate to complain was a risky affair, particularly when he did it for the benefit of the whole group. A worldly wise person would most certainly avoid drawing attention to himself. Sasakawa observed that there were few men of such spirit among the detainees. He noted that both "young and old tried to cut a deal at the expense of the others."[101]

Inevitably there were awkward incidents from time to time. One day an American warder singled out Tojo Hideki, the former prime minister, for the arduous task of cleaning the prison passageway before breakfast. Kodama Yoshio, according to his own account, challenged the warder, saying that it was not proper that an ex-prime minister should be forced to do such a menial job. According to Kodama, the warder, who was a captain, asked him why it was always the same two, he and Sasakawa, who complained about the treatment in prison when there were other Class A prisoners who spoke English.[102]

This episode brings to mind the popular belief that Kodama and Sasakawa acted like twins within the prison, and were forever challenging the American guards and getting into mischief. Yet as far as I know, the inmates regarded the two men quite differently. Kodama did not enjoy their praise for his courage and self-sacrifice in the way Sasakawa did.

Some of his friends outside the prison walls advised Sasakawa to take it easy. There was no telling, they said, what the Soviets and the Americans might do to him. Sasakawa noted:

> I am grateful for their warm friendship, but I care nothing for my own life or death. All I care about is to defend justice and righteousness and discourage evil, and save our people and my country and ultimately mankind. Heaven has assigned me this great mission and I do not intend to back off, even for the friendly admonitions I receive. Let them cut me down if they must. Kill me if they must. I shall only rejoice for being able to serve my fellow human beings. I have nothing to fear, for with me are the war dead in their millions and the two billion who are living on the planet.[103]

To be sure, there were many problems that cropped up in the course of daily life in the prison. There was a terrible scarcity of food outside and the shortage impacted on the prison all the time. Food was not fairly distributed and some grumbled. The detainees decided to submit a complaint to the warden. Immediately, some beat a retreat. Lieutenant General Wachi Tsunezo and Colonel Hirano refused to put their names to a joint letter. Instead they pushed a younger man to append his name. Sasakawa was irate at their cowardice and he raised his voice against them. "Those who shirk responsibility do not deserve to eat."[104]

The contentious issue drew in some of the most dignified detainees such as Admiral Takahashi Sankichi. He went so far as to ask Sasakawa to stop hungry young Class B and C detainees from begging for leftover food. At that time Sasakawa was not close to the admiral and, to judge from his diary, could scarcely contain his disgust.

> Here is an old man nearing seventy who flatters the guard and receives more rations than the young men, but refuses to attach his name to a general request they had written asking for an increase in rations. He wants the young men to do the hard work while he reaps the reward. Japan was beaten because of corrupt and sly officers like him.

Sasakawa continued:

> I was told that even Admiral Shimada Shigetaro asked people in the cells on our side of the passageway not to request more food because he feared that the rations on his side might be cut. Our younger men muttered that the admiral was a selfish beast. He should really be asking for increased rations on behalf of the

younger men regardless of which side of the passageway they had their cells.

We lost the war, they said, because we had a man like him as minister of the Navy. The admiral should have committed hara-kiri to take responsibility for the defeat but instead he lived on in disgrace. He had no intention of making any self-sacrifice. He just wanted to play it safe and get out of here.[105]

That was not all. Sasakawa heard that Dr. Okawa Shumei and General Matsui Ishine had handed to the guard a letter addressed to the chief warder complaining, without any evidence, that "some people on the other side of the corridor are stealing our food." Sasakawa's reaction was to decry their meanness of spirit, but he also criticized them for poor tactics:

> They are bad negotiators. They should have just said we should get as much food as the other side. But to complain that the others stole their food was bad tactics.... Really clumsy! Quarreling should be one's last resort.[106]

In Sasakawa's eyes Class A inmates were crude and unskillful in handling their affairs — in everything from building their strategies in court to demanding better treatment in jail. Not that he despaired. Reality, however daunting, only strengthened him.

As we have seen, he was not averse to going to the top. Sasakawa wrote critically a number of times to President Truman and to General MacArthur urging that the Tokyo trial be conducted with greater fairness. This was risky. Indeed, if he wanted to save his skin he should not, in the first place, have acted as he did to make sure that he would be detained as a Class A war criminal suspect. Sasakawa had taken it on himself to speak for the other inmates and they counted on him.[107]

A ringing declaration

When the US prosecutors questioned Sasakawa for a third time on 21 December 1945 he had a statement ready to make to the Occupation authorities based upon what he had heard at the previous two interrogations. He had kept a record of this detailed written declaration, as recorded in *Sugamo Diary:*

> I love America. My wish is to see world peace established and to save humankind forever from the scourges of war. To this end the Japanese must become true peace lovers. You have my cooperation to achieve this objective. Allow me, though, to speak my

mind frankly.

First, members of parliament should not be detained when parliament is in session, even in the present exceptional circumstances, without special authorization by the emperor. I expect the United States to have greater regard for the elected representatives of the people. On what legal grounds did the United States, with its avowed respect for the individual, arrest me, a member of parliament, without even an indictment? Why did America not postpone my detention, as a politician representing his constituency, until the session was over? I am sad for the United States.

He continued:

Second, now is the time to stop personal attacks based on lies, such as the accusation brought against General Tojo Hideki of accepting a gift of 10 million yen. These irresponsible accusations will only make the Japanese people lose trust in America.

Here, Sasakawa made reference to an allegation by the Allied Powers — later withdrawn — that the Mitsui *zaibatsu* made a donation of that amount to Prime Minister Tojo during the war.

Third, it is said that the Occupation censorship [of the press] is worse now than at any time under the Tojo government. The United States stands for freedom and equality and must be consistent in what it says and what it does, and not restrict freedom just because we are a defeated nation.

Fourth, what do you say to giving the Japanese government a free hand in conducting its affairs, without your direct orders?

Fifth, the greatest concern of the Japanese people is how the war criminals will be punished. Some say the United States will conduct a fair trial, because it has respect for the individual, while others fear that the trial will be only a formality, doing away with witnesses and stenographic records and merely punishing those who displease America. Since the outcome of the trial will have a grave impact on the establishment of peace and our trust in the United States, it must: (a) call witnesses, (b) have stenographic records taken of the statements of defendants and properly translated to ensure correct understanding, (c) not enact new laws with the purpose of punishing the defeated, (d) restore the honor of those acquitted so as not to leave behind bitter feelings, and (e) if the United States is serious about building goodwill between our two countries, then remove those who curry the favor of the Occupation headquarters, and listen to the frank opinions of the acquitted about the future of our two countries and the world.

Today, Japanese who truly love peace are not frequent visitors to the Occupation headquarters. If I were in the position of the United States I would have the neutral powers, and not the victors, conduct the trial. Were that done, people everywhere would assume the trial to be fair, even if it were not. If the victor tries the vanquished it will be seen as unreasonable even if it is fair — or regarded as such here because of the loser's inferiority complex. If the loser believes the trial was unreasonable there will be bitterness.

Where there is bitterness there is no true or lasting peace. I say this out of my love for Japan and America. I beg you to convey this statement of mine to General MacArthur for his active consideration, the matters I state being so important."[108]

There is no doubt that these remarks by Sasakawa were duly received by the Occupation as recorded in his *Sugamo Diary*. A document no. 2048, dated 5 January 1946 and attributed to the US Army Counter Intelligence Pacific Region Chief Office, is found in Volume 24 of the Minutes of the IPS. This same document is the English translation of the statement Sasakawa had submitted, and its outline is not different from the entry in *Sugamo Diary,* quoted above.

Not that the two records are identical in every respect. In fact, Sasakawa omitted reference to what would have been for him an absolutely key part of his statement. He made remarks, it is apparent from document #2048, on the subject of the imperial system. His comments on this subject do not feature in the relevant part of *Sugamo Diary* at all. The crucial part of document #2048 states as follows:

> The Japanese people are relieved that the Allied powers have acknowledged the need for the continuation of the imperial system. There is a rumor, however, that some in the US Occupation authority hope to destroy our imperial system with the support of the communists. If the imperial system is to be changed then it should be left up to the Japanese people to consider how. Leftist parties, particularly the Communist Party, must not be openly used to destroy the imperial system.[109]

All of the above passage is missing from *Sugamo Diary.* On the other hand, the English language text #2048 does not record items 5-a to 5-d that Sasakawa says in a diary that he had stated before the prosecutors. Furthermore, the text of #2048 is much shorter. However, the brevity of the IPS text may be accounted for by compression in the translation.

In conclusion, we can safely assume that the two documents, if not identical, constitute a full record when put together.

Keeping the Chrysanthemum Throne

There is a puzzle, a conundrum. Why did Sasakawa leave out of *Sugamo Diary* any reference to the imperial system and the possibility of reforming it? Did he hesitate in writing of this matter even in his diary? Or was it his intention to put the main emphasis on saying that it should be up to the Japanese people to decide how the imperial system would be changed? He may have intended his remark that "it is all right to change the imperial system" to be heard as a rhetorical flourish leading to the main message — and then the IPS gave it prominence beyond what he had in mind. Whatever the truth of the matter as regards this record, from Sasakawa's point of view the imperial system would not change drastically come what may, as long as the issue was left up to the Japanese, since the great majority of them were in favor of maintaining it unchanged.

Spirits of the dead calling

Back in Sugamo, meanwhile, Sasakawa occupied himself once more with good-housekeeping issues. He had negotiated successfully with the head of the jail to take on the cleaning and other chores from the elderly detainees, because he was indignant that they had been assigned as much work as the younger inmates.

> The chores, including cleaning the baths, passageways, and washbasins, were all right. I could handle this."[110] In Japanese jails, detainees under trial do not have to labor, unless they volunteer. Here we are worked fully. On the thirtieth, I cleaned the large concrete passageway with soap barefoot, and on the thirty-first I was ordered to scrub the communal bath. I worked hard at it until I had many blisters on my hands.

Not that he complained to his jailors:

> While I am hard at work it is paradise. It makes me forget how cold the water is.[111]

I cleaned even round the gallows, a task that everyone particularly disliked. At such times I happily told myself that the spirits of the dead were calling out to me, and so I worked even harder until the scaffold was clean.[112]

Four cigarettes a day

In truth, these were arduous labors. Soon after entering Sugamo Prison, Sasakawa wrote an open letter dated 18 December 1945, addressed to "My dear friends." In it he stated:

> Life in Sugamo is not as comfortable as some newspaper articles have claimed. Taking the plus side, we receive a daily ration of four cigarettes, which we are free to smoke in our cells. This is the only thing that is better than in a normal Japanese jail. The rest is worse than the pain that I experienced in Osaka when I was imprisoned there ten years ago.
>
> This discrepancy — between what we experience and what the newspapers have reported — is due to irresponsible reporters who choose to paint our life here as if we are treated as honored guests leading a pampered existence. I beg you not to tell lies, because it is the warders and we inmates who suffer when false reports are made about us.[113]

There was, of course, no heating in the cells. Sasakawa recalled this aspect of the prisoners' lives in *Expressions of Sugamo*. There, he noted that:

> It is bad enough to have to fight the cold, but that is not the whole story. We are forced to work on the coldest winter days. On mornings when the ground is covered with snow or frost, we are up at five when it is still dark and while our parsimonious sun goddess is still asleep. We finish breakfast by six.
>
> Then the cleaning of the passageway begins. With soap and a scrubbing brush we scrub away in the passageway, barefoot. The moment I enter, stinging cold creeps up my limbs. My fingers are red and numb. In this state the cold hurts. It is like being pierced by needles.... It is easy to imagine the pain that senior bureaucrats and businessmen must suffer as they are put to work in their old age. These are men who lived most of their lives protected from the heat of summer and the cold of winter, living in the comfort of their villas. I begged the authorities here to spare them this hard labor and I was successful in that regard.

I was greatly relieved. I set aside the pain, even as I glimpsed Kuzuo Nobuhisa of the Black Dragon Society, now in his seventies, sitting in his cell quietly reading some papers while being spared our chores.[114]

This same Kuzuo, it may be noted, was most probably the grand old "Mr. K" mentioned earlier as having expressed concern that Sasakawa's letters to President Truman and General MacArthur could make the inmates' position worse. Sasakawa had harsh words for the old man, given his cowardly attitude, but his natural inclination was to be sympathetic.

Trying to be a good boy

Sasakawa, no doubt, stood out a mile among the detainees by his boldness and openness. He was popular among the American guards as well as among the Japanese. Sasakawa insisted that his frank remarks stemmed from his love of both Japan and America and such comments did not fall on deaf ears. In fact, the American prosecutors and the jail authorities listened to what he had to say about the US Army in Japan, both by way of passing on remarks made to him by the general public before he entered prison and by commenting on what he read in the newspapers once in jail. It must be their own open attitude, Sasakawa noted about Americans, that made their country what it is.[115]

He recorded that:

> I was blunt with the jail authorities as well as the guards in giving them a piece of my mind. Cheerful by nature, as they are, the Americans who got to know me became a most friendly group. Even an army surgeon who had little contact with me came by my cell just to say hello on one of his visits he made nearby.
>
> Trying hard to be a good boy does not get you anywhere. If one is absolutely free of selfish motives and wishes only good for others, then love prevails in the end no matter how much they may dislike you at first.[116]

That did not mean that everyone in authority in the jail was favorably disposed to Sasakawa. There was still some deep sense of hostility and ill feeling among Americans toward the Japanese due in part to the wartime anti-Japanese propaganda. In addition, there was naturally a sense of superiority on the winning side, looking down on the loser:

> Americans use us for unproductive purposes, as if they would incur loss if they did not use us. They tell us to scrub clean with

wire brushes the dirty white paint on the concrete. Of course, the more one scrubs the worse it looks because the dark concrete is exposed. I therefore asked through interpreter Asano whether they wanted us to remove the soiled paint in order to apply fresh paint later. Apparently not. I told the overseer that scrubbing was useless because it only exposed the concrete underneath. They want us to keep scrubbing. I don't understand.

On this basis they have no right to bring up complaints about the Japanese Army exploiting their prisoners of war.[117]

The work was hard for Sasakawa, whose injury to his right arm when young had permanently impaired him, though he very rarely refers to this in his record of Sugamo:

In the course of the morning they made me scrub with a brush and soap for two hours without a break some 2,600 square feet of concrete passageway, even though my right arm is crippled. In the afternoon they made me clean cobwebs high above the passageway. This is cruelty. If the Japanese treated Americans in this way during the war they would have been condemned to death by the war crimes trial.[118]

These were the sort of things that went on openly inside Sugamo Prison.

Warder Kurosaki

Worse was to come. A second-generation Japanese American called Kurosaki (or Kurisaki, see note 119) served as a chief warder at Sugamo from late 1945. Reports conflict as to his rank. It would appear according to *Sugamo Diary* that on his arrival he held the rank of second lieutenant and was later promoted to first lieutenant. What is not in doubt is that he had enough authority to make himself extremely unpleasant toward the detainees if he so chose. In time, something triggered a flood of aggression in him toward the prisoners, especially Sasakawa. "After the second lieutenant arrived, to our dismay, we were all treated with insults and cruelty," Sasakawa said.[119]

Everyone took note of the untoward development:

The chief warder from late 1945 was a stout Japanese American First Lieutenant who went by the name of Kurisaki. During his one-year tenure he never smiled and he treated us Japanese as if he nursed a strong antipathy toward us. One day in October 1946 we were all told that we could keep only a limited amount of belongings with us.

The next day (Kurisaki) came around with a few guards and threw our personal things out into the passageway. He then stripped us naked and conducted a physical examination. He did this with obvious hatred, which staggered even his subordinates.

Without exception, all of us felt indignation. His method of handling us became a routine so that we spent a most unpleasant time for four or five months.[120]

These circumstances were rare but not unheard of. Such a show of hatred toward people of one's own ancestry, while not unusual, crops up among second-generation nonwhites in America, who try to surpass others and to be more American than the Americans. Such aggressive behavior indicates insecurity about one's own identity and it may stem from discrimination suffered by nonwhites. The manifestation of ill will by the second-generation Japanese American guard may well have been the flip side of his self hate, which he then took out on his own kind. In fact, during the Pacific War many Japanese Americans were sent off to detention camps for the duration of the war, even with no time allowed them to gather up their belongings. Many suffered enormous hardships. At the same time, second-generation Japanese Americans in the camps were drafted to fight in the US Army. Some of them, not unsurprisingly, had extremely strong anti-Japanese feelings.

One theory within the prison, according to Ishihara, was that "Lieutenant Kurosaki" was not Japanese at all but of Korean ancestry.[121] If true, this would or could raise another complete set of cultural generalizations and possible oversimplifications. After Japan's defeat in 1945, when Korea regained its independence after thirty-five years of colonization, some Koreans living in Japan were deeply hostile, having suffered from discrimination in what they regarded as their own country. The rumor that Kurosaki was Korean may itself have arisen partly from prejudice — a sense on the part of the detainees at Sugamo that the only way to explain their jailer's extraordinary hostility toward Japan was that he was after all Korean. However, if as rumored Lieutenant Kurosaki was a second-generation Korean American it would have been highly unlikely for him to have used a Japanese name after Japan's defeat.

"Those eyes!"

Be that as it may, the junior officer in question took a dislike to Sasakawa, a war criminal suspect who stood up to the US authorities in asserting Japan's position with grace and composure. One day Lieutenant Kurosaki learned that Sasakawa had written a letter to the prison director criticizing his (Kurosaki's) attitudes and requesting that letters addressed to the director not be opened "as other detainees failed to come forward to complain for fear of retaliation."[122]

A very nasty situation arose. Lieutenant Kurosaki proceeded to take out his wrath on Sasakawa:

> 12 October 1946: I found Lieutenant Kurosaki standing in front of my cell and greeted him politely, whereupon the lieutenant pulled me roughly by the collar and punched me in the chest, removed my *geta* [wooden clogs], pulled me to the *tatami* mats, struck me again with his fist, and made me to sit on my heels.
>
> Then Kurosaki ordered me to stand up, and when I did so he punched me three more times in the chest and once to the jaw. I did not know what was happening, so I told him that I did not understand English. He showed me a note I had given to the guard. I admitted it was my writing. He asked if I was a service-man and I said no.
>
> I asked for Mr. Sasaki, an interpreter. He told me what the lieutenant was saying. "Don't stare at me with those eyes," was the gist of it. "Or would I like to be struck again?" I had little choice. I told him to strike me as much as he pleased.
>
> My jaw did not hurt much but my chest did.[123]

On 13 October, the following day, the violence was resumed.

> Everyone took note of the incident and expected that I would receive an apology befitting the United States. It never came. Instead, after the daily walk ended at 9:30, I was told to clean 900 square feet of passageway alone as a disciplinary measure....
>
> I developed blisters on my hands and perspired. It must have surprised Kurosaki that I did as I was told in spite of the pain in my chest. After lunch I was ordered to wash the stairs between the first and second floors.[124]

On 14 October Sasakawa noted cryptically in his diary, "Lieutenant Kurosaki is as persistent as a serpent."

On 15 October Sasakawa was threatened again. His diary entry reads: "Where does the fatty's [Lieutenant Kurosaki's] cruelty and world-class cold-bloodedness come from?"

The next day, 16 October, Sasakawa wrote, "He said he would give me the toughest chore of all, scrubbing the wall. I worked an hour and forty-five minutes right up to 4:15 p.m."

On 17 October matters were no better:

After breakfast I was singled out again. It was work for cruelty's sake.... I was forced to labor again from 9:35 a.m. I expected him to let me off when I had completed the job, so I worked until I was worn out. But he kept me at it without rest until 11:45 a.m.

Lieutenant Kurosaki continued to press the next day:

Today...I cleaned the windows for two hours and forty minutes, from 1:35 to 4:15 p.m. The guard kept checking and I had not a minute of rest."

The forced labor routine continued for twelve days until 24 October 1946. On the previous day Sasakawa had written: "My hardships are many times worse than the humiliation suffered by the Han Chinese general Kwan-shin (died 196 B.C.E.), who was forced to crawl between the legs of his captors."

Sasakawa lost his appetite and suffered headaches and chest pains. By 16 October, halfway through the beatings, he had lost so much weight that he "could now easily do up my pants' buttons."

An eyewitness summed up Sasakawa's ordeal in these terms:

Sasakawa Ryoichi was punched by Kurisaki for one reason or another during our work periods. Although he suffered pains in his chest for the next two weeks Sasakawa was not seen by a doctor, and the warder insisted on cruelly putting this sick person to work, day after day.[125]

"No use brooding...."

Forever patient, self-confident, and above all optimistic, Sasakawa did not lose heart over this episode. Kurosaki, he noted, took the opportunity "to test the extent of my physical endurance." He added: "The cruelty and insults heaped on me helped me to cultivate my virtues." Moreover, Sasakawa had the assets of humor to match the situation. "If I were asked to be a back-scrubber in a public bath, I would resolve to be the best scrubber in the world."[126]

On 26 October, two days after the last of his beatings, he wrote the following:

I won the battle by returning virtue for Mr. Fatty's violence. I wonder if there is something wrong with my chest. It would shame him if due to his violence I am hospitalized and the incident becomes public and he is punished. He has just been pro-

moted. I must try hard to get well. Of course, the incident must
be brought to the attention of the US Army but I want to do this
without having him punished. Mr. Fatty, who is the ultimate in
cruelty, would probably not understand my feeling.

This is a great opportunity to help America improve its ways,
regain the trust of the Japanese and promote Japan-US goodwill.[127]

No matter how brutally the warder behaved Sasakawa had the
big-heartedness not only to forgive, but to put himself in the other's
shoes, while keeping his commitment to nonviolence and non-appease-
ment. Class A war criminal suspect Sasakawa had won a complete spiritual victory over Lieutenant Kurosaki, who had behaved so abominably
using the authority of the victor nation.

On 28 October 1946 Sasakawa wrote to Shizue, his wife:

It is no use brooding over things one cannot help.... One must
return violence with virtue. It is not worth burning oneself up
inside with thoughts of vengeance. One suffers for it, and even if
one were to get one's revenge one day, all it would only start a
vendetta. There would never be total victory or defeat. It would
all be so meaningless. If only one side exercises patience, we
will be saved from the pain of a vendetta.

Exercising patience does not mean defeat. Formally I may have
lost, but spiritually it has been a total victory. To cope with this,
one should be unconcerned with the praise or criticism of others,
and stay the course against the ill wind of slander. Let the enemy
realize the uselessness of ill will, and be discouraged from further
mischief. Without this firm determination, one would forever be
an easy target of unpleasantness and contempt.[128]

This was a precious piece of advice, coming from one who had survived
the physical abuse and who followed the biblical injunction, "Love your
enemies and pray for those who persecute you." (Matt. 5:44).

Events moved swiftly thereafter. At the end of 1946 Lieutenant
Kurosaki was transferred from Sugamo and put in charge of catering.
Four months later he was court-martialed for some wrongdoing and was
sentenced to ten years in prison. He was given an additional seven
months for injuring Sasakawa.[129]

According to Kodama Yoshio, there was a little known background
to these events: "Kurisaki had kept a woman by secretly appropriating a
great portion of the food intended for the detainees in Sugamo and re-
moving it in a US Army truck for sale on the black market.[130]

This may explain why the food at the jail had rapidly deteriorated after Lieutenant Kurosaki became head warder in 1946.

VI

Sasakawa, we have seen, was very different from the other inmates in Sugamo. Unlike the bulk of the Class A suspects he felt an ongoing responsibility for the state of the nation. Feeding the people came first. Ordinary Japanese were acutely short of food in the aftermath of the war and right up to the end of the Occupation in 1952. There were many other issues to contend with. Inflation was rampant and the economy needed an expert hand to guide it back to the path of stable growth — but the lack of food was the most vital problem.

Troubles did not come singly. Sasakawa was concerned about the safety of millions of compatriots still in foreign lands. We have seen how with the courage of a Don Quixote he had written to President Truman and General MacArthur imploring them to provide food assistance and to curtail the inflation. He also communicated with Japanese leaders. On 3 June 1946 Sasakawa wrote to Prime Minister Yoshida Shigeru, with whom he probably was not personally acquainted: "In order to build a new Japan, economic breakdown must be prevented and our 75 million brothers must be saved both from rampant inflation and death from starvation."[131]

On 17 December 1945 Sasakawa noted:

Awake or asleep, my mind is preoccupied with the Communist Party problem, the general starvation and the safety of our compatriots scattered abroad. Victorious Americans, please, just think of our situation. Loving your family and your relatives as you do, please consider that we are all the same. Will you not make our families happy by bringing home their loved ones on your ships? At the moment, the rice we purchase cannot be transported because there are no ships. Will you not put yourself in our shoes and send us rice?

The best way to make the Japanese true peace-lovers is not by taking our arms away. Rather it is to be a doctor who cares for his patients, setting aside the fact that we were your enemies. I would gladly give my life if I could save our helpless and pitiable fellow countrymen. Dear Americans, think what you would feel, if you were the defeated people. Believe me, our resentment at having had our homes burned and our brothers killed will instantly dissolve if you act with compassion. We will forever respect the United States of America as our big brother and will not forget our gratitude.[132]

Sasakawa chiefly feared expansion within Japan of communists and their sympathizers. This was for a number of reasons, among them his strong resentment of the inhuman regime of the Soviet Union, the home of communism, and its policy of external aggression. He opposed Marxism, and of course the avowed aim of Japanese communists to end the monarchy in Japan.

Above all, he believed that the food policy of the Japan Communist Party (JCP) was obstructing food aid from America:

> It is futile for the JCP to mobilize people to mount a food dem-
> onstration outside the Imperial Palace [in Tokyo]. There is no
> rice to be had, and the demonstration will only make people
> hungrier. Such action is contrary to what the party purports to
> stand for. Its groundless propaganda and its claim that the JCP
> has unearthed hidden food supplies make them feel good and
> self-righteous.
>
> Are they themselves living only on meager official rations by
> any chance, and not buying on the black market? It is easy for
> them to point a finger at others while deceiving us claiming that
> they are the only true saviors. A plague on them! They are sabo-
> taging General MacArthur's goodwill offer to import rice by al-
> leging that somewhere there is 3.42 million tons of rice hidden
> away. This cruel deceit is driving the Japanese people to starva-
> tion. How can the JCP claim to be compassionate? The party
> talks of humanity and justice but it behaves like a wild animal.[133]

Praying for the rice harvest

Sasakawa was furious with the communists. They were playing dice with the lives of the people they purported to represent. He was a country boy. Thoughts of the harvest began to fill his mind. A good harvest that year would help. He was well informed, based on what his constituents told him of the desperate lives they led. His strongest critics acknowl-edged Sasakawa's qualities. For example, Royama Masamichi, a profes-sor turned journalist, while having denounced Sasakawa to the US Counter Intelligence Corps, also noted:

> Sasakawa is a talented and eloquent orator and is extremely
> good at winning the hearts and minds of the destitute and
> lower-class people. He is particularly popular among blue-collar
> workers with little education.[134]

Sasakawa's diary for 1946 frequently mentions the weather in relation to prospects for the rice harvest:

The weather these days makes me worry that there will be a poor harvest. (8 May)

The wheat needs sun round this time of the year. But it is fine one minute and cloudy the next. Weather like this spells a bad harvest. (14 May)

Got up at 5 a.m. and prayed for better weather and a bumper crop for the sake of the victims of the war. (15 May)

It makes me happy to have this long-awaited spell of good weather. Prayed today for a rich harvest. (29 May)

At the height of summer, he continued to make notes on the weather:

This fine weather and the heat should be good for the rice harvest. For the rice cool evenings are the best thing to hope for. I say it is worthwhile to pray. (14 July)

It is good weather, and if we have this heat for some more days it will be good for the rice harvest. If I should die in this steamy heat the rice will do well. (15 July)

I waited for the typhoon thinking that it could feed the rice, but it never came. (19 August)

Am still waiting for the typhoon but it never comes. (20 August)

By 10 September 1946 his spirits had risen:

It is the 220th day of the lunar year, which is normally the peak of the typhoon season, but thank goodness there is only token rain. It will be a good harvest. I thank heaven and earth.

After all his anxiety about the weather it was only natural that Sasakawa was beside himself with joy when he came across a newspaper article forecasting a bumper crop in 1946.[135]

Give peace a chance

At the same time that he was beset with these home country concerns, Sasakawa was worried about the international situation. He had been concerned from prewar days for the whole world, and not just for the Japanese people. Before the war he believed that if necessary Japan should use military force to undermine Western colonial domination of Asia and thereby bring about the liberation and independence of non-white peoples in the region. After the total defeat of Japan in World War Two his thinking underwent a complete change. He dreamed of re-nouncing the world's arms to save humankind forever from the scourges of war. There was a clear link, as noted earlier, between the prewar slogan "Hakko Ichi'u" (Eight Corners of the World under One Roof) and the postwar ideal of "the world is one family." Sasakawa wrote soon after he entered jail: "In defeat we have the important obligation and responsibility to exert our best efforts to establish peace."[136]

Particularly noteworthy is the development of his thought soon af-ter his detention commenced. He wrote that "the peoples of the world are all brothers [and sisters]." He launched an appeal, even from jail as he noted in *Sugamo Diary* (p. 104), to "start a movement right here in Sugamo for the salvation of humankind and to save our brothers [and sisters] all over the world." It was certainly ambitious, if not ridiculous, for a detainee — a Class A war criminal suspect, no less — to dream of starting a new peace movement from within the four walls of a prison cell. Others were certainly not in the mood for it.

Yes, it may have seemed absurd to others at the time, but Sasakawa was in earnest. He shared his thoughts in an open letter that began "My Dear Friends," dated 25 December 1945:

> The leadership that will save our people eternally from the scourge of war and enable them to live free and happy lives as true peace-loving people will not come from those opportunis-tic bystanders, but from those who will be acquitted after endur-ing hardships as war criminals.[137]

In another "My Dear Friends" letter dated 18 February 1946, he emphasized the consistency of his ideology before and after the war:

> I have always fought against loveless power, and worked to build a paradise on earth. With the end of the Great East Asian War my thoughts turn to the need for Japan to become a god-dess of peace based on the realization that killing people is the worst evil on earth. That is why George Washington admonishes that putting an end to war is the first of the three great American principles to be observed.
>
> In spite of this, constant warfare has victimized hundreds of millions of people. While the survivors yearn for the eradication of war and the salvation of humankind from its scourges, they

have no voice. A better memorial for these noble victims, rather than at altars with incense and flowers, will be by building a paradise on earth through the establishment of a permanent world peace and ensuring that all peoples live as brothers in peace and harmony.

To achieve that goal, the absolute basic policy must be to abolish weapons and redistribute food, clothing, and shelter worldwide. I declare this will be much more effective than organizing any number of United Nations organizations.[138]

In March 1946 he drew up an "Initiative," as he called it, on everlasting peace worldwide and sent it by mail to Shizue, his wife, with the following instructions:

I have drawn up the "Initiative" as a prayer for the souls of the war victims and must be read by as many as possible. It must be printed and distributed widely. Those who wish to develop virtue can reproduce it and send it to their friends as a postcard for happiness. The worldwide famine is a proof that the souls of the war victims have yet to be laid to rest in peace. The war dead did not die in vain, and their spirits are still troubled.

The document read thus:

The Initiative

The cruelest thing is killing and the worst is in war.
Since time immemorial many have worked to prevent war.
Nevertheless, we have known incessant wars with hundreds of millions wasted in carnage.

These noble victims yearn to put and end to war and save humankind forever from its horrors, but they do not have voices.

The best service we can perform in their honor is to establish eternal world peace, save humanity, and so build a paradise on earth in which we can all live happily as brothers and sisters.

I therefore declare that I shall be the mouthpiece and the messenger of these victims, and work tirelessly to achieve the grand objective through global disarmament and the distribution of the essentials, such as food, clothing, and shelter.

Anyone who does not support this movement is a coward and his sons and heirs shall not prosper. Those who oppose the initiative are enemies of humankind and invite misfortune for posterity. Those who support the proposal and cooperate will be assured of their reward in future generations.

The victims of war will long live in the minds of men and in eternal union with nature, and the families they left behind will be protected. I offer this initiative to the gods and Buddha and all the spirits and I beg that they watch over us and protect us so that we may expeditiously achieve our objectives.

— Initiator, Sasakawa Ryoichi

[seal][139]

Sasakawa explained his "Initiative" to his friends in a letter dated 18 May 1946:

Those of us detained here by the US Army have no fear of starvation, but I worry my head off night and day for compatriots who are doomed to suffer under the vicious inflation and to be tormented by starvation because of cowardly and irresponsible politicians. The strength of my anger can shake the walls of my cell, but what can I do from inside jail?

I pray before every meal for the peace of the spirits of the war dead and for a rich harvest by reciting the Initiative to myself, thereby renewing my commitment before the gods and Buddha and all spirits, known and unknown, to global disarmament and distribution of food, clothing, and shelter for the ultimate goal of eternally rescuing humankind from the scourge of war.[140]

Sasakawa, as we have seen, had attended a Buddhist place of instruction, the local temple he went to in his mid teens, scrubbing the floors in the early hours of the morning. That education showed in those months when he faced life inside Sugamo and rubbed shoulders with Japan's war leaders on a daily basis. No other person in detention there had the temerity to dash off peace appeals, letters to world leaders, appeals to the prime minister and prayers for peace.

Two decades later, Sasakawa was much of the same mind — to uphold the cause of peace. In April 1964 he used his enormous private funds to construct a "Memorial Dedicated to the Victims of All Wars" in Ibaragi in Osaka Prefecture. In August of the same year he also established a foundation called the "War Memorial Association for the Victims of All Wars." The memorial is in the form of a large sphere made at great expense of duralumin to withstand rusting and the destructive power of typhoons.[141]

Sasakawa's multifarious activities as a global philanthropist, starting in the 1970s are extensions of the "Initiative" launched from Sugamo Prison under conditions that must now seem all but indescribable in terms of their squalor and suffering.

Everything began there.

VII

Freed

On 24 December 1948 Sasakawa was discharged from Sugamo Prison with other Class A war crime suspects, including Kishi Nobusuke and Kodama Yoshio. None of them had been charged. After his release Sasakawa lost no time in providing support for the families of those who had been executed and families whose members were still serving out their terms in prison. He never abandoned them.

Once out of prison, he was a veritable one-man powerhouse when it came to caring for those who were still inside. He did so against a broad background of concern over current events. Sasakawa had repeatedly made mention in his diary of the crucial importance of providing redress and relief to the victims of war.

> Hate sin, and not the sinner. What do we do for the families of the war criminals? One cannot speak of humanitarianism without considering this point. This applies alike to the United States, Japan, and the world.[142]

On 12 February 1946 he noted:

> We must help families not to lose their means of livelihood. Lawyers must be encouraged to help win relief for the suspects. The Communist Party puts up a front that it is a humanitarian organization. It appeals to the public as a people-loving party. In reality, it is doing its best to make war criminals of fellow Japanese. They are liars, and it is an evil party.[143]

On 14 May 1946 he returned to the subject:

> Human beings are selfish. In war every country treats its men in uniform and their families well, and bereaved families too. But once the war is over both the winning country and the loser forget all about compensation for their fighting men and the injured. What can we say about Japan? After 15 August 1945 even official burials were conducted according to military rank. What defamation of the war dead! Given this sort of attitude, how can victims of war be able to rest in peace?[144]

There was no end to his lament, as he wrote in this entry made on 15 May 1946:

> During the war the dead heroes and the families they have left behind, as well as the fighting men themselves, are treated well, but as soon as the war is over they are given the cold shoulder. This ungratefulness is common to both the victor and the defeated. It is particularly inexcusable where the dead are concerned. Japan would do well, in defeat, to conduct memorial services for the dead. Why hesitate?... Those of you outside, pick up your courage. Don't be cowards. Let us all, the winners and the losers, remember the dead and offer our eternal respect to the bereaved families and those who died for us.[145]

Four months later he wrote:

> Those who fail to put themselves in the shoes of those who are in jail and to consider their anxious families are beasts, not men. Neither rank nor birth can change that.[146]

Newspapers, radios, and record players

The first thing Sasakawa did after his release in 1948 was to send in newspapers, radios, record players, and records to the men who were still detained. He wrote constantly comforting and encouraging letters in spite of all the many tasks he had to attend to. He visited Sugamo frequently, and when he was not available he sent members of his family to talk to those still serving sentences in prison. Shibuichi Mitsuo, who worked under Sasakawa for a long time, told me that sending in the newspapers alone cost Sasakawa 30,000 to 40,000 yen a month.[147]

Sasakawa was tireless. He petitioned the US authorities to reduce the sentences imposed, covered the travel expenses of their families living in the countryside to visit Sugamo, and gave them financial support. He bore in mind others who were still detained overseas. Thus Sasakawa remembered those Class B and C war criminals detained in Muntinlupa Camp in the Philippines. There, the conditions were far worse than in Sugamo.

The Sasakawa family received thousands of thank you letters from those still held in jail and their families. The family has kept the letters to this day. They speak of Sasakawa's exceptional kindness and their profound gratitude to him. Then, as now, society tended to treat war criminals as villains rather than as victims. It was risky for Sasakawa to have assisted them or to help them in regaining their honor. Knowing this, the prisoners were all the more grateful to Sasakawa for his dedication.

In time recognition came his way.

Yamaura Kan'ichi, a well-known commentator, had this to say in an article he wrote titled "War Criminals Released." Published in the *Tokyo Shimbun* on 21 June 1952:

> To the best of my knowledge, Sasakawa Ryoichi started the movement to free the war criminals and to support their families. He too was detained in Sugamo as one of the suspects but on the very day he was released he began this campaign.
>
> It was difficult to openly undertake it in those days, for unlike today the United States held strong views about the war criminals, to the extent that any Japanese who would initiate a movement of this sort was labeled anti-American and faced the danger of being sent back to Sugamo.
>
> Sasakawa gave up smoking and drinking and dedicated himself to the cause he supported. He involved his family, notably his seventy-seven-year-old mother, his wife, brothers, and employees.
>
> Since this man, the initiator of the support and release campaign, is a former right-wing leader it is easy for those who seek to criticize to associate what he has undertaken with such causes as Japan's rearmament and anticommunism. But that's being jealous. A good deed is a good deed regardless of who does it.[148]

The letters

Some of the letters Sasakawa received from thankful prisoners and their families appear below:

Letter 1

> I am most grateful for your frequent letters. I learned with great emotion from men working at the golf course about your recent visit to Mr. Saito with your kind and gracious wife....
>
> During my interview the other day with Mr. Tsukamoto, head of Sugamo Branch Prison, he spoke of you saying, he wished that there had been even one more, if not five, like you among the Class A men who were let free. Mr. Yoshimura of the Ministry of Foreign Affairs also said that you were the only one who visited the Ministry to talk about helping those still serving sentences.[149]

Letter 2

Thank you for your generous gift of the record player, which men in every ward and on every floor have in turn enjoyed. We were also deeply moved to learn that you had generously supported our amateur performances on 26-27 September. We know only too well that there must be many things that occupy you now that you are free.

You have not only generously sent each of us comforting presents but your own good mother and wife have also shown the same warm understanding.

I am without words to express my profound gratitude.[150]

Letter 3

I thank you for your welcome letter received today. I have nothing but gratitude for you and your whole family for working for us in so many ways.... Indeed, soon after you left the jail you wrote to many of us and I wanted to write to tell you how moved I was, but not knowing you in person I hesitated, and now a postcard has arrived from you, written by your wife. I deeply regret my earlier idleness.

All of us have ingrained in our memory a deep gratitude and respect for you, sir. How many of the former leaders, classified as Class A and B, are working for us? Indeed when most of them are merely concerned about defending their own interests and thus bending their long-held beliefs my respect for you makes me feel especially close.

I am sorry I cannot adequately express the depth of my feelings.[151]

The punishments of December 1948

Events, it may be noted, had followed their course at Sugamo. Tojo Hideki and six others had suffered the supreme penalty. They were executed on 23 December 1948.

For the others: All Class A prisoners not charged were released by 24 December. Twenty-five Class A war criminals were indicted and found guilty. Seven leaders were hanged and the remaining eighteen were given either life sentences or very long prison terms. There were many Class B and C war criminals as shown in Table 1. Defendants under US jurisdiction were all interned at Sugamo from the beginning. But those tried, sentenced, and executed by other countries were kept in jails overseas under far worse conditions.

This broad picture is evident in table 1:

Table 1. No. of Class B and C war crimes suspects by country of detention and trial

Country	No. of Cases	No. of people	Death	Life impri- sonment	Fixed term	Not guilty	Others
The USA	456	1,453	143(3)*	162(2)*	871	188	89
The UK	330	978	223	54	502	116	83
Australia	294	949	153	38	455	267	36
Netherlands	448	1,038	236(10)†	28(1)†	705	55	14
France	39	230	63(37)‡	23(4)‡	112(2)‡	31	1
Philippines	72	196	17	87	27	11	27
China**	605	883	149	83	272	350	29
Total	2,244	5,700	984	475	2944	1,018	279

Note: "China," as found in the table above, refers not to the Communist but to the Kuomintang government of China. Numbers in the column marked "Death" includes execution by firing squad and hanging carried out by the United States, Britain, Australia, and the Philippines. Imprisonment for an indefinite period includes imprisonment for life. The "Others" column includes cases in which an indictment was withdrawn, the case dismissed, the judgment overturned, or cases of repatriation for reasons of sickness, or escape, and unknown outcome.[152]

* Numbers in brackets denote sentences commuted after conviction.
† Numbers in brackets denote sentences commuted after conviction.
‡Numbers in brackets denote those not arrested but tried in absentia.
** "China" refers not to the Communist government but to the Kuomintang government of China.
Numbers in the "Death" column include execution by firing squad and hanging carried out by the United States, Britain, Australia, and the Philippines. Imprisonment for an indefinite period includes imprisonment for life. The "Others" column includes cases whose indictment was withdrawn, the case dismissed, the judgment overturned, or cases of repatriation for reasons of sickness or escape, and unknown outcome.
Source: Tokyo Saiban Handobukku Henshu Iinkai [Tokyo Trial Handbook Editorial Committee] ed., *Tokyo Saiban Handobukku* [Tokyo Trial Handbook] (Tokyo: Aokishoten, 1989), 219.

Some countries chose to send their prisoners back to Japan rather than keep them in detention. Some 121 prisoners of France, serving sentences overseas, were repatriated to Sugamo in May 1950; and 693 prisoners of the Dutch were returned to Japan in December the same year. Seventy prisoners held by Britain and Australia, and serving their terms in Hong Kong were repatriated to Sugamo in May 1951; and 231 more from Singapore on 14 August 1951.

However, the repatriation of prisoners in Kuomintang Chinese and Soviet custody, as well as those held under Philippine jurisdiction and in Australian custody on Manus Island had to await the final realization of the San Francisco Peace Treaty in 1952 or even later.[153]

A cruel twist: Article 11

Japanese independence, as realized by the San Francisco treaty signed in September 1951, had immediate implications for Sugamo. Following the signature of the treaty the operation and management of Sugamo Prison was transferred to the Japanese as of 15 February 1952. After 28 April 1952, the day when the peace treaty came into force, the prison came under the jurisdiction of the Japanese government both in name and fact, and its name was changed from Sugamo Prison to Sugamo Keimusho in Japanese. At the time, there were 111 Japanese detained in the Philippine Muntinlupa jail and another 206 in the Australian Manus Island jail. Their custodianship was transferred to Japan in July 1953 and August 1953 respectively.

With Sugamo back under Japanese custodianship prison conditions improved substantially. It was established, as juridical practice, that war crimes would not be considered as "previous offenses" under Japanese law. Moreover, prisoners were entitled to cast absentee ballots in elections and to do so from the prison. Food rations improved as well. While ordinary jails in Japan allocated 50 yen a day per head for food, Sugamo had a budget of 120 yen per person. Inmates were given free access to newspapers and library books, and were served tea and coffee. Five cigarettes a day were distributed. Baths were available every day. There were no longer any restrictions on visitors. Forced labor without compensation as practiced under the Occupation management ceased; labor was now compensated and prisoners were offered a choice of working or not. Prisoners were allowed to enjoy outings on parole. After February 1953 public employment agencies started offering them jobs outside.

With these changes for the better Sasakawa's relief activities gained momentum. In addition to his regular visits to the prison he arranged to speak to the men to encourage them, while Shizue played her *biwa* (Japanese lute), and recited classical Chinese poetry. With the thought of preparing the men for employment after they were released, Sasakawa donated an automobile and made arrangements with the police so that the men could get driving licenses while still at Sugamo.

There was a problem, however. Prisoners were still not actually released even after Japan recovered its independence. This was in accordance with Article 11 of the San Francisco Peace Treaty, which stated in part:

> Japan will carry out the sentences imposed thereby upon Japanese nationals imprisoned in Japan. The power to grant clemency, to reduce sentences and to parole with respect to such prisoners may not be exercised except on the decision of the Government or Governments which imposed the sentence in each instance, and on recommendation of Japan. In the case of persons sentenced by the International Military Tribunal for the Far East, such power may not be excercised except on the decision of a majority of the Governments represented on the Tribunal, and on the recommendation of Japan.

During the period when Sugamo Prison was under the de facto control of the US Army, commutation and parole were readily implemented. But after Japan achieved independence in 1952 these matters were subject to diplomatic negotiation, making the release of prisoners more difficult.

Prisoners of their own country?

Naturally, this development was unexpected and disappointing for most of the prisoners. They had hoped for speedy release after independence. Under the circumstances they were all the more grateful to Sasakawa for his support. Their letters speak for themselves.

Letter from Hoshino Naoki, 29 May 1952

> Thank you so much for visiting us with your wife. It was indeed thoughtful of you, and timely, to have brought the great Mr. Machino.[154] I believe that it is very effective to bring elected representatives as you do to Sugamo. I also believe that the grand venture of liberating Sugamo has advanced a step and I express my sincere respects for your efforts.
>
> Thanks to you, those who were depressed after the peace treaty, particularly the young, have felt their morale boosted, and their faces brightened yesterday for the first time in many

weeks. As I listened to your good wife recite a Japanese poem I could not control my tears.

Due to lack of resourcefulness, and above all their negligence, the government and diplomats have committed one blunder after another [a reference to the government's approval of Article 11 of the peace treaty]. Liberation of war criminals has become a challenging venture requiring enormous legal maneuverability and power. There is no one else besides you. It is not an exaggeration to say that tens of millions depend on you alone. I can only beseech you to keep working at it.[155]

Letter to Sasakawa Shizue from an old family friend

Allow me to write you a letter of gratitude. You have graciously taken the trouble and time to visit us today at Sugamo Prison for which I have no adequate words to express my appreciation.

On that occasion I thoroughly enjoyed myself listening to your exquisite recitation of poems and music on the *biwa*. They were the kinds of entertainment I had wished for all along and I deeply enjoyed the passionate rendering of your program, as did all the others as you saw. It would be redundant for me to describe their excitement here for fear of spoiling your memory. Please let me express all my emotions by just saying thank you.

I knew your father and your brother rather well during my time in China, and every time your name was mentioned it brought back many a fond memory. Since then your husband has written frequently to encourage us and you can imagine how his few but warm words have been music to the sensitive emotions peculiar to us war criminals.

Your husband continues to work untiringly for us with the zeal of family and kin. For seven long years since the end of the war, from the time when few paid attention to us (or if they did, it was anything but hospitable) you and your husband have shown us consistent sympathy and understanding, rare in our populous country where even family planning is necessary.

The way you shower indiscriminate blessings on us like the sun and the moon is unparalleled and wins our unbounded gratitude. The unquestioning respect and love we have for you, young and old without any exception, as for our own mother and father and without any of the cynicism that colors our times, can only be the fruit of the inspiration you give.

I am concerned in my heart of hearts that in today's rough

world you must face many difficulties, particularly where material things are concerned. The chivalrous spirit of your husband was a national asset even in prewar times, but to see him boldly and without vacillation obeying his firm convictions under the present circumstances and to have you there supporting and encouraging him with your benevolence has been a source of hope to us. We are gratefully reminded of our enormous debt to you as we enjoy the daily gift of your newspaper.[156]

Letter to Sasakawa

I have no adequate words to thank you for visiting us with your wife the other day. Indeed, I have nothing but admiration for your untiring devotion and efforts on behalf of all of us in Sugamo. A few years back, when some of us on occasion organized an in-house entertainment, you generously supported us each time. Later, when I created Sugamo Gakuen [an educational initiative started voluntarily by the inmates in April 1949, whose lectures were given in turn by the prisoners] and were even short of chalk for the blackboard, I turned to you without any introduction for assistance. How delighted we were when you responded with your characteristic generosity and supplied us with ten boxes of chalk every month. There is no one at Sugamo who fails to be grateful for your constant kindness through the newspapers you provide, the private visits you make and the many encouraging postcards you send.

I now learn that as a consequence of your passionate persuasion of Mr. Machino Takema and political leaders and parties, including even the communists, preparations are underway for parliament to adopt a resolution for our release. We marvel at the greatness of your vision and the innovative ways you work for us.[157]

Letter from Segawa Masumi

I admire my respected *sensei* everyday as an incarnation of the great Saigo Takamori (1827-77).[158] On 3 June you were accompanied by the honorable Maeda Ikuo, an elected representative from my home town of Kagoshima. Being easily moved, I quietly wiped away my tears with a yellow cloth I had, the moment the two of you entered the auditorium. I shall make sure that this emotional encounter will be remembered forever by my sons and their sons.

There are voices among us at Sugamo to urge Sasakawa *sensei*'s candidacy for a seat in the House of Councilors from a nationwide constituency. There is no word to adequately thank you for your most pure compassion and sincere commitment with which you have undertaken to salvage us war criminals. Through each word of this inadequate letter I have tried to convey to you my profound sense of gratitude.[159]

Letter from Kawaguchi Kiyotake

I thankfully acknowledge receipt of your six-page letter dated 11 July, which arrived on 16 July. I am most grateful that you continue to work energetically for us at the height of summer. You have personally brought top political party executives and over one hundred members of both houses of parliament to Sugamo, and convinced their obstinate and disinterested minds to have both Houses pass the resolutions concerning the release of war criminals. The saying "An act of sincerity moves heavens" literally applies to you. Please accept my sincere respects.

Everyone at Sugamo, as well as those who were detained in overseas jails, promised without exception to do their best for the war criminals once they got out. No doubt they meant what they said but when they came to it there was a lack of will and passion so that their impressive promises usually ended up in disappointment. By contrast, you presented a motion in the Diet and roused public opinion in our favor, although you are still under the shadow of a public purge. There was a common understanding among those who had been purged to keep quiet in order to speed up the end of the purge. I bow my head to you.

You did not stop there. You went on to organize a Parliamentarians League for the Release of War Criminals, while enlisting one hundred and twenty-plus members from the Liberal Party [Ji'yu-to] alone to effect the release of all prisoners, both in and outside of Japan. We are truly indebted to you.

I learned that on 25 June, the anniversary of the outbreak of the Korean War, communists and Korean student demonstrators assembled at Machikaneyama in Osaka. Fifty of them broke from the group and, while on their way to Suita via Hattori,[160] forced their way into your home where your mother lives, swearing and shouting that releasing war criminals was proof that Japan wished to restart the war. Your seventy-seven-year-old mother stood her ground and told off the hooligans, bravely saying that she regarded their attack as proof of the success of her son's work. Like mother like son! I was deeply impressed.

I shared your precious letter with those serving time and life sentences (wearing red prison clothes) as well as those on death row (in their blue uniforms). All were deeply moved and I know that some have written directly to thank you. We admire your noble spirit and willingness to sacrifice yourself, undeterred by death, for a moral rebirth. The country needs someone like you, a selfless man of action. Please look after yourself well, and be careful not to sacrifice yourself unnecessarily, for we want you to hold out till the end.[161]

VIII

With the transfer of Sugamo Prison to Japan in 1952, the prisoners held there, eager to see some forward movement and loath to spend more years sequestered in jail, organized what they called a Sugamo Release Committee (Sugamo Shakuho Iinkai), later renamed the Sugamo Steering Committee (Sugamo Un'ei Iinkai). At the same time, they launched a campaign for their release. In April of that year, three months after the San Francisco Peace Treaty took effect, the following petition was sent by the representatives of Class B and C prisoners to the prime minister, the foreign minister, the justice minister, and the chairman of the Central Rehabilitation Committee, a body that had the authority to recommend countries concerned temporary discharge and release of prisoners.

This petition read as follows:

In the light of the nature of war crimes and the principles of peace and reconciliation, all prisoners serving war sentences should have been released with the coming into force of the peace treaty in April 1952.

It is regrettable that the government not only failed to realize this, but continues to hold us in custody more than ninety days after the treaty came into force.

We, therefore, earnestly request that the government immediately recommend to the governments concerned the general release of Class B and C detainees, based on its ex officio examination so that we will be discharged between 15 August (the anniversary of the end of the war) and 8 September (the anniversary of the signing of the San Francisco Peace Treaty).

Copies of this petition were sent to the speaker of the House of Representatives, president of the House of Councilors, the president of the Japan Federation of Lawyers, the president of the Supporters' Organization of the War Convicts, Fujiwara Ginjiro, the director of Sugamo Prison — and Sasakawa Ryoichi. Sasakawa was the only person sent the petition who held no official post. This suggests the extent of the trust the prisoners placed in him.

In fact, he had up his sleeve what he called "an atom bomb" of a strategy for their release. He wrote:

It would require enormous time and expense to mobilize organizations to collect 10 million signatures.

However, the war convicts and their families cannot endure further delay. Since the government has signed Article 11 of the peace treaty, it would be difficult to obtain immediate release without an atomic bomb-like scheme. I have, after much thought and deliberation, often lying awake in the middle of the night, devised a well-thought-out plan that has in part already been acted on.

1. To move the Diet, the representative organ of the Japanese people, to submit a resolution requesting immediate release of all war criminals.

(a) To negotiate with the secretaries-general of each political party concerning the submission of the resolution. Negotiation took place on 19 May with Secretary General Masuda Kaneshichi of the Liberal Party and Secretary General Miki Takeo of the Kaishin-to (Progressive) Party. Likewise I had a negotiation with Mizutani Chosaburo, acting secretary general of the Right-wing Socialist Party, on 21 May.

Negotiations were held on 22 May with Nomizo Masaru, secretary general of the Left-wing Socialist Party. In addition, I have an appointment next week with Representative Kazahaya Yasoji of the Communist Party.

(b) To work on the leading politicians of each political party to encourage their secretaries general as well as to convince their fellow representatives to adopt the resolution concerned.

(c) To accompany top party leaders to Sugamo to call on the prisoners from their home towns to remind them of the plight of those from their constituencies.

Those whom I had already taken were Miki Takeo of the Progressive Party on 21 May, Mizutani Chozaburo, policy council chairman of the Right-wing Socialist Party on 23 May, and Murakami Isamu, standing member of the Liberal Party's General Affairs Committee on 24 May. Future plans include visits by Shi'ikuma Saburo and Yoshida Yasushi, executives of the Progressive Party on 26 May, Kanda Hiroshi, Executive Council member, and others from the Liberal Party on 27 May. Among others I took on 29 May were Hirai Yoshikazu, Executive Council member, and other executives such as Uda Jiro and Konishi Toramatsu of the Liberal Party, and Arita Ki'ichi, an executive of the Progressive Party.

2. To work on every prefectural assembly to submit the same resolution demanding immediate release of the prisoners. This may seem superfluous but has the desired effect of enlisting public opinion.

3. To aggressively mobilize governors of the prefectures for the purpose of comforting the prisoners and supporting their families.[162]

Characteristically, Sasakawa moved forward on several fronts at the same time. *Sasakawa Ryoichi Kankei Bunsho* (Sasakawa papers) contains a copy of a letter he sent to prefectural governors, and to mayors of cities, towns and villages throughout Japan to achieve his strategies (2) and (3). This courteous alert read as follows:

Dear Sir,

As we approach summer I trust this finds you in good health and successful in your endeavors.

Let me alert you to a situation I think you may wish to be informed about. Many of our war criminals are misunderstood as being consummate villains due to the misinformation of their enemies. Some of these prisoners had overreacted, angered at having their homes bombed and family members killed. They may have killed, but only under orders. The victors, however, have also overreacted by imposing the maximum penalty on their former Japanese captors in revenge even for slight offences such as being slapped in the face or refused a cigarette. Our enemies have committed their own atrocities on war criminal suspects since the war and even after the excitement of war had cooled. I for one was detained in Sugamo as a Class A war criminal suspect and was acquitted and released on 24 December 1948. During my three years in jail I have been punched in the face and chest for impertinence. As a result, on one occasion, I ran a high fever. The next day I was ordered back to hard labor and eventually fell ill. They gave me a pack at night, but dragged me out of bed to force me back to work the following day. If the enemy could do this even after the frenzy of the war had passed, how would they have behaved had they found themselves in the same dire conditions as the Japanese troops?

Our war criminals are national victims who deserve our sympathy. They and their families had believed that, with the peace treaty, they would all be released, but now they find themselves living ignominiously in jail even after its ratification. This has to be rectified by what I think of as an atom bomb-like expediency. I beg you, therefore, to show sympathy for the war criminals and their families and adopt by unanimous consent a resolution requesting their immediate release. I would make this request to you in person but because of the urgency of the matter I must ask your understanding that I appeal to you by letter. I shall also be appealing in writing to prefectural, city, and municipal assemblies to adopt a resolution similar to that passed by the Diet and to deliberate on taking appropriate measures to comfort and support the detainees and their families.

Yours sincerely,[163]

Leaving no stone unturned, Sasakawa even drafted an appeal to the Throne. The following draft of a letter intended for the Showa emperor in his own handwriting is kept at the Nippon Foundation:

In the face of the unparalleled disgrace and the first surrender since the beginning of our history, the people were moved by Your Majesty's proclamation to end the war and found strength and comfort in your presence. Having said this, there is a matter of great import for which I must beg your indulgence and bring before your attention, namely that a great number of war convicts languish in jail even after the restoration of our independence.

Today there is much deliberation, even in the countries that were victorious, as to whether war trials are legally and morally justifiable. Some legal experts say that trials do little more than gratify the victors' desire for revenge, and make a show of power. They contend it represents a shame to civilization and is the worst blunder of the recent war. The process and substance of the recent trial were clearly marred by injustice and unreasonableness, and those sentenced were "victims of the worst injustice," to quote Dr. R.B. Pal, one of the panel of judges at the Tokyo International Trial.

With the peace treaty in place and independence recovered, common sense dictates that all war crime detainees should be released. Having experienced the worst of the war, they are well qualified to be the apostles of peace. Their families, too, suffer distress and sorrow instead of the honor and protection they deserve for offering their loving husbands, sons, and brothers for Your Majesty and their country.

I write because your people know of Your Majesty's deep concern for them. At this critical time a concrete expression of this by Your Majesty in behalf of the suffering families and the immediate release of the detainees would be profoundly appreciated by all your subjects.

It will win the hearts and minds of all Japanese and preserve the beauty and strength of the imperial system.

I humbly beg Your Majesty's august consideration.

Whether this letter was ever presented at the palace and, if so, whether it reached the Showa emperor is unknown. Even if the letter had been presented to him, given the negative mood against war crime convicts, it would have been unrealistic to expect the emperor to take any action for the prisoners' release, and it might well have been counterproductive, as the Left would have been quick to portray any such move as a sign of the resurgence of the prewar imperial system. But still, this letter indicates Sasakawa's passionate commitment.

It took until 1958....

Efforts to free the war criminals grew into a nationwide campaign. With the support of many people a War Convicts Supporters Group (Senso Jukeisha Sewa-kai) was established on 10 May 1952. Between 12 June 1952 and 19 July 1955, the House of Representatives passed no fewer than six related resolutions, while the House of Councilors passed three of its own. It took until 30 May 1958 for the authorities to bring about a final result. The last eighteen convicts still being held were then granted "temporary discharge" as required by the United States. By 29 December their sentences were reduced, and finally, with the exception of those imprisoned in Communist China, the last war criminals were free.

Sasakawa continued to organize memorial services for those who had been executed as war criminals, and found ways to help their families carry on daily life. There was much to do. In March 1953 the bereaved families had formed an association called the White Chrysanthemum Society (Shiragiku Izoku Kai) with Yamashita Hisako, the widow of General Yamashita Takebumi who had been executed in the Philippines, as its first president. The society erected a Guardian Deity of Peace (Heiwa Minoshiro Jizoson) in Gokokuji, a temple near Ikebukuro in Tokyo. Buddhist memorial services were held regularly for the 1,068 men who were executed.

When the memorial services at Gokokuji were discontinued, Sasakawa offered his home in Sengoku, Tokyo, as a place to hold services on the eighteenth of each month. These services continued up to 1971 and altogether were held 241 times. When no home could be found for the stone Guardian Deity of Peace, Sasakawa made space for it at his own home. In due course, the venue of the memorial services moved to the tenth floor of the Japan Shipbuilding Industry Foundation's building, where from 1972 the ceremonies were held twice yearly, in January and September, to make it easier for family members, many of whom were now elderly, to attend. Finally, on 18 January 1993, the White Chrysanthemum Society was dissolved, and the services were discontinued. All along it had been Sasakawa who had kept them going. He urged banks and corporations to make donations as "incense money" to cover the society's expenses. In due course, Kimura Kaho, the widow of General Kimura Heitaro, succeeded Mrs. Yamashita as the second president of the association. She was said to have commented that the White Chrysanthemum Society, even with the membership of 1,068 bereaved families of executed Class A, B, and C war criminals, would not have continued had it not have been for Mr. Sasakawa's support since it lacked financial resources.[164]

An eyewitness record

Onishi Hajime, who was detained in Sugamo as a Class B war criminal, has described how Sasakawa devoted himself to the prisoners and their families, and how he was respected by them:

> Sasakawa Ryoichi spent three full years in Sugamo as a suspect at the Far East International Military Tribunal from December 1945 to the same month in 1948 when he was released. We can never forget how he constantly maintained friendly communication with the young detainees who found themselves blown by circumstances into the prison like small abandoned boats, encouraging them with warm sympathy and strong leadership and providing us with a sense of purpose in life. At a time when people tended to be apologetic in their dealings with the US authorities Sasakawa was true to his convictions and demanded fearlessly what he felt was our right, which left us in awe of him. He had once led a political party and showed a capacity for orga-

nizing people.

After his discharge, he and his wife continued to comfort men in the jail, all the while encouraging and supporting their families including those whose members had been executed. He deplored the way society looked down on the detainees, which he put down to US Army propaganda, and he took it on himself to influence powerful politicians to come to their rescue. On many occasions Sasakawa brought them to Sugamo, affording us opportunities to give them true accounts of the war trials. Today, most citizens look at us with sympathy in place of disgust, thanks largely to the efforts of Mr. Sasakawa.

In 1950 a religious group called the White Water Lily Association (Byakuren-sha) was established to conduct memorial services for those who were executed and to comfort the detainees. When the association was dissolved two years later the White Chrysanthemum Society (Shiragiku Izoku-kai) was left without a sponsor, Mr. Sasakawa lost no time in offering his home for the bereaved families to continue their memorial services each month. The services are still held regularly today. It has become customary for many political and former military men to pay respects to the dead at the invitation of the survivors' association and Mr. Sasakawa.

These monthly meetings have given immeasurable hope and courage to grief-stricken families. Family members who just wept each time they saw each other are more relaxed today and they are beginning to engage in animated conversation, often for long hours....

Mr. Sasakawa's high-mindedness and achievements are refreshing in today's morally corrupt world and he has our singular respect.[165]

Who knows of these services?

Sasakawa's endeavors in behalf of war criminals and their families are barely known outside circles close to him. This is partly due to Sasakawa's dislike of self-advertisement, but it seems to me to have something to do with the overriding concern people have for protecting themselves against taking any kind of risk — even of assigning praise where it is due.

When the White Chrysanthemum Society was dissolved in 1993, the Tokyo Broadcasting Station put together a special program in which it simply stated that the memorial services had been held earlier at the

Sasakawa home, and the last service was hosted by "that Mr. Sasakawa." It would not have taken much investigation to learn that Sasakawa's contribution was decisive to the existence of the association. This is another example of the formidable hold the Sasakawa taboo had on the media and on intellectuals.

Teru's part

Incidentally, Sasakawa's mother, Teru, kept up until 1957 her daily homage at a Shinto shrine, rain or shine, to pray for the early release of the convicts. She died at the age of eighty-two on 17 January 1958. Before her death she called Sasakawa to her bedside and instructed him "not to give me a funeral until everybody is released from Sugamo."[166] In fact, Teru's funeral did not take place until 17 June 1958, a month after the last person had been formally discharged from Sugamo Prison.

Sasakawa made his position known in many ways, large and small, regarding the lingering issue of the detained war criminals. Thus, he refrained from smoking and drinking, not to speak of taking no part in politics, until all the convicts were freed. When he finally invited to his home the last eighteen men from Sugamo, he downed a glass of beer with great gusto.[167]

Honoring the war dead

This was not the end of Sasakawa's commitment to honoring those who had suffered on the Japanese side. During World War Two many Japanese soldiers and civilians died in East Asia and the Pacific islands, and 1.5 million failed to return home. In 1975 the Japan War-Bereaved Association (Izokukai) planned to send a delegation composed mainly of the children of the war dead to collect the remains. Sasakawa and his Japan Shipbuilding Industry Foundation (JSIF) supported the project generously, and Sasakawa himself led the delegation to the South Pacific islands, paying expenses from his own pocket. In that same year the governments of Japan and the Philippines agreed to erect a war memorial in the Calamanian Islands.

The JSIF provided the funds for a twelve-hectare memorial park, including a Japanese garden, around the cenotaph. In addition, the association has since 1978 provided subsidies for memorial events held annually to cherish the memories of the civilians who died in air raids and bombings.[168] During all this time, Sasakawa was continuing to play a leading role in helping convicted war criminals and conducting memorial events for all those who died as victims of the war.

IX

One of the salient characteristics of Sasakawa was that he did not hesitate to criticize the United States openly when he felt it was deserved. At the same time he kept an open mind, free from the inferiority complex that he feared had become the hallmark of his compatriots. In one of his letters addressed to "Dear friends" he compared the way Japanese and American prosecutors carried out their investigations.

When I was detained without being convicted ten years ago [in Osaka, from 1935 to 1938] I often shared my candid views regarding the state of our justice system out of my love of the country and respect for the law. My openness was repaid with bitterness. I did not have a single happy memory of those interrogations. Yet all l did was ask for a comprehensive investigation of myself and others in order to search the truth of the matter. Still, those [Japanese] investigators treated me cruelly and despotically. By contrast, interrogations by the US Army were quite pleasant.

Out of my respect and goodwill, I often spoke boldly and frankly, articulating on behalf of the Japanese people, and pointing out where the Americans had contradicted themselves. Not once were my comments received with displeasure, nor was I ever treated badly. My interrogators were gentlemen. Those in authority in Japan would do well to learn from them. I pray that the day will come, hopefully soon, when the cowardly and self-seeking power holders in our country who swim with the tide and bow to the money and military might of the US forces, will be replaced by true Japanese who will be called upon to rebuild a peaceful Japan.[169]

One of the arrows in Sasakawa's quiver was humor, if necessary of the bawdy variety. When the US Army prosecutors asked him about his relationship with Kawashima Yoshiko, Sasakawa replied as follows:

Relations between men and women belong after dark. What takes place after dark is a private matter. I am an upright man above my waist but I give no guarantees below it. I beg you not to ask questions on such matters.

This response caused his questioner to burst out laughing. Sasakawa later wrote about this incident:

It is desirable for both interrogator and the interrogated to have a bit of latitude. When you have a stern and uptight Japanese investigator, and a Japanese defendant who can't crack a joke — well, the truth may not emerge so easily. Japanese prosecutors, in particular, have a lot to learn. They take things too personally and they bear grudges. In that regard I thought the American prosecutors were so much more human. One may pound on the table to make a point but they do not hold things against one. Frankly, they were disinterested and free of self."[170]

On the sincerity of lawyers

Among the papers kept at the Nippon Foundation are some letters exchanged between Sasakawa Ryoichi and Kawashima Yoshiko. Sasakawa refers to himself in this correspondence as "icchan" (part of his name "Ryoichi" in child's language) and Kawashima calls him "onii-chan" or "my big brother." It appears that Kawashima, used by the army and in constant danger of assassination, lived a lonely and dangerous life but trusted Sasakawa.

American lawyers left an indelible memory on Sasakawa for their sincere defense of Japanese who were accused or under suspicion.

It may be difficult for Japanese to understand their mindset, but I imagine it to be the fruit of the nobility of mind that accepts truth as a matter that supersedes all ethnic groups and national borders. Is it at the same time the reflection of a truly democratic state? A person can be cynical about the international war trial but he cannot but at the same time bow unconditionally to the sincerity of the American lawyers.[171]

Sasakawa was the last person to seek to ingratiate himself to the US Occupation forces or the prosecution in the war crimes trial. In fact, he did not hesitate to criticize any behavior he thought was contradictory to American democracy. Yet, "Americans who claim to respect freedom, equality and human rights do not treat me accordingly," Sasakawa wrote in his diary.[172]

And again:

Americans are easygoing about their own misdoings and tough on others, thus severely punishing the Japanese for their misbehavior. It is a white lie that Americans respect human rights....[173]
They are clever. They pretend to treat you with respect but torment you mentally. The Japanese does not torment you men-

tally but does not treat you with respect either. Which is the greater evil?[174]

Admiral Yamamoto and the Americans

As described above in Chapter 1, Sasakawa thought like Admiral Yamamoto Isoroku in that he was reluctant to launch war against America. But once the war began he threw himself into the cause with all his strength. He was not shy to declare himself the number one war proponent of war in the country.[175]

Yet after the war his cool-headed judgment made him see that the world would evolve around a confrontation between the United States and the Soviet Union. He therefore devoted his energy to building close relations with the United States. At first glance this may appear inconsistent, but there was logic to it. He gave priority to national interests and ample consideration to realpolitik.

Here is how Sasakawa described his state of mind after the war:

As Yamamoto Isoroku's foresaw, we would not be able to sustain our national strength if the war lasted more than eighteen months. Japan surrendered, overwhelmed by American might, after spilling the last drop of its blood. It was an inevitable outcome. In such circumstances, the warrior of the past met his death honorably. He accepted his fate, without cursing others or harboring bitterness against them, but simply blaming his own lack of skill and inexperience. That was my feeling toward America. In war each side fights with all its might and the weaker loses. This is logical. It is not reasonable to hold a grudge against the victor. Having fought fairly on the battlefield it is no time to be dishonorable afterwards. That is the wisdom coming from both Japanese Bushido [the warrior's chivalrous sense of honor] and the American sense of fair play. I felt no bitterness or grudge against America, but I had a mountain of things to say against a certain other country.

(The "other country" mentioned here was the Soviet Union. At the time he was preparing his book *Expressions of Sugamo* for publication, he wished to make this reference ambiguous since Japan was still under Allied Occupation, including the Soviet Union, and to criticize one of the Allies could jeopardize publication.) He considered that his final contribution to his country was to spill out his feelings regarding the Soviet Union at the trial.[176]

In all of this, a point to recognize or to restate is the consistency of Sasakawa's thinking before, during, and after the war. We have seen how his prewar notion of "Hakko Ichi'u" (Eight Corners of the World under One Roof) had developed into the concept of the world as "one family" in the post war years and how his prewar populism evolved into post-war democracy.

This is not to say that the defeat and the ensuing years in Sugamo Prison had little or no effect on him.

> My three years in prison gave me the time and the opportunity to reflect on myself.... Throughout my detention, and the ensu-ing years until all the war convicts were finally released, my mother made daily visits to the shrine to pray for us in spite of the poor state of her health. It was her devotion that changed my whole life and way of thinking, I would have to say, and enabled me to face the postwar years. I vowed then to devote myself the rest of my life to the construction of a new Japan and to the less fortunate among us.
>
> There was a time in my life when I was ambitious and wanted fame, and to boost the family name. And then there were times when I wanted to give myself to a just cause. I went through ups and downs in fortune and had to grapple with contradictions in my own life. After the war, I learned all about human beings in Sugamo and I don't know whether to call it enlightenment, but I lost all selfish desires.[177]

As to the war and the defeat:

> The years in Sugamo made me realize the utter stupidity of the war crimes tribunal. Without the experience of Sugamo and the crushing defeat of Japan I might have continued to tout milita-rism and be a warmonger, while enjoying the spectacle of the weak going to the wall. If, as a consequence of Japan's defeat, Asian peoples were truly liberated and able to enjoy independ-ence, the result is good and our sacrifice may not have been in vain.[178]

Sasakawa was not one of those who made a volte-face after the war or jumped on the bandwagon. However, he had "died" once — with the defeat of Japan. There is no doubt that the defeat was the most stagger-ing reverse of his life. But true to his character he fought hard to come back. He had found a purpose in life when he declared while he was still in Sugamo: "I have the power to move others because I act not as

Sasakawa Ryoichi but as a messenger of the uncountable victims of war, with a mission to free all people from its misery forever."[179]

Sasakawa, on his own account, had "died" along with the Empire of Japan and was then reborn as a larger man, thanks to his mother's self-sacrifice and "the myriad spirits of the war victims." In the next chapter we discover how he had a business inspiration while in prison in Sugamo. Its success enabled Sasakawa to build what became the world's largest private grant-giving foundation. The spiritual basis of the philanthropy for which he was destined to be widely known was nurtured during the Sugamo days.

Notes

1.   See Chapter 2, p. 136, Table 1.

2.   Sasakawa Ryoichi, *Sugamo Nikki* [Sugamo diary] (Tokyo: Chuokoronsha, 1997), 124.

3.   Nosaka Sanzo was a leader of the Japan Communist Party who returned to Japan from China after the war ended. He had engaged in anti-Japanese propaganda during the war, basing himself at Yenan, the operational center for the Chinese communist leadership under Mao Zedong.

4.   Ishikawa Tatsuzo (1905-85) was a novelist and winner of the Akutagawa Prize. He was known for his work on the 1937 "Rape of Nanking," as an instance of large-scale arson, plunder, and murder of civilians and surrendered Chinese soldiers by Japanese forces.

5.   Sasakawa, *Sugamo Nikki*, 143. *Konnyaku* is a jelly-like food made from taro.

6.   Ibid., 276.

7.   Ibid., 37.

8.   Ibid., 405.

9.   Ibid., 288.

10.   Ibid., 311-12.

11.   Ibid., 66.

12.   Honma Masaharu, commander of the Japanese 14th Army, directed operations in the Philippines from 1941 onward and was sentenced to death after the war by a tribunal held in Manila as the commander responsible for the "Bataan Death March."

13.   Sasakawa, *Sugamo Nikki*, 101. Yamashita Takebumi was a supreme Japanese commander in the Philippines.

14.   Sasakawa Ryoichi, *Sasakawa Ryoichi no Mita Sugamo no Hyojo* [Expressions of Sugamo, as seen by Sasakawa Ryoichi: Secret records of a "war criminal suspect"] (Osaka: Bunkajinshobo, 1947), 89.

15.   Sasakawa, *Sugamo Nikki*, 329.

16.   Sasakawa Ryoichi, *Sasakawa Ryoichi Kankei Bunsho* [Sasakawa papers], unpublished documents kept at the Nippon Foundation, dated 18 May 1946.

17.   Sasakawa, *Sasakawa Ryoichi no Mita Sugamo no Hyojo,* 32-33.
18.   Sasakawa Ryoichi, unpublished documents, submitted to International Prosecution Section (IPS), nos. 6, 9, and 10, date unknown.
19.   Yamaoka Sohachi, *Hatenko Ningen Sasakawa Ryoichi* [Sasakawa Ryoichi: Record-breaking man] (Tokyo: Yuhosha, 1978), 231-32.
20.   Awaya Kentaro and Yoshida Yutaka, eds., Vol. 24, *Kokusai Kensatsukyoku (IPS) Jinmon Chosho* [Official records of interrogations by examining prosecutors] (Tokyo: Nihon Tosho Center, 1993), 221.
21.   Ibid., 126, quoting Civil Intelligence Section (CIS) records, *Minkan Joho Kyoku,* 4 December 1945.
22.   Ibid., 201, quoting US Army General Staff Section 11, G-2 "Top Secret" document, 4 July 1947.
23.   Paula Daventry, ed., *Sasakawa: The Warrior for Peace the Global Philanthropist,* 2d ed. (New York: Pergamon Press, 1987), 56.
24.   Sasakawa, *Sasakawa Ryoichi no Mita Sugamo no Hyojo,* 39-44.
25.   Yamaoka, *Hatenko Ningen Sasakawa Ryoichi,* 236-37.
26.   See Counter Intelligence Corps, 90th Army Post Office 660, unpublished document no. 4, declassified by Occupation Authority on 26 November 1990 (10 December 1945).
27.   Ibid. Awaya and Yoshida, Vol. 24, *Kokusai Kensatsukyoku,* 143.
28.   Awaya and Yoshida, *Kokusai Kensatsukyoku,* 143-44. Royama Masamichi was the influential editor-in-chief of *Chuo Koron,* a liberal magazine founded in 1899 that reached a peak during the Taisho Era when democracy flourished. Publication halted in 1944 as paper was in short supply and resumed in 1946.
29.   Kokushidaijiten Henshu Iinkai [The Editorial Committee of the Encyclopedia of National History], ed., Vol. 2, *Kokushi Daijiten* [Encyclopedia of national history] (Tokyo: Yoshikawa Kobunkan, 1980).
30.   Abe Shinnosuke, ed., *Gendai Nihon Jinbutsuron* [Contemporary Japanese personality portraits] (Tokyo: Kawadeshobo, 1952), 260.
31.   Kodama Yoshio, Vol. 2, *Fu-un: Kodama Yoshio Chosaku Senshu* [Winds and clouds: The collected works of Kodama Yoshio], ed. Kurihara Kazuo (Tokyo: Nihon Oyobi Nihonjinsha, 1972), 176; and Vol. 3, *Fu-un,* 360. Kodama returned from China just before the end of the war with a planeload of commodities and gold — a fortune that he donated to Hatoyama Ichiro, a leading conservative politician. The latter used this treasure to fund the Liberal Democratic Party, the group that has ruled Japan continuously since 1945 either in its present form or in a coalition of the two political parties that created the LDP by joining forces in 1955.
32.   See Awaya and Yoshida, Vol. 24, *Kokusai Kensatsukyoku,* 229-30.
33.   Sasakawa Ryoichi, "Fukkokuban Hakko ni Yosete" [Introduction to the reprinted edition], in Sasakawa, *Sasakawa Ryoichi no Mita Sugamo no Hyojo.*
34.   Sasakawa, *Sugamo Nikki,* 113.
35.   Ibid., 154.
36.   Sasakawa, *Sasakawa Ryoichi no Mita Sugamo no Hyojo,* 202.

37.   Sasakawa, *Sugamo Nikki,* 129-30.

38.   Ibid., 138.

39.   Ibid., 139.

40.   Ibid., 141.

41.   Ibid., 296-97.

42.   Ibid., 312.

43.   Ibid., 439-40.

44.   Sasakawa, *Sasakawa Ryoichi no Mita Sugamo no Hyojo,* 143-45.

45.   Sasakawa, *Sugamo Nikki,* 120.

46.   Document no. 10, dated 8 January 1946. The English text is contained in IPS official records of interrogations by examining prosecutors. See Awaya and Yoshida, Vol. 24, *Kokusai Kensatsukyoku,* 154.

47.   Sasakawa, *Sugamo Nikki,* 409-10.

48.   Sasakawa, *Sasakawa Ryoichi no Mita Sugamo no Hyojo,* 146-47. The *moso* bamboo alluded to in the poem is the strongest, broadest-stemmed species of bamboo, found in southern parts of Japan.

49.   Sasakawa Ryoichi, *Jinrui Mina Kyodai* [Human Beings Are All Brothers and Sisters] (Tokyo: Kodansha, 1985), 35-36.

50.   Kishi Nobusuke et al., *Kishi Nobusuke no Kaiso* [Memoirs of Kishi Nobusuke] (Tokyo: Bungeishunju, 1981), 303-4.

51.   Kodama, *Fu-un,* 273-74.

52.   Sasakawa Shizue, interviewed by Sato Seizaburo, 14 August 1997.

53.   Sasakawa, *Sasakawa Ryoichi no Mita Sugamo no Hyojo,* 31.

54.   Ibid., 41.

55.   Document no 10, dated 8 January 1946. This Sasakawa statement partially translated into English and contained in Awaya and Yoshida, Vol. 24, *Kokusai Kensatsukyoku,* IPS, 154-65.

56.   Ibid.

57.   Samuel Healey, "Fairu Dai 185" [File no. 185]. Unpublished memorandum, dated 13 April 1946.

58.   Shioda Michio, *Tenno to Tojo Hideki no Kuno* [Anguish of the emperor and Tojo Hideki] (Tokyo: Nihon Bungeisha, 1988), 189-90.

59.   Awaya, numbered 25 in a series of portraits. Awaya and Yoshida, Vol. 24, *Kokusai Kensatsukyoku,* 41.

60.   Sasakawa Ryoichi, "Kokumin no Giwaku wo Isso no Gen'an" [Proposed ways to dispel the misgivings of the people]. Unpublished document, submitted to Occupation authorities, document no. 10.

61.   Pacific US Army GHQ Intelligence Section. Samuel Healey, "Fairu Dai 19" [File no. 19]. Unpublished document, dated 8 January 1946.

62.   Document no. 10, 8 July 1946.

63.   "Sasakawa Ryoichi Jinmon Chosho" [Records of Sasakawa Ryoichi's interrogation]. Unpublished document, dated 18 January 1946.

64.   Awaya and Yoshida, Vol. 25, *Kokusai Kensatsukyoku,* 1993, 431. Kodama had himself not been indicted up to this point, a year and a half after his incarceration. Like Sasakawa he was never to be indicted.

65.   Sasakawa, *Sasakawa Ryoichi no Mita Sugamo no Hyojo,* 190-94.

66.   Awaya and Yoshida, Vol. 24, *Kokusai Kensatsukyoku*, 312.
67.   Sasakawa, *Sugamo Nikki*, 391-93.]
68.   The International Prosecution Section, Supreme Command of the Allied Forces, unpublished documents, dated 4 August 1947.
69.   Awaya and Yoshida, Vol. 25, *Kokusai Kensatsukyoku*, 428-31.
70.   "Kodama Yoshio Jinmon Chosho" [Records of Kodama Yoshio's interrogation]. Unpublished document, 20 June 1947.
71.   Healey, "Fairu Dai 185," 21 July 1947.
72.   Yamaoka, *Hatenko Ningen Sasakawa Ryoichi*, 219-21.
73.   Awaya and Yoshida, Vol. 25, *Kokusai Kensatsukyoku*, 427.
74.   "Sasakawa Ryoichi Jinmon Chosho" [Records of Sasakawa Ryoichi's interrogation], unpublished document, dated 10 April 1946. The English translation of this part of the record is contained in Awaya and Yoshida, Vol. 24, *Kokusai Kensatsukyoku*, 293.
75.   Awaya and Yoshida, Vol. 24, *Kokusai Kensatsukyoku*, 232.
76.   Sasakawa, *Sugamo Nikki*, 277-78.
77.   Ibid., 279.
78.   Ibid., 311-15.
79.   Ibid., 284-86.
80.   Ibid., 174.
81.   Ibid., xx.
82.   Sasakawa, *Sasakawa Ryoichi no Mita Sugamo no Hyojo*, 176-77.
83.   Ibid., 57.
84.   Ishihara Hiroichiro, Akazawa Shiro, and Awaya Kentaro, eds., *Ishihara Hiroichiro Kankei Bunsho* [Ishihara Hiroichiro and related papers] (Tokyo: Kashiwa Shobo, 1994), 263.
85.   Ibid., 338.
86.   Ibid., 375.
87.   Ibid., 335.
88.   Kodama, Vol. 1, *Fu-un*, 401.
89.   Kodama, Vol. 2, *Fu-un*, 363-64.
90.   Takahashi Shin'ichi, ed., *Waga Kaigun to Takahashi Sankichi* [The Navy and Takahashi Sankichi] (Publication site unknown: Takahashi Shin'ichi, 1970), 106.
91.   Ibid. 114-15.
92.   9 January 1946. See Sasakawa, *Sugamo Nikki*, 66.
93.   15 January 1946. Ibid., 74.
94.   Sasakawa, *Sasakawa Ryoichi no Mita Sugamo no Hyojo*, 106-8.
95.   Ibid., 71.
96.   Ibid.
97.   Sasakawa, Sugamo Nikki, 79.
98.   Ibid.
99.   Sasakawa, *Sasakawa Ryoichi no Mita Sugamo no Hyojo*, 116.
100. Ibid., 72.
101. Sasakawa, *Sugamo Nikki*, 103.
102. Kodama, Vol. 2, *Fu-un*, 261.

103. Sasakawa, *Sugamo Nikki*, 213.
104. Ibid., 120.
105. Ibid., 125-26.
106. Ibid., 128.
107. Ibid., 103.
108. Ibid., 44-5.
109. Ibid., 152.
110. Ibid., 40.
111. Ibid., 377-78.
112. Sasakawa, *Sasakawa Ryoichi no Mita Sugamo no Hyojo*, 117.
113. Sasakawa, *Sugamo Nikki*, 247-48.
114. Sasakawa, *Sasakawa Ryoichi no Mita Sugamo no Hyojo*, 59-61.
115. Sasakawa, *Sugamo Nikki*, 265.
116. Sasakawa, *Sasakawa Ryoichi no Mita Sugamo no Hyojo*, 116-17.
117. Sasakawa, *Sugamo Nikki*, 191.
118. Ibid., 212.
119. Ibid., 216. As to the name of the officer, he is identified in *Ishihara Hiroichiro Kankei Bunsho*, Vol. 1, p. 400, as First Lieutenant Kurisaki; Kodama Yoshio refers to "Kurisaki" in his memoir "Wind and Clouds," Vol. 2, p. 284. Kurisaki is probably correct.
120. Ishihara et al., *Ishihara Hiroichiro Kankei Bunsho*, 400.
121. Ibid.
122. Sasakawa, Sugamo Nikki, 216.
123. Ibid., 215-16.
124. Ibid., 216-27. Sasakawa's references to the maltreatment are on pp. 218, 219, 220, 221, 222-23, 227. and 220.
125. Ishihara et al., *Ishihara Hiroichiro Kankei Bunsho*, 400.
126. Sasakawa, *Sugamo Nikki*, 223.
127. Ibid., 230.
128. Ibid., 360.
129. Ishihara et al., *Ishihara Hiroichiro Kankei Bunsho*, 400.
130. Kodama, Vol. 2, *Fu-un*, 284.
131. Sasakawa, *Sugamo Nikki*, 298.
132. Ibid., 38-39.
133. Ibid., 291.
134. Awaya and Yoshida, Vol. 24, *Kokusai Kensatsukyoku*, 143.
135. Sasakawa, *Sugamo Nikki*, references to the weather and the 1946 rice crop are found on pp. 142, 146, 149, 179, 182, 194 and 202.
136. Ibid., 84.
137. Ibid., 250.
138. Ibid., 259.
139. Ibid., 268-69.
140. Ibid., 290-91.
141. Tsurumaki Yasuo, *Kaikaku no Jidai* [An era of reform] (Tokyo: IN Press, 1989), 19.
142. Sasakawa, *Sugamo Nikki*, 68.

143. Ibid., 100.

144. Ibid., 146.

145. Ibid., 147.

146. Ibid., 201, entry on 7 September 1946.

147. Shibuichi Mitsuo, interviewed by Sato Seizaburo, 5 February 1998.

148. Yamaura Kan'ichi, "Senpan Shakuho" [Releasing war criminals], *Tokyo Shimbun*, 21 June 1952.

149. Numajiri Shigeru, letter to Sasakawa Ryoichi, 3 August 1949, addressing Sasakawa as principal of Sugamo School.

150. Taniguchi Gosuke, letter to Sasakawa Ryoichi, 3 October 1948.

151. Hayashi Yoshinori, letter to Sasakawa Ryoichi, 10 October 1949.

152. Tokyo Saiban Handobukku Henshu Iinkai [Tokyo Trial Handbook Editorial Committee] ed., *Tokyo Saiban Handobukku* [Tokyo Trial handbook] (Tokyo: Aokishoten, 1989), Table 1, 219.

153. Ibid., 140.

154. The given name of the Mr. Machino referred to was Takema. A former officer in the Japanese Army, he served overseas as an adviser to Zhang Zuolin (1873-1928), a Chinese warlord killed in 1928 when his train was blown up by the Japanese Kwantung Army. He was a notable figure who had served as an adviser to Prince Konoe (1891-1945), politician, prince, and prime minister.

155. Hoshino Naoki, letter addressed to Sasakawa Ryoichi. 29 May 1952. There was no longer any trace, in their relationship, of the confrontation that took place between Sasakawa and Hoshino, when the latter was serving as chief cabinet secretary under General Tojo Hideki.

156. Ochiai Jinkuro, letter to Sasakawa Shizue, 29 May 1952.

157. Numajiri Shigeru, letter to Sasakawa Ryoichi, 30 May 1952.

158. Saigo Takamaori (1827-77), a Satsuma clansman and politician of the waning days of the Edo Period and the early Meiji Period, who worked to bring about a bloodless "Meiji Restoration." He was killed by government forces in a showdown in Kagoshima.

159. Segawa Masumi, letter to Sasakawa Ryoichi and Sasakawa Shizue, 3 June 1952.

160. These are names of towns.

161. Kawaguchi Kiyotake, letter to Sasakawa Ryoichi, 28 July 1952.

162. Sasakawa, *Kankei Bunsho*.

163. Ibid.

164. Yamaoka, *Hatenko Ningen Sasakawa Ryoichi*, 264.

165. Onishi Hajime, "Sugamo no Oya" [Parents of Sugamo], *Sakuraboshi* [Cherry Blossoms and Stars], 1 June 1956, 11.

166. Yamaoka, *Hatenko Ningen Sasakawa Ryoichi*, 265.

167. Zenkoku Motaboto Kyosokai Rengokai, ed., *Motaboto 30 Nenshi: Topikkusu hen* [History of thirty years of motorboat racing: Topics] (Zenkoku Motaboto Kyosokai, 1981), 38.

168. Zenkoku Motaboto Kyosokai Rengokai, ed., *'81-'90 Motaboto Kyoso Nenshi: Kyotei Gannen karano Ayumi* [History of motorboat racing, 1981-90] (Zenkoku Motaboto Kyosokai, 1991), 116-17.

169. Sasakawa Ryoichi, "Shin'ainaru Shokun" [My dear friends], 15 April 1946, in Sasakawa, *Sugamo Nikki*, 274-75.

170. Sasakawa, *Sasakawa Ryoichi no Mita Sugamo no Hyojo*, 113-14.

171. Ibid., 153-54.

172. Sasakawa, *Sugamo Nikki*, 198.

173. Ibid., 203.

174. Ibid., 207.

175. Sasakawa Ryoichi, *Kono Keisho wa Nariyamazu* [The alarm bell never stops] (Tokyo: Shirakawashoin, 1981), 44.

176. Sasakawa, *Sasakawa Ryoichi no Mita Sugamo no Hyojo*, 29-30.

177. Nihon Gin Ken Shibu Shinkokai, [The Japan Recitation, Dancing, and Fencing Association], *Sasakawa Ryoichi Kaicho to Zaidan 25 Nen no Eiko no Kiseki* [Chairman Sasakawa Ryoichi and twenty-five years of the glorious history of our association] (Tokyo: Nihon Gin Ken Shibu Shinkokai, 1993), 6.

178. Sasakawa, *Kono Keisho wa Nariyamazu*, 44.

179. Sasakawa, *Sugamo Nikki*, 119.

Chapter 3

A New Role as a God of Wealth:
From Motorboat Racing to Philanthropy

I

S ASAKAWA RYOICHI emerged from Sugamo Prison in the autumn of 1948 with hardly a penny, and little to declare but his genius at making money. A book published in 1951 sums him up:

> Sasakawa had been detained as a war criminal (suspect) immediately after the war, but he conducted himself admirably while in prison. Even after his release he did so much to help those still in detention that there is not a soul in Sugamo even today who does not know his name. At fifty-two, he is in the prime of life, and based upon his rich experience to date, he is ready to make a fresh start. He will electrify the world.[1]

The forecast proved right. But that's hindsight. When he came out of Sugamo, it was not a hospitable world that awaited him. Japan was flat on its back. The Allied bombing of Japan had destroyed the main cities, the nerve centers of the nation, especially Tokyo. Hardly a single building stood in 1945, at least in the center of the city. Three years later, the worst of the winter famines was past, but the nation was still struggling to get to its feet, and was being battered by hyperinflation.

In addition, Sasakawa himself and his wife, Shizue, had another battle on their hands. He had owned a fair amount of property in the city; these were holdings that he had built up before World War Two. Almost all of these real estate holdings had been blown away, mostly by asset depreciation due to the postwar inflation, but also because his subordinates in the PPP had helped themselves to them. This was particularly true in Tokyo. Most of the land there had been sold off to cover living expenses and to help friends of the PPP. Shizue recalled: "Those were hard times. We had no money, just one big idea."[2]

We shall come to that "idea." Meanwhile, the one blessing was that his real estate holdings in the Kansai, the Osaka region, had survived. So he had something to start up with again. Thanks to his business acumen Sasakawa again amassed an enormous fortune in stocks in a short period of time. The Tokyo Stock Exchange was getting back to its stride, and enormous profits could be made there, not least by one with contacts and personal acquaintances at the top in business.

Teru's stand

Not that money sufficed to command respect, then or now, in Japan. And Sasakawa had an image problem. To have been a war criminal suspect carried a social stigma, especially in those days. Such was the way Japanese society worked. To be accused of a crime in this culture is to be guilty. For most Japanese there was no difference between an actual convicted war criminal and a suspect. Sasakawa was released from prison without indictment, so his friends knew, but most people were unaware of the distinction. To have been found guilty or not guilty did not come into the equation for him, because "not guilty" was a status that could only be acquired after going through a legal process. As we have seen, he never stood trial. This vague status led to a situation where the public regarded him as one of those reprehensible war criminals. In other words, he was a social outcast.[3]

The gravity of his situation was compounded by the purge order issued by the Allied forces. This meant that he could not accept public office or engage in any activity that met the public eye. On top of this, the fact that he led a right-wing organization before the war made matters worse.

Personal circumstances combined to hem him in within his family as well as in the world outside. His mother, Teru, told Sasakawa, when he emerged from Sugamo: "Son, you are not to go into politics. Your first job is to win the release of all war criminals. I will be sure to make my daily homage at the shrine."[4]

He respected his strict mother and kept his word to her, to concentrate on helping those actually convicted, and still held in Sugamo, to get out of prison; and to alleviate their sufferings until this happened. We have seen, in the previous chapter, the enormous efforts he put into such activities. His promise to his mother, the strongest influence in his life, meant that he had no choice but to obey. He could not consider entering politics, even after the Occupation purge was lifted.

On turning the pages of *Life* magazine

Given his irrepressible nature, Sasakawa was not daunted. He committed himself passionately to finding ways to support those detained in Sugamo. At the same time he looked for ways and means of embarking on a new business venture that was to be in money terms the biggest project of his life. Conditions were bad in Japan. The economy was not in working order, shortages existed on all sides, and daily life was hard.

Yet those were also times when dynamic new business ventures sprang up. An entrepreneurial mood gripped Japan. In short, it was a wonderful time to launch a great new idea. Sasakawa had one. He had found an inspiration that would bring him untold wealth, and at the same time allow him to pursue his passions in the decades to come — the reconstruction and development of Japan, and world peace. His idea? It was to create a new "public sport," motorboat racing, to be legalized for betting, thereby to attract the general public in swarms, like horse racing.

This idea came to Sasakawa, while he was in prison; he was in his cell one day browsing through a copy of *Life* magazine when he came across an image that grabbed his attention. It was a photograph of a motorboat. The article set bells ringing in his head:

> It was stated that over there (in America) motorboat owners enjoyed a higher status than owners of automobiles. Just at that time Lieutenant Admiral Fukudome Shigeru, one of the Class B war criminals held in Sugamo, recounted how he witnessed a test in Leyte Bay in the Philippines during the early stages of the war. Some weapons researchers had frontloaded a small motorboat with explosives, set the steering, switched on the engine, and sent the boat shooting into an obstacle. It exploded noisily. Fukudome took this idea to the Navy Ministry, but they had no time for it. It was the heyday of the big guns and mammoth battleships. If only he had had his way, the admiral said, the Battle of the Philippines could have taken a different course. That story was the first seed of the vision of motorboat racing that now began to develop in Sasakawa's mind.[5]

When Sasakawa was released from Sugamo Prison in the winter of 1948, the copy of *Life* magazine was among his few possessions.

A new sport is born

Motorboats interested him, for reasons that are now obvious. In occupied Japan (1945-52) the airplane industry, his old passion, was ruled out for anyone Japanese. The United States had put the aircraft industry off limits in the hope that Japan would never again rise as a military power. Island country that it is, Japan still needed access to the world in order to live. The Americans controlled all air routes. That left the sea as the sole channel of communication with the rest of the world. Thus, the development of the nation's maritime industry became an overriding priority and a linchpin of the postwar reconstruction of the country. Shipbuilding technology held the key. Motorboat racing could contribute to its advancement by pushing engine development. This was to be Sasakawa's mission and destiny.

He wasted no time once he had earned his freedom. In less than two months beginning in February 1949 he made contact with the major political parties, with central government ministries in Tokyo, and with individuals who knew about legalized gambling. Legislation was required. The main thing was to establish a motorboat racing law.

Without legislation, nothing could be done. That was why he contacted the political parties first of all. Politicians and civil servants would determine the outcome.

An après-guerre phenomenon

At the time, motorboat racing did not exist as a professional sport in Japan, or anywhere in the world. Sasakawa was proposing a new departure. The idea of racing identical-looking small, high-powered boats around a closed circuit, with spectators in the stands and bets placed simply had not occurred to anyone else in the world as far as we know. It was therefore difficult not to be skeptical about its future prospects.

Sasakawa, however, had a strong hunch about the potential success of the uncharted venture, and he acted on it. His reasoning was not difficult to follow and he explained it, as he made the rounds in Tokyo, calling on politicians and civil servants and friends, or receiving their visits. In postwar Japan, there had to be entertainment on offer, as anyone could observe, watching the way public bicycle, horse, and auto races were all of a sudden boom pastimes. This après-guerre need for fun broke into the open very quickly after peacetime conditions were restored. As early as October 1946, when a large part of the population was living below the poverty line and facing the prospect of a bitter winter, Sasakawa learned while still in prison that horse racing (*keiba*) had started up again and had caught the popular imagination. The public was starving for diversion.

A bicycle race in Kokura

When horse racing caught on, reasoned some in Tokyo with an eye out for new business opportunities, could other "public sports" managed by local governments be far behind?

As money was involved, and the lure to the public was the dream of winning a fortune, there were certain requirements even in the newly flexible postwar era. Such activities had to be regulated in the interests of the general public and civic order. This meant, as noted, that new laws had to be introduced for the new public sports.

In August 1948, just months before Sasakawa was released from Sugamo, a bicycle race law was enacted. There can be little doubt that this event served to focus his mind as he prepared himself for new ventures. This new law qualified competitive bicycling as a public sport, with appropriately high-minded and worthy objectives in mind. One objective was the "promotion of the bicycle industry," another was the need to get the economy going. A third objective was to buttress local government finances with a portion of the proceeds.

Local government finance, like the cities themselves, was in ruins. In November 1948, with the new law in place, the first bicycle race was held amid great public enthusiasm in Kokura city in Kyushu. The success of the Kokura event was immediately noticed around the country. A fad was born. Local governments, mainly at the prefectural and big city levels, competed to attract bicycling industry aficionados and investors to hold races.[6] Stadiums had to be constructed. Officials had to be hired. All this became possible after the new law was enacted. The Kokura race, it may be noted, was held just one month before Sasakawa emerged from Sugamo.

A fiesta in Zushi

Meanwhile, in May 1950, right in the middle of Golden Week (the holiday season that precedes the summer), a Japan-US Motorboat Racing Competition was held in Zushi, a seaside town about seventy minutes by train from Tokyo. Attracting up to one hundred thousand visitors, the event proved a great success.

Most of the spectators had never seen a motorboat racing competition. Such frivolities had taken place before in Japan but not in wartime, not since 1939.

Peace shattered, but...

[A month after the Zushi event war broke on the Korean peninsula. Japanese industry, in support of American involvement in the war (though technically part of United Nations forces) surged. Orders poured into Japan for matériel, for trucks, for food, and even beverage supplies. Companies that had been starved of business for five years following the end of World War Two suddenly found their order books filling up overnight. Money flowed into Japan and Japanese pockets. The US Occupation, which continued, would place no obstacles in the way of holding further events like the motorboat competition in Zushi.] A second Japan-US Motorboat racing competition was held, this time on the Edogawa River in Tokyo. Once again, the event drew immense crowds.[7]

Amateur motorboat racing, from that point on, was sure of a future in Japan. The two events, in Zushi and Tokyo, had shown there was a community of fans.

Sasakawa and those working with him on the motorboat-racing project went into top gear. He and his team wrote a draft law modeled after the *Bicycle Race Law* and took it to the Ministry of Transport. He went there with two companions of long standing, Yatsugi Kazuo and Fukushima Yone, a friend who knew all about motorboats and loved them. This trio, bowing deeply, requested the ministry to shape their draft into a well-phrased bill, spiced with all the appropriate civil servants' jargon, and place it before the Diet. Sasakawa, for his part, worked on ruling party politicians.

It was how one got things done in Japan — by making a parallel approach to the civil service and to leaders of the ruling Liberal Party. Sasakawa's bill reached the floor in the winter of 1950-51 and was submitted to the Transport Committee of the House in March. It was to all intents and purposes his, though it was in fact sponsored jointly by interested members of the three major parties, Liberal, Democrat, and Socialist. The bill declared three objectives, couched in high-flown rhetoric to convey good intentions:

1. To build a maritime industry, to serve as the foundation of the Japanese economy…to encourage technological innovation in the shipbuilding industry, and to improve the performance of ships' engines.
2. To disseminate maritime science, to focus attention on the importance of the sea, and to promote tourism.
3. To contribute to local government revenues through the distribution of a proportion of the proceeds from betting.[8]

Cogent objections raised

Sasakawa may have thought that the bill would sail through, given the support of members of the three main political parties. However this was not the case. The bill hit choppy water immediately. A number of cogent objections were raised by vigilant and outspoken members of parliament, based in part on prior experience with bicycle racing. Some members expressed opposition to legal gambling, noting that while bicycle racing had proved immensely popular, the placing of unsuccessful bets had broken up some families, arousing public opinion against these events. The public worried about opening new doors to the passion for gambling, or so some MPs said. To stir up trouble by tempting more breadwinners to the races was highly undesirable, said critics.

Was it proper, asked others, that national and local finance become dependent on revenues from gambling? Wasn't this wholly inappropriate? A nation should not become one of official gamblers, trumpeted some.

Kikukawa Takao, a Diet member, was one of those who spoke against the proposed bill. He noted: "Setting aside for now whether motorboat racing is more or less harmful than horse racing and cycling, one should not forget that local race meetings like these have come under fire from thoughtful citizens, precisely because they are connected with gambling."

Kikukawa maintained that rather than increasing these types of gambling, an opposite course of action was desirable; they should be curtailed:

> If the government endorses this gambling, there will be no end to it. Already, a dog-racing bill has been submitted to the Agriculture and Forestry Ministry for deliberation; and according to rumors a plan is underway to submit a bill legalizing bullfighting. Indeed, I hear that there are people who are preparing a cock-fighting bill as well.[9]

Objections were raised on other grounds in a general atmosphere of skepticism. Some critics claimed that motorboat racing lacked excitement and appeal, because the outcome was predicated merely on the performance of the boats, though this flew in the face of the fact that two events already held had drawn huge crowds. Sasakawa was unhappy. Some just spoke out without any basis, he considered. What did non-experts know of the skills of racing drivers at the wheels of high-speed boats? The criticisms did not stop. Some theorized that the sport would be vulnerable to fixing and to the rigging of results, and was therefore the least desirable form of public gambling.

Would not the boat with the best engine always win, asked Suzuki Naoto, one of the skeptical Diet members. That wouldn't be any fun at all. So could an upset result or some kind of fake accident not be arranged? That would, of course, be cheating. But who would know? More than one Diet member, Nadao Kimikatsu among them, spoke out about "fixing" as a possibility. Engine failure, he said, could ensure that a participant was defeated, but spectators would be unable to tell if the failure was genuine or faked. That could arouse the public. There could be agitation. There could be protests even worse than those seen at bicycle races, where fixing was suspected. There was a still greater chance of skullduggery when it came to motorboats. Or so it was said.[10]

This was not an end of the torrent of criticism. Skeptics said that this odd sport could never possibly break even, let alone make a decent profit. Diet member Kozakai Yoshio said that he had taken soundings, and had established, albeit tentatively, that motorboat racing was unlikely to have a future. It wasn't based on a strong business plan.[11]

There seemed, at first, to be no end to the objections lodged by the elected representatives of the people. Some doubted, openly, whether this new sport could make any difference, good or bad, in the realm of shipbuilding technology. What had little boats, such as these racers, to do with ocean-going vessels? They belonged to different worlds. Diet member Okada Nobutsugu raised this point. He had another criticism: it would be hard or impossible to find suitable venues. Then, he said, there were still other issues. How would the races proceed given the unpredictability of the weather? Would this not restrict the number of occasions when they could be held?[12]

There seemed no end to the chorus of doubts. Some raised the specter of intervention by organized crime. What would happen if *yakuza* (gangsters) appeared on the scene? Surely this new form of gambling would be attractive to them. All in all, that would have "negative educational impact" and "awful consequences brought about by the undesirable involvement of local bosses."

Diet member Tamaoki Shin'ichi mentioned the "negative experience" encountered in bicycle racing, which as everybody knew, "had an extremely bad effect on public morals." National newspapers and the media had exposed "the involvement of unsavory characters," meaning petty hoods, and other race goers bent on mischief.[13] Diet member Kosakai Yoshio said he shared such concern. He had heard that a certain "boss" or don of the shady variety — he preferred not to mention his name — had a grip on bicycle racing, and he feared that such a person might extend his territory to the new sport.[14]

Sending in the warhorse "Fuji"

In short, Sasakawa ran into heavy legislative weather. He experienced a major frustration. "His" motorboat-racing bill passed the House of Representatives, but then foundered. The House of Councilors, the upper chamber in Japan's bicameral system, threw out the bill, rejecting it at the last stage, after the draft had just struggled through the Transport Committee of the Upper House.

This reversal, however, served to put Sasakawa on his mettle. In the face of this rude rebuff he was suddenly very cheerful. Instinct told him that all would be well. Thereupon he instructed his man Fuji Yoshio, the veteran of the PPP from prewar days, to go directly and "negotiate" with Hirokawa Kozen, a pillar of the political world, who served as the secretary general of the Liberal Party, a very senior position in politics.

Fuji and Hirokawa, as it happened, were old friends and cronies, having known each other when serving in the Tokyo Metropolitan Assembly before the war. The outcome of this encounter, given their personal friendship, the indispensable glue in Japanese politics, was in itself fairly predictable. The "Sasakawa" bill was revived, with a little judicious rephrasing, and it was reintroduced to the House of Representatives and voted on for a second time. Now sailing before a fair wind to the very last stage, the controversial bill became the law of the land.

I can only conjecture that Sasakawa must have invested an enormous amount of time and resources in achieving this feat. Be that as it may, the *Motorboat Racing Law* had at last passed. This, however, was nothing more than a prelude to the main battle, as we shall see, of having the new law implemented.

II

With that somewhat vexing and messy start, it was perhaps to be expected that there would be further frustration. Sasakawa had obtained his *Motorboat Racing Law* and in theory the racing could begin, subject to prudent decisions on matters such as where, when and how, but in practice there was a lot more work to be done in building a legal foundation for the new sport. In fact, according to Shizue, "every day there was some new problem."[15]

Another crucial piece of legislation

Writing the bill into law had not erased the opposition to motorboat racing among some powerful politicians. To such people, the venture was itself essentially a gamble. Yet somehow, these opponents failed to constitute an immovable obstacle to the promoters of gambling of all kinds. A veritable sea change was in the making, as political leaders came to see what was at stake. This became apparent when a law calling for "Ad Hoc Special Measures concerning Bicycle Racing, et al." was enacted in June 1954.

This absolutely crucial piece of legislation changed the procedure regarding the handling of gambling proceeds. It was vital for that reason; it set a template to be followed in other "public sports" involving gambling.

Three percent of the take was no longer to be paid to the state, the ad hoc measures said, but to sports bodies that were under the all-observing eyes of the state. To be specific, the 3 percent of the gross proceeds from public races previously paid into the National Treasury would henceforth be paid into the accounts of these bodies (horse racing was dealt with separately):

The Federation of Bicycle Industry Associations.

The Federation of Small Car Racing Associations.

The National Federation of Motorboat Racing Associations.

The use of these potentially huge amounts of money was assigned to a body called the Central Depository of the Commerce and Industry Co-operatives, which in turn received its instructions from the ministries responsible. Each "public sport" was the purview of a different ministry: horse racing came under the powerful Ministry of Agriculture and Forestry (MOA); bicycle racing was the province of the very influential Ministry of International Trade and Industry (MITI); and motorboat racing was the responsibility of the Ministry of Transport (MOT).[16]

This all-embracing change was made upon the recommendation of C.S. Shoup (1902-) an American fiscal pundit, who had been appointed by the Occupation authorities in 1949 to head a committee looking into and investigating the workings of the Japanese tax system. He strongly believed that the national budget should depend on direct taxes for revenues, and thought that it was wrong to put gambling money directly into the coffers of the state.

The Upper House weighs in

The topic of gambling in fact raised apprehensions that were not easily laid to rest. Thus, the Upper House Commerce and Industry Committee adopted a "supplementary resolution" with the intention of making two things clear. First, that gambling was antisocial and not something to be encouraged. But, second, that under existing circumstances the government chose to make it possible. Exemptions were being offered for a period of one year for certain gambling activities, even while, as a rule, gambling was wrong!

The main points of the Upper House supplementary resolution were:

1. Exemptions were being offered to allow bicycle racing and betting thereon, and other such sports. This was because the funds thus created helped to boost industrial development.

However, the exemptions were still essentially "improper." "The Government should promptly take action to remedy the situation." In other words, gambling on these sports was treated as liable to be halted, when the situation permitted. Bans were under consideration. The activities had no guaranteed future.

2. The Government was urged to strengthen "supervision and improve the management of the Bicycle Industry Racing Association and other such bodies, as there were "not a few unsatisfactory points."

3. The *Bicycle Racing Law* and other such legislation had been put in place during the abnormal times that prevailed immediately after the war, and "should be abolished as greater stability is achieved in society and in the economy." The government should therefore "observe the degree of social stability, and as soon as possible take appropriate steps."[17]

The supplementary resolution fell short of clearly stating the Diet's view that public gambling was undesirable. But still the stigma was there, from Sasakawa's point of view. The effect of this was that motorboat racing and the other sports had a provisional air to them. The *Motorboat Racing Law* was not a time-limited legislation, but the temporary nature of the exemption, in law, had a comparable impact to making the *Motorboat Racing Law* and others into time-limited legislation. To be sure, at every deadline in the years to come, the exemption was extended to keep legalized gambling going, but people concerned were constantly under the pressure of uncertainty. The revisions made to the regulations governing their operation under time-limited legislation imposed restrictions including the number of days available for motorboat racing.

Kono speaks

Evidently, public feeling ran fairly high on this topic. One could see that from the fact that big shots in the world of politics involved themselves in the details. Thus, Kono Ichiro, one of the most powerful men in conservative politics and then minister of agriculture and forestry, announced his support for a rule that there should be horse racing only on Saturdays, Sundays, and public holidays. He made his position known in January 1955.

Kono's thinking was no doubt typical of the times. He said that it was reasonable to restrict horse racing to weekends and holidays given "the general economic pressure, as it affects people's livelihood and the need for them to work hard." He added: "This is appropriate to the new lifestyle." He went on to say that he planned to speak to the Minister of International Trade and Industry, to let the minister give his support to similar restrictions on bicycle racing. The Cabinet duly decided to introduce administrative measures with the effect of law to suppress all weekday gambling. There were no such restrictions on motorboat racing at the time. The sense was that there should be limits.

What then was the position of the Ministry of Transport, which had responsibility for motorboat racing? They had to do something, but not much, it turned out.... In due course, the ministry issued a "notification" regarding what was called "voluntary restraint" by those responsible: (1) motorboat racing should be held on three consecutive days including Saturday and Sunday plus a day before or after the weekend, or four days including the weekend, (2) holidays shall include local holidays, and (3) racing on weekdays shall be in the afternoon.[18]

Tanaka vs. Narita

Public concern over public sports gaming continued to weigh on politicians down the years. A decade later, in the 1960s, the high and mighty in the land were still under pressure on this topic.

This is a matter of public record. Thus, on 30 May 1966 two of the top politicians in the country, Tanaka Kakuei, secretary general of the ruling Liberal Democratic Party and a future prime minister, and Narita Tomomi, the secretary general of the opposition Socialist Party, faced off in a TV debate shown live nationwide. Narita took the lead. He called for an early and total abolition of public gambling for four reasons:

1. It was grossly contradictory for the government to prohibit gambling by law, on the one hand, and to enact another law citing self-serving reasons to condone it in certain designated places.
2. Some said gambling was a human instinct, but it was a big mistake to say that public sports gambling was necessary on that account.
3. As ever, irregularities and fixing in horse and bicycle racing had been repeatedly exposed, and such unwholesome activities should be discontinued as soon as possible.
4. To begin with, these special cases of public gambling had been condoned with the full knowledge of their evil nature, for the benefit of postwar reconstruction and financing of local governments. That period was a thing of the past, given the progress of the Japanese economy.

Tanaka, sounding cautious, responded by declining to condemn public sports as "unhealthy and socially unacceptable," but he did not consider them as desirable either. He therefore did not think it right that public sports gambling should take place everyday. The ideal would be to abolish public gaming, but he wanted horse racing to continue as an exception. He argued there were few irregularities in horse racing and that it had "a special nature and mission" compared to bicycle, boat, and car racing. The latter, however, as Narita said, had been set up for the avowed purpose of rebuilding shattered postwar Japan.[19]

A committee on "public sports"

Rsponding to an undercurrent of criticism, the government found it prudent to go through the motions of self-criticism. Accordingly, it set up a committee under the chairmanship of a veteran Finance Ministry official, Naganuma Hiroki, to consider the future of public sports.

The committee, which was appointed in February 1961, duly made a report, which added very little. Its anodyne introduction stated:

> Public sports are the target of much criticism, not least because of certain socially undesirable situations that their present forms of operation cause. On the other hand, one cannot ignore the role they are playing by providing subsidies to related industries and social welfare projects, and by promoting and contributing to local government revenues as well as by furnishing popular entertainment. Furthermore, it cannot be denied that the public aspect of the sports contributes somewhat to preventing greater harm.
>
> The committee is, therefore, of the view that, without providing alternative sources of revenue and programs for job relocation for those concerned, the total abolition of public sports would have enormous and unfavorable consequences, not least by opening the way to secret gambling. For these reasons the committee reached a decision to approve of their continuation, but basically not to increase the scope and frequency of these sports, more than at present, and to devise measures to prevent any resulting harm.[20]

The report was a realistic one trying to keep a balance between criticisms hurled at public gambling on one hand and the roles its proceeds are playing on the other as well as the danger that abolition of public sports would merely encourage more corruptible forms of private gambling. As we shall see, it turned out to be of epochal importance.

No rocking of the powerboat

There was in fact a powerful constituency in favor of legalized gambling in public sports. The shipbuilding and related industries saw motorboat racing as their savior. Said one expert:

> Things were at their worst in the early years, when motorboat racing was introduced in the 1950s. No bank was willing to make loans for the necessary improvements and innovation. In fact, the support of motorboat racing saved the situation.... Shipbuilding and its related industries contributed to Japan's recovery by building the world's best ships.[21]

Another top MOT official noted:

> Cash-poor "related industries" [parts suppliers] were able to go over the head of the shipbuilding industry and make their presence felt in the world. In cases where the Japan Development Bank refused to lend to them, the motorboat racing fraternity stepped in with a helping hand. This funding came from the races.[22]

Powerful politicians, Kono, Tanaka, and Narita represented the overwhelmingly negative climate against public sports at the time. The publishing of the compromise report reflected the realistic demands of the war-devastated industries. It is more than likely that Sasakawa pulled strings behind the scenes, too.

Sasakawa commented:

> No man is born without an urge to gamble....
> If motorboat racing is evil, then what about *pachinko* [pinball]?
> Most of the proceeds from motorboat racing are farmed back to society, but pachinko does nothing. The industry takes all. It does not make sense for *pachinko* to be allowed, and not bicycle, horse, car, and motorboat racing.

These were his points. He was aware of the criticism that public gambling broke up marriages and destroyed family life, but those were the consequences, more than anything else, of "weak will," he said. On the other hand, Sasakawa was realistic enough to accept that people could be led astray. He therefore wished to dilute the gambling factor, so that fans would enjoy the racing itself more than gambling. Races must enrich their lives, as entertainment. He noted the downside of racing and he encouraged those around him to humbly face criticism and put things right.[23]

His son Yohei put it this way:

Human beings are not all pure and spotless. They have their good sides as well as their bad. When they are blended into a harmonious whole, life is a pleasure.[24]

What the JSIF achieved (I)

Earlier, we noted how the "Ad Hoc Special Measures" of June 1954, as laid down for bicycling races, established a pattern for motorboat racing as well, according to which the gross proceeds were divided up and 3 percent of the funds were allocated to the National Federation of Motorboat Racing Associations. These funds, which were to grow to extraordinary proportions with the explosive growth of motorboat racing, accrued to the JSIF run by Sasakawa Ryoichi.

How were these funds utilized? As stated, their principal use was to fund the growth of Japan's shipbuilding industry, as it grew dramatically in the 1960s to establish itself as the world leader.

One may cite Ishii Yasunosuke, chairman of Mitsui Shipbuilding and a doyen of the industry in which he was associated from 1950:

Japan's shipbuilding industry has seen splendid times, sailing along ever since the 1950s...but a ship requires an enormous capital investment and a high degree of technical precision. We started by improving engine performance, then we focused on energy saving, and then on container ships, and automobile and other carriers. With purpose-built ships we were able to avoid waste and improve efficiency. Speed was improved as well. Large carriers crisscross the Pacific today at the speed of a naval cruiser.

Japan led in technology and in innovation in this field. The leadership all came from Japan. Our ship owners expected as much. Our shipping companies were world leaders. In every field we owed so much for basic research to the JSIF. It is no exaggeration to say that the Foundation was involved in every major technological development and breakthrough."[25]

What the JSIF achieved (II)

Author Tsurumaki Yasuo gathered together materials for a study of the JSIF, in which he quotes the remarks of Ninomiya Toshimichi, senior managing director of the Japan Small Vessel Industry Association, a key executive on the smaller shipping side, relevant to the JSIF contribution:

> Our main work was to organize small ship manufacturers into groups. By pulling together we saved on management resources. Thus, firms were able to stay in business. Low-interest loans were immensely helpful in bridging operating and building funds and capital investment. Firms needed money to pay their people. Frankly, most of the money came from the JSIF. To begin with we needed 800 million yen in endowment funding to start our association. This money came from the JSIF in its entirety. Basically the association had to run its projects on its own responsibility, but there was always a shortfall, and every year the JSIF generously provided grants and subsidies. Their sum total in the last twenty-six years comes to 2,901 billion yen. In addition we received a subsidy of one billion yen for technological development programs.
>
> All told, without the JSIF there would have been no Small Vessel Industry Association. We would not have survived, and we will not survive without them.

Japan is surrounded by the sea. Its flatland is only 30 percent of its landmass. There is a limit to land transport, no matter how many expressways are built. More trucks mean more carbon dioxide, more congestion, and a shortage of drivers...maritime transportation is the answer. In particular, coastal shipping. Japan needs small vessels. Without its coastal and ocean-going shipping it would not last a month.

The small vessel shipyards have inferior equipment compared to large-sized shipyards. Their technology is behind. This has to be rectified somehow. We must improve working conditions as well as the working environment to attract the best people. Without them the industry has no future.

For this purpose low-interest loans were provided through the banks. Many small and medium shipyards escaped bankruptcy by having access to this money, to cope with their immediate need of operating funds or for upgrading facilities. This sort of funding should be borne by the government or by local autonomous bodies, but they said they did not have the money and refused to help.

Well, the JSIF almost single-handedly provided us with funds to cover our needs. We were probably too naïve to these facts.[26]

Ginza vs. Kabuki

One at a time, Sasakawa addressed the problems that reared up in his path down the years. For him, it seemed, the sailing could never be as smooth as for the shipbuilding industry itself. Very early on, there was a battle for leadership in the motorboat-racing field. Sasakawa was the man who had succeeded in getting the *Motorboat Racing Law* enacted, as everyone knew, but he had a rival.[27]

Maeda Takashi, chairman of the House of Representatives Transport Committee at the time of the passage of the bill, was an old friend. He had even visited Sugamo Prison to comfort detainees with Sasakawa. But Maeda wanted to control motorboat racing as soon as he saw its possibilities. He had an office near the main Kabuki theatre in downtown Tokyo, while Sasakawa continued to work at his prewar office in the Ginza, and the ongoing strife between the two of them became known as the battle of the "Ginza" vs. the "Kabuki" factions.[28]

This feud came to a head very early on. The original *Motorboat Racing Law* of 1952, it may be noted, provided for the establishment of a National Federation of Motorboat Racing Associations, a key body for the industry. But this body was in fact not set up until 19 October 1952, four months after the enactment. The delay in establishing the Federation was said at the time to have been caused by internal feuding and the need to coordinate the two warring parties.[29]

Sasakawa had been prevented by the purge from taking any public office. And he had scruples about taking a front seat in the Federation, having played a central role in the enactment of the law. So others had to take the main posts when the new body started off. The first chair was Adachi Tadashi, president of the Japan Chamber of Commerce, a very prestigious post, and its president was Takiyama Toshio, the first director general of the Ships Bureau of the Ministry of Transport. The executive committee chairman was Yatsugi Kazuo. The latter individual was responsible for the actual management, and belonged to the "Ginza faction." He was a Sasakawa loyalist, and he worked with him closely.

Thus Sasakawa ensured that he was in charge. However, for years he refrained from letting his name go forward for a top position. He accepted the position of "racing chairman" when it was created later. He also became vice-chairman of the Federation only in 1953, some time after he had been officially "de-purged" with the coming into force of the San Francisco Peace Treaty in April 1952. He then served as "acting chairman," and in the following year he was de facto chairman. However, he waited until 1955 before formally taking the title *kaicho*.

His strength of character, and his experience in dealing with rough diamonds, was needed at times. As one might surmise, the power struggle within the newly created motorboat racing industry had come to the attention of organized crime — of gangster groups with an interest in gambling. According to Kageyama Yukio who was an employee of the Federation from the very beginning, there were times when he felt his life was in danger. But Sasakawa skillfully settled such undesirable relationships.[30] Along with his commitment to rule out any suspicion of fixing, Sasakawa made a considerable contribution to the development of motorboat racing as healthy entertainment.

III

Motorboat racing, contrary to Sasakawa's expectations, did not have a smooth start in business terms. Far from it, in fact. The first race meet, held in the Omura arena in Nagasaki in April 1952, did not meet the sponsor's expectations either as regards the take or the number of spectators.[31]

In fact, right up to 1957, the sport was in the red. Far from contributing to local finances, it took losses. Those in the line of duty were distressed. There were local operators, notably in prefectural governments, who suggested scrapping the whole enterprise, as they seemed to be spending money rather than earning it. A fiasco threatened.[32]

To compound the difficulty, most of the local governments with a large population base and an interest in public sports were operating bicycle or car races, and had taken on these commitments ahead of motorboat racing. This was a very difficult situation, according to the same source.

> There really was no need to take a risk with the unfamiliar sport of motorboat racing.... Therefore, apart from the well-endowed regions or municipalities, say with a large lake or a calm bay, only relatively small towns and villages, lacking a minimum population base of 30,000, were interested in serving as sponsors. They, of course, hardly had the capacity to scrape up funds to build racing arenas.[33]

Minoo City

Sasakawa stepped forward. He took on the unenviable job of visiting local governments to persuade them to continue sponsoring motorboat races. He even promised to pay out of his own pocket if they incurred losses. Nakai Buhei, the mayor of Minoo City, Sasakawa's birthplace, worked assiduously for motorboat racing, and he remembers:

> There were two opposing factions on the City Council. One group wanted to scrap the plan, and one supported its continu-

ation.... Sasakawa told the Council he would reimburse the city if it incurred losses. If there were profits from this venture, such gains would belong to Minoo City. When it came to a vote as to whether or not to continue the races, the motion to continue carried by one vote.[34]

Sasakawa helped some self-governing bodies raise funds needed to build racing arenas by providing personal guarantees on the loans.[35] As already mentioned Sasakawa had amassed huge assets of his own through stock and commodity trading, and he used these resources to get motorboat racing going.

Other difficulties that had to be overcome were public outcries against foul play, clumsy management from inexperience, and frequent premature starts due to the lack of training of competitors. The latter, in particular, agitated the crowd. In the face of this situation Sasakawa devoted all his energies to improving the skills of both racing drivers and referees, and in strengthening their commitment to ethical principles. He did everything to eliminate the unsavory influence of local *yakuza*. For him, the fans came first.

Sasakawa had this to say to those involved in the sport professionally:

> The important thing is to be aware that we are entrusted with the precious money of 100 million people. Most of the proceeds are used for social welfare. Ours is a noble mission, including for those of us who are working in the background to raise the needed resources. I want you to have pride in what you do, and to do your utmost to brush up your skills and enjoy fair competition.[36]

More thoughts of Sasakawa Ryoichi

> The principle that operates in our world is survival of the fittest.... The gambling world solemnly represents that principle. Referring to motorboat racing, we have set a strict rule to prevent fixing. Any sibling or parent of a driver or any of us associated with racing will be punished if we purchase a betting ticket. But if you compete fairly and win you are rewarded with big prize money.[37]

> In motorboat racing, we had the smallest number of incidents of fixed races compared to other public sports, and the lowest number of fatal accidents to drivers. Out of some 10 million or more racers fifteen have been killed in competition in the last twenty-seven years, the lowest figure among public sports. This

is a result of successfully inculcating throughout the sport the stern truism that "human rights mean above all respect for life." The results speak for themselves. "Violation of human rights" in our sport cannot be compared with other sports. We have strict rules. Drivers are forbidden to talk to outsiders, even on the phone, during the last twenty-four hours prior to a race. Their friends and acquaintances are watched, and drivers must not drink. They must turn out their lights at a fixed time. Our way is stricter than the prewar military. There are criticisms against this "disregard of human rights," naturally. Well, I took a decisive step in favor of "respect for human life" at the risk of a "disregard of human rights." This resulted in solemn discipline, with no room for cheating and wrongdoing. Above all, please note, we reduced the number of fatal accidents to drivers.[38]

A training center on Lake Biwa

Training racing drivers proved to be challenging, both technically and spiritually. In the beginning, the training arenas were located in Omura, Wakamatsu, and Ashiya. Immediately following the enactment of the *Motorboat Racing Law* in August 1951 Sasakawa opened an International Training Center for Motorboat Racing Drivers and Referees on Lake Biwa.

Whenever regular training sessions took place, Sasakawa was there preparing drivers for their jobs and breathing into them the required spirit. He had a powerful appeal, according to Aki Yoshiharu, one of the early trainees. He was a successful racer, who entered the field early on, in 1952, and served as chair of the Japan Motorboat Drivers Association. Sasakawa's two-hour lectures were laden with an unsparing and severe but caring message, so much so that Aki never felt the sessions were long.[39]

A notice to all drivers

In June 1952, the Federation put out a "notice to drivers" in what may have seemed somewhat old-fashioned language to some among them. It encouraged racers to act as models among their peers — "to be leaders, to be international sportsmen with a boatman's pride, and to be gentlemen at all times." The notice admonished each driver to be law-abiding, to be cooperative, and to study. "Be above all a sportsman who wins respect." It explained the position of the motorboat industry in many respects and urged each athlete to be fully prepared for the challenges ahead.[40]

The notice to drivers was put out many times. Picking up some more admonitions from among only the earlier ones clearly brings out Sasakawa's philosophy. "Motorboat racing means a lifetime of hard training" (July 1952). "Do not disgrace a boatman's honor" (September 1952). "Apply yourself unremittingly" (September 1953). "There is more to racing than just winning and losing" (April 1954). "Take care to avoid pileups" (August 1958). "Behave yourself in private life" (September 1960). "Be accountable for your actions" (March 1964). "Learn from your errors (bad navigation) as drivers" (August 1967).[41]

Troublesome rumors arise

In spite of these efforts there were continuous rumors of irregularities in motorboat racing. In June 1952, the Federation set up an inspection office headed by Fuji Yoshio to give guidance, and to carry out investigations. As a consequence it was learned that:

> The rumors about foul play by drivers were not unfounded, certainly in some instances. At that point all could see that the future of motorboat racing depended on taking appropriate countermeasures.... A regular drivers' course was established for this purpose, and the first course was held on 20 January 1953 at Omi Shinto shrine near Lake Biwa. The training, which centered on spiritual education, was carried out in groups of fifty at a time. From early in the morning to late at night....The drivers' lecture course was later made compulsory, and served as the base of the strong solidarity of those engaged in the motorboat racing industry.[42]

Furthermore, a Self-disciplinary Study Group was organized in December of the same year, to counter ugly rumors concerning racers' unruly behavior. Leading drivers, selected by the Federation and the Athletes' Association, took part in a study of what is truly expected of a motorboat racer. At the outset the Federation made a presentation on the background of the *Racing Law,* the responsibility of the Federation and the status of drivers.

This was followed by free discussion among the drivers, and frank exchange of views with the Federation directors to define the next steps. The drivers returned to their respective regional associations, and called ad hoc general meetings to report on the decisions taken at the study group. All drivers were asked to take the issue to heart and to commit themselves to a collective improvement where discipline was called for. They agreed to work with the next group of drivers to participate in the second study group to keep up the momentum, and to raise the level of collective awareness.[43]

They must be gentlemen

This continued for years. Then, on New Year's Day 1957, the Federation made public its core program. This centered on a commitment "to make gentlemen out of motorboat drivers." The gist of the "Principles of Motorboat Drivers" announced at that time was as follows:

> The Federation will provide proper guidance to drivers whose racing attitudes, aptitude, character, and daily behavior leave much to be desired.

> The Federation will conduct special training to improve skills of those drivers who have high accident rates and poor results.

> Drivers who fail to attain the required standards will be disqualified as having impeded the objectives of motorboat racing.[44]

The Principles were strictly enforced. As a result, the number of absentee racers increased, as some, for example, avoided difficult courses set up in order to avoid accidents. The Federation was quick to point this out in one of its messages to racers. The notice deplored rash and self-serving behavior and pronounced it unacceptable.[45]

To become a professional driver a candidate had to pass the Federation's registration test. Sasakawa decided to have this test rigorously conducted. In other words, the maximum standard under the regulations was applied. As a result, out of seventy-six candidates who took the thirty-fifth registration test in September 1956 only twenty-seven passed the written examination. Seven of these failed the physical examination that followed. The first stage of the exams left twenty applicants in the running.

> The candidates were then subjected to tests of practical skills including steering, maintenance, and repairs, all the while considering their suitability for group living. Fifteen passed this stage and were then put through five days of aptitude tests. Four were eliminated, leaving just eleven successful final candidates.[46]

The drivers' training period was originally two months long. But it was extended to three months in 1960, then five in 1965, and finally to a full year in 1970. Originally, the drivers paid for the training, but to go without any earnings for a year and paying out of their pockets was too heavy a burden. The Federation therefore decided to bear all necessary costs of training. A full- fledged training arena was opened at the Motosu Center in 1966, and contributed in no small measure to the drivers' qualitative improvement.

One of Sasakawa's great aims was to make certain that all irregularities were eliminated from the sport. To this end, "He packed drivers into dormitories during races, prohibited contacts with the outside world, and forbade drinking and mahjong."[47] These efforts worked and incidents of irregularities plummeted. It is no longer a problem today.

I noted earlier how in a 1966 TV debate with Tanaka Kakuei, the ruling party's powerful personality, Socialist Party Secretary General Narita spoke in favor of the total abolition of public gambling, citing the frequency of fixing as a major problem in horse racing and bicycle racing. By then the proceeds from motorboat racing had shot up and exceeded those from horse racing as operated by the Japan Racing Association, but still lagged behind cycling revenues. Narita's neglect to mention motorboat racing as an example of fixing is unlikely to have been an accidental omission or simple forgetfulness on his part.

World-class drivers

A lot of hard work went into bringing about these results. For example, Sasakawa improved the rewards to racing drivers. Accident compensation was institutionalized in 1953, and winning drivers were given a sharp increase in award money as well as in retirement allowances, starting in 1959.

These measures helped to give the world-class drivers they were aiming to produce a handsome income, in addition to the development they sought in the motorboat racing industry in general. In 1976 one motorboat athlete earned in excess of 60 million yen, the highest income in all public sports. Today it is not rare for a relatively young athlete to earn 100 million yen a year. The combination of better treatment and strict punishment for irregularities has been effective in eradicating foul play in motorboat racing. Aki Yoshiharu, chair of the Motorboat Drivers' Association told me:

> If foul play was discovered a driver lost his qualification, found himself without a job and forsook his retirement benefit. From a purely economic point of view foul playing was not worth it.[48]

Building wholesome personalities

Those who were associated with boat racing at the time invariably referred to the strictness and thoroughness of Sasakawa's guidance to drivers and trainees. Tsuboi Kurotsuna said the success in eradicating foul play was thanks to "Mr. Sasakawa's commitment to disallowing irregularities." Amari Koichi pointed out that, "In addition to masterful management Mr. Sasakawa's other achievement was fostering drivers. There are no problems with the drivers in motorboat racing. That is because his training covered not just practical skills but character building."[49]

Not only did the Federation impose strict training and discipline on drivers but it spared no efforts in improving the quality of inspectors who were in charge of maintenance and inspection of the boats. During the first two years of operations, unlike referees, there was no registration system or certification for inspectors. The Federation initiated a system to certify inspectors in 1953 and at the same time created a rule that two inspectors were needed at each race.

Inspector applicants were tested for general knowledge, practical maintenance skills, and boat operation, and by oral examination:

> Practical skill tests required an applicant to reassemble the parts of a Mercury-type boat, install them, and operate the boat once around the racing circuit. Unlike today, when there are ample opportunities to play with engines, this was a high-level examination, and those without experience would be sure to fail.[50]

IV

Motorboat racing started its life in adversity, and in the beginning the sale of admission tickets and gross revenues did not increase all that much. But the high economic growth of the 1960s had a positive impact on revenues, which then grew at an astounding pace of 30 to 40 percent a year. The number of spectators increased as well. In 1975 motorboat racing overtook bicycle racing in yearly revenue. It had become the number one public sport.

This success had at last earned recognition for the sport from the society at large. In June 1955, it was granted a two-year extension beyond the first legal deadline. In 1957 it earned a further three-year extension.[51]

Finally, in April 1959, the wording of the *Motorboat Racing Law* was changed so that assistance from racing proceeds could now be given to the shipbuilding industry at large. To be specific, assistance might be provided to improve "motorboats and other vessels," rather than the former narrowly defined "improvements to motorboats, ship engines, and ship gear and export promotion."[52]

In August 1960, the Federation also received an extension of an extra year to the privilege of receiving part of the proceeds of races in grant form, set in 1957 for a period of three years. When the deadline came the following year it was then extended for a further year.[53]

1962: The law is revised

The most dramatic change to the *Motorboat Racing Law* was brought about with its revision in April 1962. This took place at the recommendation of the Naganuma Investigating Committee organized the previous year. Its main point was to remove the time limit placed on the grant receivable by the Federation. The motorboat industry was at last liberated from the threat of discontinuation, and able thereafter to devise a long-term business plan.[54]

The second major change was that the sport was allowed thereafter to give grants, in addition to conventional purposes, for "physical training and promotion of other enterprises that have as their objective development of the public good."[55] The third change was that the grant-receiving body was changed from the conventional recipient — the Federation of Prefectural Associations of Motorboat Racing — to the newly established JSIF.[56] The Naganuma Committee report,

> initially intended a "special-status corporation" to be the new recipient.... But Chairman Sasakawa took the strong view that a government corporation with special status meant that rigid management would prevail instead of flexible methods. He preferred to make the recipient body an organization infused with private sector vitality. In the end that body was defined in the wording of the law as a "public-service foundation" or a "legally incorporated foundation."[57]

The JSIF

Thus, whereas grants from the proceeds of horse, bicycle, and car racing are distributed by special-status corporations under the control of the relevant ministries, the motorboat racing proceeds are distributed by a private, therefore, freer organization, the JSIF. "Deregulation" and "privatization" have become household words in Japan today, but at the time this was done setting up a private organization for the purpose of distributing grants was a novel idea.

Sasakawa was twenty years ahead of his time. In Japan deregulation and privatization became buzzwords in the 1980s, as experts faced the consequences of the government's mismanagement of the economy and the ballooning of public debt, not yet in the 1960s. An ad hoc committee was set up under the chairmanship of Doko Toshiwo, a leading businessman, to consider the situation. Meanwhile, as a result of the second major change in the law, the beneficiaries of the motorboat racing grants were no longer limited to the shipbuilding industry and to maritime interests. Had Sasakawa not insisted on getting his way, there would have been a special-status corporation in receipt of the huge grants; and had he not also pushed to get the scope of potential beneficiaries expanded we would not see today that philanthropic body now known as the Nippon Foundation.

Sasakawa Yohei sees "1962 as our second birthday, if 1951 was our first."[58] It was indeed a milestone year in as much as time-restriction was removed for good. In that same year, the vision of Sasakawa Ryoichi ensured that the use of the grant was diversified, and meanwhile the grant monies were to be distributed not by a special-status corporation, but a foundation. As a result, the second "birthday" became a springboard for a dramatic leap.

Watch out for "migrating birds"

A special-status corporation has tax and other advantages. But its downside is its tendency to encourage excessive dependence on the government. The Ad Hoc Administrative Reform Council's avowed intention was to surgically operate on that very point as special-status corporations are retirement destinations for high-ranking bureaucrats. Every year the Public Workers Union publishes the number of bureaucrats who "descend from heaven" to eighty-one such corporations. As of October 1984, of a total of 480 directors, 379 or 79 percent were ex-bureaucrats. These privileged former high-ranking civil servants again receive enormous retirement bonuses (20 to 40 million yen) after short periods of service.

They then go on to other organizations like migrating birds. I knew that if our organization became a special-status corporation this would happen. If the top executive posts were occupied by retired bureaucrats as representatives of vested interests wasting their time until they were replaced by another lot, employees would have no incentive to work hard.

Emerging from the ashes of the war it was the private sector volunteers who built the motorboat racing enterprise. They should, therefore, be left to manage it. Indeed I wanted to see how different we can be compared to the bureaucrats, and that is why I chose to set up a juridical foundation based on civil law.[59]

A de facto lifetime chairman

In those days Sasakawa was criticized for allegedly misappropriating JSIF resources. Ino Kenji, for example, had this to say:

Horse racing, bicycle racing, and auto racing were all organized into special-status corporations. For example, the president, vice president, executive manager, and members of the operating committee of the Horse Racing Association were all appointed by the minister of agriculture and forestry for a maximum term of eight years exclusively, and forbidden to hold other jobs.

Ino observed critically that the JSIF alone was a juridical foundation and that this allowed Sasakawa to use the grant money at will as a de facto lifetime chairman.[60]

Not a single yen for the chairman

This point was brought up in a tête-à-tête with Miki Yonosuke in 1983. He asked Sasakawa:

The Second Administrative Reform Council's efforts have provided an opportunity to focus on special-status corporations, and they had come under fire as a result. That does not apply to Japan Shipbuilding Industry Foundation because it is in a separate bracket as an incorporated foundation. As its chairman, what thoughts do you have?

Sasakawa replied:

We have no misgivings at all. We are all for "administrative reform." In fact, I encouraged Doko Toshiwo, the Council's chairman to go all the way, not half way. I said I will cooperate with him with all my strength if he was prepared to stake his whole life on the reform. I can say this because our foundation has in a sense graduated from the administrative reform. Our accounting and books are as transparent as a glass house and are open to the public. People too often misunderstand how our grant money is used because they do not know how the mechanism works.

Actually I could not get a single yen for myself, even if I wanted to. In other words, the distribution of the grant monies must go through an exhaustive investigation process by the examination department, and then the advisory committee makes the final decision. The organization is managed strictly on six principles: justice ("encourage the good and punish evil"); survival of the fittest ("the superior wins and inferior loses"); punishment and reward ("reward good conduct and you will punish evil doing"); simplification and rationalization; management by a select few; and the right man in the right place.

There, Sasakawa broke out laughing.[61]

A lean craft

In fact, even today, the management of the JSIF, generally known as the Nippon Foundation, is extremely simple and flexible compared to that of other grant managing organizations such as the Horse Race Association and the Bicycle Industry Association. While proceeds from motorboat and bicycle races are about the same, the Nippon Foundation has a staff of eighty-nine, with its chairman and president serving without remuneration and with only a few of its directors paid. By contrast, the Bicycle Industry Association has a staff of two hundred and twenty.

The Horse Race Association has almost double the proceeds of both motorboat and bicycle racing, and has a staff of nineteen hundred. Its chairman, president and directors receive high honoraria. Needless to say, most of them are former government officials who have parachuted from the ministry responsible for monitoring the Horse Race Association, the Ministry of Agriculture and Forestry. Moreover, as special-status corporations whose expenditures are set by annual budgets, they are incapable of responding flexibly and promptly to unforeseen incidents, unlike the Nippon Foundation. In other words, rather than being a full-fledged private grant-giving organization they are no more than auxiliaries of the ministries that preside over them.[62]

That said, it cannot be denied that Sasakawa Ryoichi had a large impact on the disbursement of the grants. It probably was not easy for others in the organization to oppose his initiative given their boss's vision, insight, flair, and exuberant personality — and the central role he played in the evolution of the motorboat race enterprise. To be sure, outsiders have equated the Foundation with a "Sasakawa Empire," no doubt because of the inevitable and excessive loyalty that he has attracted.

Jimmy Carter testifies

Still, he was no tyrant. He had no autocratic authority over the disbursement of grant monies. The foundation's decision-making system, as described by Sasakawa to his interviewer Miki, was not a mere formality. Former president Jimmy Carter, a friend of Sasakawa who worked with him in fighting famine in Africa (under the Sasakawa Global 2000 Project), told me: "Because of the opposition of other members of the [board of the] foundation, not all of what we [Sasakawa and Carter] wanted to do was realized."[63]

The JSIF structure did not allow Sasakawa to move even a single yen at his whim. Certainly, its system of management is open and transparent. Yet, generally speaking the existence of a charismatic leader can infect others and lead them to support him without question. It is often hard to distinguish between the will of the leader and those working under him, particularly when his performance has almost always proven successful. Perhaps it was unavoidable that people had the impression that the Foundation had been hijacked by Sasakawa.

For his part he was convinced that:

> No one is readier to listen to the staff more than I, to share their thoughts with the board, and to have them adopted as the decisions of the organization. This is the secret of the success of everything I undertake.[64]

Interestingly, Sasakawa's subordinates endorsed this principle.

The problem, however, lay in the fact that his employees' interests were from the beginning identical with Sasakawa's. They seemed to align themselves automatically. It may be added that there is little clear distinction between free and flexible management and an arbitrary one under a charismatic leader such as Sasakawa. The question was whether or not the performance was up as a result; and also, how much the outcome contributed to the public good. On both scores the result was the yardstick; in both respects the JSIF passed with flying colors.

How to avoid corruption

In fact, Sasakawa himself was fully aware of the fine line between a flexible management style and an arbitrary one. And he was clear on how managers should avoid being corrupted.

> Human beings are weak. On the one hand, we are troubled by our conscience but on the other we want to make a profit. This exposes one to the risk of corruption. It is a risk anyone could face in business. I am faithful to the principles that keep me away from temptations and on the right track. I must be clear whom I am working for and what I am living for. The work I do today is for the company. So if I am approached by people I should know that they are interested in my position and the power it represents.
>
> It is clear that I must not usurp that power. If I am clear that I owe what I am to my family, then I cannot possibly do things

that will make my parents or wife and children unhappy. The higher one climbs on the corporate ladder and the greater the success and responsibility one enjoys, the greater in turn are one's power and authority — and as a corollary of that, the greater the risk of corruption. To escape this trap and fulfill one's responsibilities, one must constantly keep in mind how one should relate to society, and to whom one owes one's existence. For this purpose I should earnestly pursue a virtuous life.[65]

Unfortunate conventions

The JSIF was also criticized for its "arbitrary management," simply because it was controlled less by the ministry concerned compared to other grant-giving public sports organizations. Such criticism was the product of the unfortunate Japanese custom of making much of government and little of the people. At the base of such thinking was that public works should be left to the public domain since the private sector was only concerned with profit-making and not in promoting the public interest.

In order to understand things properly, it is helpful to independently consider the two opposing concepts of government versus civil society and the public versus private domains. A simple figure may be useful.

Figure 1. Relationship of government, civil society, public, and public domains.

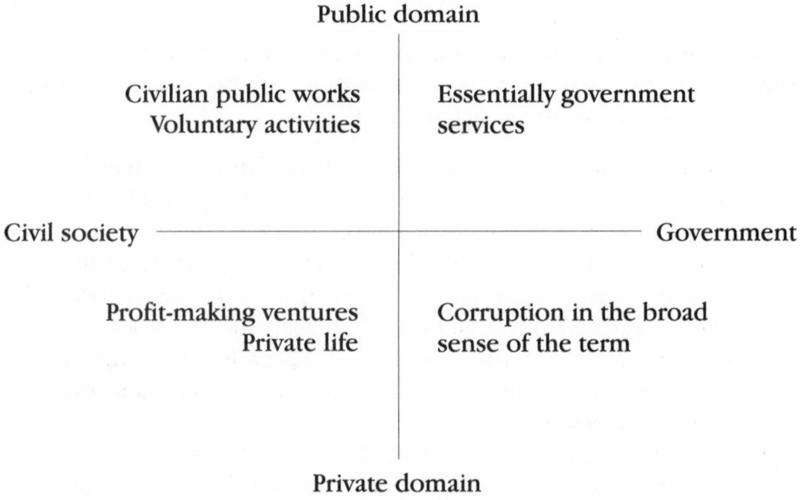

Public domain

Civilian public works Voluntary activities	Essentially government services

Civil society ——————————————————— Government

Profit-making ventures Private life	Corruption in the broad sense of the term

Private domain

There are four categories in the figure to show how government and civil society and the public and private domains relate to each other. In postwar Japan, until quite recently, the dominant pattern was for the government and the public sector to occupy the same sphere while the civil society and the private sector occupied another, excluding, as a consequence, other types of relationships. In fact, any other combinations were discouraged or forbidden.[66]

Frequent bribe taking by politicians and the corruption of officials stemmed from the unduly close relations between government and business. A bureaucrat is a private individual, but a government organization must remain in the public domain. This does not mean that civil society naturally inhabits only the private domain. These days, the emphasis given to the topic of "the corporate social responsibility" is based on the notion that private enterprise should not pursue merely its profit-making mandate but also endeavor to enhance the public interest. The emergence in Japan in the 1990s of nonprofit organizations (NPOs) and nongovernmental organizations (NGOs) providing public services suggests diversification of the patterns of relations between the four domains shown in the figure have reached a new level. In this, Sasakawa was a pioneer. The JSIF is a forerunner of today's NPOs and NGOs in Japan and is still today the largest in the field.

Parasites heaven

Sasakawa was convinced of the need to break with the unenviable Japanese convention of accepting the dominance of bureaucrats over private individuals and slighting the people:

> Japan is a heaven for government officials. Notwithstanding that the sovereignty of the people, equality, and justice are guaranteed under the Constitution, the lamentable custom persists of putting government above the people. The public is disgusted with our politicians — these *sensei* [an honorific meaning literally teachers] who look down on the voters, and with government officials who abuse their authority. In the field of the economy our "Japan, Inc." model of the past still persists. What we have is an industrial structure headed and led by government departments, bloated with officials who "parachute" into the private sector. In Japan there is a preponderant economic regime under which bureaucrats are the dominant players. This system is reflected in the people's persistence in revering officials at the expense of themselves....

> How do we rid ourselves of this conventional way of think-

ing? The first priority is for the civil society to wean itself away from immature dependence on government. Unless we sever our dependence on politicians and on those bureaucrats in times of need, we have no right to censure government officials for their unreasonableness or to lament their haughty behavior toward people.[67]

Keep them out

"Let's not be ruled by those weird government officials," Sasakawa told Doko Toshiwo, the veteran business leader formerly with Toshiba, who served as head of the Second Administrative Reform Council, "and let us go right ahead and do what we can."[68]

Follow the JSIF

Sasakawa asserted that other public sports corporations, with comparable responsibilities for dispensing large grants, should follow the example of the JSIF and subsidize not just their specific field of industry, but diverse social services. For that purpose, he was convinced revision of the present legislation was necessary:

> Horse racing is supervised by the Ministry of Agriculture and Forestry, bicycle and auto racing by the Ministry of International Trade and Industry, and motorboat racing by the Ministry of Transportation. The three ministries should align their respective policies on public sports. Right now, the law restricts the use of proceeds from horse racing: almost all proceeds have to go directly to the livestock industry. The other three public sports can make donations to public services. Subsidies by bicycle and auto racing associations may be restricted by regulation to a maximum of 50 percent of the project budgets of their beneficiaries. In contrast, the motorboat racing associations can give up to 80 percent of beneficiary-project budgets. That is why we [JSIF] are swamped with approaches from sports and welfare organizations.
>
> I propose that this imbalance be corrected, and that the Ministry of Agriculture and Forestry revise its relevant laws and regulations so that proceeds from horse racing can be donated, as much as ours, for social causes, physical education, and other public projects.[69]

Gathering of five thousand barbers

Here, we may look back and note how it was that Sasakawa pledged a great part of his active life to motorboat racing and philanthropy, when earlier a career in politics had beckoned.

When the Occupation came to an end in 1952 and purges of senior Japanese, decreed under the Occupation, were ended, Sasakawa was approached by many people urging him to return to public life, i.e., to politics. Sasakawa made his personal position clear in a letter to Shige-mitsu Mamoru dated 6 May 1952, soon after the San Francisco Peace Treaty went into force, ending the Occupation.

> I have at the moment three offers from people who want me to present my candidacy, but I have turned them all down. I have explained my position: I will not stand in any election until there is a definite schedule for the release of all war criminals from prison. As a result of taking this position I have earned a reputation that I take my responsibilities seriously. And that meant that more people asked me to return to politics and stand for office. On 12 May the governor of Osaka, the mayor of Osaka and I have been asked to speak at the city's main public hall to address a convention, attended by no fewer than five thousand barbers. I have been told that people want to hear a frank talk from me and not just formal speeches from the top officials such as the governor and the mayor. I will be appearing on a public platform for the first time in seven years.[70]

Opting out of politics

Sasakawa had no intention of returning to politics until everyone had been freed from jail. Those convicted at the War Crimes Tribunals were then still detained in Sugamo. He had made a promise to his mother Teru not to run for public office until such time as every last war criminal had been released. Years later in May 1958, the last of those detained had completed their sentences, including those on parole. At that point Sasakawa was in still greater demand. He thereupon expressed his in-tention to stand in the House of Councilor's election in 1959 from the national constituency.

However, there was a problem. The situation surrounding the mo-torboat racing industry was at that time still precarious — meaning that at least in theory the public sport of motorboat racing could be abol-ished at any time. Reflecting on this and reconsidering his position,

Sasakawa withdrew his candidacy, thinking it would be irresponsible of him, after all, to fight an election campaign under such circumstances.[71]

In effect, Sasakawa decided to opt out of politics as it happened, forever, and to give his all to the development of motorboat racing. "I stake my life on fostering the public sport of motorboat racing, and managing this as an enterprise," he liked to say. This was no mere conceit.[72]

V

Motorboat racing had won a permanent place as a popular pastime in Japan, ensuring the JSIF's financial base. The proceeds skyrocketed. And Sasakawa's interests expanded from promoting the development of the brilliantly successful shipbuilding industry to spreading sound maritime thinking and to preventing disasters at sea — and later to health, hygiene, fire prevention, and firefighting. In due course he widened his horizons to international philanthropy, to help in eradicating famine and combating disease and promoting international goodwill. Japan's shipbuilding industry had by then set the world's top standards in both technology and in scale, but Sasakawa remained strongly interested in shipbuilding and related industries. The JSIF did not relinquish its support of shipbuilding.

By the 1970s, however, the motorboat racing industry seemed to hit a plateau after leapfrogging upward for many years. Sasakawa was alarmed. He proposed that 1981, the thirtieth anniversary of the start of motorboat racing, be treated as the first year of a new era. He warned his associates that the next thirty years should not be an extension of the previous thirty years. He called for a change in mindset and a new policy. Sasakawa could not take his eyes off his motorboat racing enterprise — well, not yet.[73]

Going forward

To devote his life to others, and to society, was his consistent commitment throughout his life. This was the motive behind Sasakawa's devotion to the motorboat racing industry. To expand the sphere of activities of the Foundation was a preordained step toward his final objective. Here, it is hardly possible to describe, in concrete detail, the large-scale and colorful activities of Sasakawa himself and the Foundation.

By the 1980s the JSIF had overtaken the Ford and Rockefeller Foundations, hitherto considered the largest in the field, in terms of operating funds. The JSIF had grown to be the world's largest grant-giving private foundation providing grants and subsidies larger than those of the two American foundations combined. It had abundant funds to support a great range of immensely varied activities. For details of JSIF activities the reader is kindly referred to the *Thirty-Year History of the Japan Shipbuilding Industry Foundation* (Nihon Senpaku Shinko-kai Sanju nen no Ayumi) and to Tsurumaki Yasuo's most informative book, titled *Undisclosed JSIF's Real Image* (Daremo Kakanakatta Nihon Senpaku Shinko-kai no Jitsuzo) and *The Foundation's Economics* (Zaidan no Keizai-gaku).

Giving Carter a hand

I shall use the pages remaining here to describe the outstanding features running through Sasakawa's activities in new fields.

First and foremost, Sasakawa dedicated himself, with his disinterest in either praise or blame, to serving the most unfortunate. In the United States it has become a practice for retired presidents to raise money to establish a memorial center or a library. President Jimmy Carter, too, visited Japan after his retirement to raise money for the Carter Center. Japanese politicians and businessmen who paid respect to him during his time in office turned a cold shoulder after his crushing defeat in the election.

When Sasakawa learned of this he volunteered to cover part of the construction cost:

> We Japanese keep our word. Those who promised you support must have reasons for not having been able to do so today. Please do not hold it against them. I will help you in their place.[74]

By Jimmy Carter's own account:

> Sasakawa Ryoichi visited me at my home in Georgia. As he stepped in, the first words he uttered were: "How is it that a man who served as president lives in such a simple home!" Right then and there he pledged half a million dollars for the Carter Center. I had been busy collecting ten dollars here and a hundred dollars there until then. It was the first large donation.[75]

A leaning gatepost

Incidentally, according to Sasakawa, Carter asked to stay with Sasakawa when he was visiting Japan and offered his home in turn when the latter was in the United States. Sasakawa recalled:

> I declined the offer because my home is, unlike what many think, unsuited to putting up guests. Mr. Carter seemed to take

it that I did not like the whole idea. He asked if I would at least invite him to lunch. Mr. Carter visited us in July 1983. He was surprised to find that while the neighbors on either side of us had huge homes, ours had a leaning gatepost and the house itself was shabby. "How many villas did I own?" he asked.

He expected me to be spending weekends in the country, away from the city as many American politicians do. I replied. "Up to today, at eighty-four, I have never had one. There are too many unfortunate people in the world who have no food to eat or home to sleep in, and if they fall ill they die because of the lack of treatment. When I think of them I cannot afford luxury. I live very simply to avoid malnutrition, and as a result I need no reading glasses and enjoy health and long life." My answer seemed to satisfy Mr. Carter.[76]

Helping the WHO

Sasakawa gave assistance to the needy on a worldwide basis. Among such programs the most successful were the eradication of smallpox and relief for Hansenite patients. At its May 1980 General Assembly, the World Health Organization (WHO) declared that smallpox had been eradicated. Humankind was liberated from one of the most feared diseases. The JSIF had donated a total of $2,861,880 dollars to WHO's smallpox eradication program from 1975 to 1979. It was the largest donation by a private organization.

At the same General Assembly, WHO Secretary General Halfdan T. Mahler sent a special invitation to Sasakawa to honor him with a certificate of appreciation. "It is a happy occasion that we are able to declare smallpox eradicated," Mahler told the assembled guests and delegates.

> In particular, the cooperation of the Japan Shipbuilding Industry Foundation, and the leadership of its chairman Sasakawa, have been a great light of hope for smallpox eradication. The assistance provided by the Shipbuilding Industry Foundation was given at the most crucial period of the eradication, and was timely and truly effective.[77]

As the secretary general pointed out, the large donation for smallpox eradication starting in 1975 was indeed significant in its timing. At the time smallpox had more or less died down, even in Africa. This meant, however, that at the same time an increasing number of people did not have immunity or resistance to smallpox. In other words, if smallpox recurred at that stage, there was a high danger of another explosive epidemic, given the poor state of public health in the countries of Africa. Essential to the total eradication of an epidemic was the final massive push. In that sense the Foundation's assistance was most timely.

The memory of a beautiful girl

Hansen's disease had long been considered an incurable disease requiring the social isolation of patients. In his childhood Sasakawa had a terrible memory of a beautiful girl in his neighborhood from a family one of whose members had been afflicted. She could not marry a man she loved, and she had run away in despair. All his life Sasakawa had pondered ways to eradicate leprosy.[78] It happened that the WHO tropical disease special research group had developed a leprosy vaccine reagent in 1961.

Sasakawa volunteered that year-end to be the first subject to be vaccinated, to prove its safety. Said he: "I want to show the world the vaccine is safe, and ensure its smooth distribution."[79] Vaccination meant implanting diluted pathogen in one's body. Agreeing to be the first person to be vaccinated against leprosy took courage, hardly an act of self-advertisement.

In 1974 for the purpose of improving leprosy vaccine, Sasakawa established a Memorial Health Foundation in his name, and became its chairman. He visited Hansenite hospitals in Japan and in developing countries as much as he could. He took meals with patients and went to their bedsides to shake hands and talk with them.

One patient who had lost his fingers to the disease shared a meal with Sasakawa, shed tears of joy, and told him:

> It's been forty years since I was stricken. Many people have come with presents. But you are the first person who ate with me. I had my best meal today.[80]

"I want to shake your hand"

When Sasakawa extended his hand, most patients hesitated to take it. Sasakawa patiently waited, his hand extended, smiling into the eyes of the patient.

> I say, "I want to shake your hand." At first suspicious, the patient gives in and timidly puts out his. I take his hand with a firm grip. "At last we are friends," I say, and he returns the grip. Tears streak down his cheek and I can hear him saying thank you in so slight a murmur.[81]

This was not a matter of putting on a bold face or his philanthropic spirit. He had studied leprosy and knew it well. He never tired of saying:

> Leprosy has a latent period of fifteen to twenty years, but with modern medicine the infectious disease can be treated fully in half a year. Patients under treatment do not transmit the disease, and there is no danger of contagion. People who are afraid are simply caught in an archaic convention and groundless discrimination. There is no need to fear once one learns the truth.[82]

His idealism was underpinned by scientific knowledge.

One hundred Chinese students a year

Medicine was an area of particular interest to Sasakawa. He started a project in 1987 to host annual visits by one hundred Chinese students to study in Japanese medical schools. To date, one thousand Chinese medical students have received training in medical schools, hospitals, and research institutes in Japan, and contributed to advancing the level of medicine in China and greatly improved relations between the two countries. Sasakawa and the JSIF provided assistance to a broad range of research fields, making a large donation to the Cancer Research Group (Gan Kenkyu Kai), a representative cancer research institution in Japan; he made grants to build and donate ships with medical facilities on board, to make rounds between distant islands in Japan; he offered support to fighting AIDs worldwide; he constructed welfare facilities for senior citizens and mentally and physically challenged people; and he supported the training of health and welfare services providers.

For those with nothing to eat

Relief to refugees displaced by famine and wars was one of the major projects of Sasakawa and the JSIF. Between 1984 and 1985 Ethiopia was struck by a devastating famine, leading to mass starvation and an outpouring of refugees. Sasakawa and the JSIF embarked on efforts to resolve food problems in Africa. He explained, "We were convinced that we should make it an objective to help Africans help themselves to fight hunger by increasing food production and winning independence from foreign assistance."[83]

To start with, three men — Jimmy Carter, Dr. Norman Borlaug, a University of Texas agricultural specialist who worked for the Green Revolution in Asia and Central and South America; and Sasakawa — organized a World Famine Conference in Switzerland, bringing together concerned persons from around the world. Most of the expenses were covered by the Foundation. A decision was made at the conference to target Sudan, Tanzania, Zambia, and Ghana for an African Green Revolution. This was known as the Sasakawa Global 2000 (SG 2000) project.[84]

Details of the Green Revolution in Africa are provided in Yamamoto Eiichi's book. Here I will simply state that a straightforward reform in agricultural technology doubled the average harvest of maze in Ghana from 1.2 tons a hectare to 2.5 tons and that of sorghum from 0.5 tons to 2.5 tons.[84] The Green Revolution yielded remarkable harvests in other African countries as well.[85]

According to Agriculture Minister Steve G. Obimpeh of Ghana:

> Japan's official development assistance (ODA) has made a huge contribution. SG2000 and ODA from Japan have played complementary roles. If the Japanese government had not provided chemical fertilizer to farmers, SG 2000 would not have escaped having an adverse impact.
>
> It was possible that the project would have been unable to follow the guidance of the field instructors. Without ODA pesticides and spraying machines, locusts and clouds of grasshoppers could have stopped the project itself. However, official assistance alone could not have yielded such a result. We were able to increase production because the SG 2000 project was already in place.[86]

"We are not Santa Claus"

Indeed SG 2000 worked well, guided by the spirit of helping farmers to help themselves. Ku Jeng Un, a Korean researcher under Norman Borlaug, who headed the SG 2000 project as the regional director, knew where to draw a line. When a Ghanaian village head requested funds for him to purchase a tractor, fertilizer, and seeds, Ku had this to say:

> We are not Santa Claus. We are not here to give you presents. I want you to please understand this point. We have seen too many projects ultimately fail when they were just about providing machinery and equipment. What we are here for is to work with you and perspire with you. We believe the best assistance and cooperation is to help you make your country stand on its own feet.[87]

The international press has covered some of this work. *The Financial Times* carried an article on 2 March 1998 by Michela Long, covering projects in Ethiopia. The piece, headed "A Big Dream and Plan for Farmers," started by observing that once steady progress was achieved against famine, even the impact of an El Niño was just a hiccup by comparison. After describing a food production program in Ethiopia the writer continued that staff working on the Sasakawa project demonstrated that with the right combination of chemical fertilizer, new seeds, pesticides, and agro-technology the harvest could be dramatically increased. Some 583,000 farmers were working on the project and the number was expected to increase within a year to some 2 to 3 million.

"Energetically crisscrossing the desert"

Yamamoto Eiichi, a writer for the *Yomiuri Shimbun*, Japan's largest daily with a circulation of over 10 million, penned a vivid and moving description of what he saw in the field:

> I am not an agro-expert but I ended up recording the activities of a nongovernmental organization working at the grassroots on the Green Revolution in Africa. I happened to be at a harvest festival in a Ghanaian village. I was greeted by cheerful farmers who shared with me their happiness at being able to live a decent life. When they learned I was a journalist from Japan they asked me to relay their gratitude to my country.
>
> Their unaffected manner touched me. I was also interested in recording the efforts of the late Sasakawa Ryoichi, a Japanese who made a great contribution. I saw him marching about in Africa, already past his ninetieth birthday, energetically crisscrossing the scorching desert of South West Africa in work clothes, talking with farmers, negotiating with supervisors and calmly questioning national leaders. I saw in him a man who had outgrown Japan.
>
> During the "Pacific War" he served as a non-government-sponsored member of parliament representing his silent constituency and consistently upholding his commitment to defend constitutional government. After the war he faced the Tokyo War Crimes Tribunal and was detained as a Class A war criminal suspect but was never indicted. It is said that he volunteered to go to prison to urge other Class A war criminal suspects not to implicate the emperor in responsibility for the war.
>
> Later he worked hard as the creator of motorboat racing in Japan. He established JSIF in the service of world philanthropy, true to his belief that "The World Is One Family, and Human Beings Are All Brothers and Sisters."
>
> Large-minded and unaffected, true to his guiding principles of life, making no bones about small matters, self-possessed at

all times, and thorough in planning, he was a perfect personification of the Meiji man.

It is said that a man's worth is settled only when he is laid to rest. The fortune he left was much smaller than what was generally expected, and did not even compare with what a man of business or property might have left. It spoke vividly of his indifference to wealth.

It must have been this probity that made him pursue the grail of bringing the Green Revolution to Africa.

The revolution aroused the hopes and dreams of the poorest of the world's farmers. The late Sasakawa Ryoichi pondered ways and means to realize humankind's long-cherished yearning, advocated it, brought together collaborators, and opened the way to achieving the goal of doubling food production.[88]

VI

Sasakawa and the JSIF undertook numerous projects that had foresight and vision. Typical were the establishment in 1973 of the Blue Sea and Green Land Foundation (B and G Foundation) and the opening in 1974 of the Museum of Maritime Science. B and G Foundation built training facilities for young people on "blue sea and green land" with the object of helping them develop healthy bodies and minds. To that end the Foundation built local marine centers throughout the country; by March 1998 there were a total of 416. The B and G Foundation operated a passenger ship that provided youth with the broadening experience of foreign travel. There were also yachting, canoeing, and swimming classes, and every year a sports day was held for young people to test the success of their training.[89]

The museum with an upper deck

The Museum of Maritime Science is a unique museum built on reclaimed land along Tokyo Bay. It was a bold idea that many people regarded as reckless at the time. Today, however, the area is a fast developing, popular Tokyo waterfront. It was another case of Sasakawa's foresight. The Maritime Museum is a six-story concrete building built like a 60,000-ton passenger liner that is equipped with an upper deck, a simulated bridge, and a navigation and control room, just like a real ship. The museum display tells the history of ships, and devotes a large space to showing how they may evolve in the future, in such a way as to excite interest in marine development and navigation technology.

According to museum president Kamiyama Eiichi, Sasakawa's vision called for 20 percent of the space to cover the past, 30 percent to deal with the present, and 50 percent with the future.[90] The construction cost of the museum was borne by the Foundation, and Sasakawa also contributed 25 million yen from his own resources. A similar reference is found in *Novel: The Maritime Museum*.

In 1978 and 1979, Sasakawa and the JSIF also put together a Spaceship Science Exposition on Lot 13 at Ariake on Tokyo Bay centered on the Museum of Maritime Science. The exhibition was titled "Space — Hopes and Dreams of Humankind" [Uchu; Jinrui no Yume to Kibo] and featured the mammoth Saturn V rocket used in the Apollo and Gemini spaceships that predated the Lunar module. It also contained the Apollo moon landing vehicle and pieces of lunar rock, all furnished thanks to the cooperation of the US National Aeronautics and Space Agency and the Smithsonian Air and Space Museum. This was the first time those exhibits left the United States for an exhibition abroad. A Space and Science Exposition Association was established for the grand project with Sasakawa as its chairman. The expenses were absorbed by the JSIF.

The bridge over the river Kwai

In addition to these mega projects Sasakawa and the Foundation were involved in smaller but visionary programs. One such program was built on Sasakawa's dream of a reconciliation of Japanese and British soldiers who had served in Burma during World War II. He hoped to see them shake hands one day on the old battlefield. Gruesome battles in the Pacific War and the ill treatment of Allied prisoners of war in Japanese-run camps were still then causes of bitter enmity. In the hope of putting Japan-UK relations back on track with reconciliation in mind Sasakawa established a Great Britain-Sasakawa Foundation in 1985.

Sasakawa contacted the All Burma Veterans Liaison Conference on the Japanese side and the Burma Campaign Fellowship Group in Britain to arrange for their respective representatives to travel to Burma for reconciliation, and he supported the project.[91] John Nunneley, the editor of a book of reminiscences on the Burma campaign, commented that the project was a "strikingly imaginative" idea to bring together former avowed enemies as pioneers of a new friendship between Britain and Japan. Japanese television broadcast the moving scene of veterans shaking hands and hugging each other on the bridge over the river Kwai.

The introduction to the book concludes with a poem titled "Yesterday's Foe Is Today's Friend." It could well be the English translation of Sasakawa's own poem.

All honour to him, friend or foe,
Who fought and died for his country.
May the tragedy of his supreme
Sacrifice bring to us, the living
Enlightenment and inspiration.
Fill us with ever-mounting zeal
For the all-compelling quest of peace
World Peace and universal brotherhood.[92]

Good investment?

Sasakawa kept his private and public life religiously apart, but when necessary he did not hesitate to invest his own money in a public enterprise. "I am not a money worshipper," Sasakawa would say. "But without it, it would be difficult to carry out one's work."[93] He was strict in the use of public money under JSIF, for example, but generous in the use of his own money.

As noted earlier in this text, Sasakawa offered to compensate the operators in the event the fledgling motorboat racing arenas incurred losses. In addition, he offered his own property as security, offering surety jointly when operators took out a bank loan. Other such cases arose throughout the years.

For example, when a circus was organized with support from associated organizations worldwide as the very first event of the leprosy relief year, and then ran at a loss of one billion yen over three months due to poor attendance, Sasakawa made up the loss. It was a loss, but if the children who saw the fearless acrobats work their wonders gained courage to take on come what may in life, then it was well worthwhile, Sasakawa thought.

If as a result even one child is given courage not to run away or take his own life because he has been scolded at home or in school the loss of money has been worth it, he said.[94]

The *Nahimov* (I)

On occasion, his generosity took unexpected forms. A Russian battleship called the *Nahimov* had sunk on the high seas not far from the Japanese coast during the Russo-Japanese War of 1904-5. For a long time it had been rumored that it had a vast treasure on board. Hearing of this, Sasakawa embarked on a quest "to solve a problem that no one else dares to tackle." The project cost a small fortune but he put up 3 billion yen (roughly $25 million) of his own money to recover the ship. Originally, the cost was estimated at 3 billion yen, but it was said that he ended up pouring 5 billion or even 10 billion yen into the project.

Sasakawa explained:

> If we succeed in recovering a huge treasure, we might be able to spend one trillion yen a year for twenty years on combating leprosy, two trillion yen a year for twenty years on the eradication of parasitic worms, and even two trillion yen for twenty years on bringing to an end forever war and to its incalculable losses.
>
> I put up 3 billion yen. If it is lost, it is entirely my loss. If there is a profit to be had let it all be used for the benefit of humankind in addition to the purposes mentioned above. I have no intention of taking a single yen for myself. Even if I lose that 3 billion yen, that's just seventy cents a head given the global population of 4.4 billion. If I fail to pull up a treasure horde from the ship, we can all have a good laugh! Laughter brings luck and your circulation will benefit. It is a good investment.[95]

The *Nahimov* (II)

This was not the whole story, however. There was another reason for Sasakawa to have spent heavily on the recovery of the *Nahimov*. And here he briefly reentered the realm of politics and statecraft, or tried to. His idea was to encourage the return to Japan of "the northern territories," the four small islands off the coast of Hokkaido seized by the Soviet Union in 1945 at the end of World War Two. Rightly or wrongly, foolishly or otherwise, Sasakawa is said to have believed that the territorial question should be settled, both as a matter of historical justice and to improve Japan-Soviet relations. Sasakawa was passionately interested in having the "northern territories" returned, and in his mind perhaps, naively, the salvage of the ship could be a good step toward getting these islands back.

"What must be done to unify national opinion and focus the world's gaze on the return of the 'northern territories?'" Sasakawa asked.

> I believe that the *Nahimov* provides a golden opportunity. But if all goes well with the salvage operation and we succeed in recovering the treasure, the Soviets will most certainly insist that it belonged to them and demand its return.

Sasakawa had thought of an answer to that. "The *Nahimov* is considered a trophy of the Russo-Japanese War," he said, noting that the Soviets had made no claim at the time of an earlier attempt at salvage by prewar politician and financier Kuhara Fusanosuke (1869-1965) and others." Sasakawa was prepared to negotiate on a quid pro quo basis.

> The *Nahimov* reputedly carried a vast cargo of gold ingots to cover the Russian Grand Fleet's costs while sailing round the world from the Baltic to challenge Japan. If we are able to recover its treasures I would be happy to present them to our Soviet "brothers and sisters" to help in solving their food problems. In exchange, I would urge the return of the "northern territories" they took from us in 1945.

Sasakawa believed that the salvage of the *Nahimov* would bring the Soviets to the bargaining table, and invested his own resources to start the project.[96]

The anchor that cost billions

As regards Sasakawa's motivation, it is difficult to fathom which explanation is true. Both interpretations may serve to illustrate Sasakawa's romantic nationalism and at the same time his ultimate lack of interest in amassing personal wealth. He was scrupulous in the matter of public funds. But, by contrast, he was careless when it came to his own money, and it seems that some who sought his influence cheated him. In the end, the salvage venture failed and apparently all he could recover was a rusted anchor. This item, "the anchor that cost Sasakawa billions of yen," is exhibited in the Museum of Maritime Science. In sum, the *Nahimov* venture was a rare illustration of Sasakawa's sometimes ill-conceived intentions.

Those who worked with Sasakawa for a long time almost without fail pointed out that on occasion he was cheated.[97] In fact, there was no one more prone than he to being cheated. It was not just a matter of the *Nahimov,* according to his staff.

Sasakawa, according to Yamamoto Eiichi, in spite of his reputation for being a man of immense wealth, left very little property when he died. In fact, mainly as a result of the unsuccessful *Nahimov* salvage operation, the family was left not with property but enormous unpaid debts. Ironically enough, I think, Sasakawa's generous use of his own money for the public interest became a cause for suspicion. It may well be beyond anyone's comprehension that an individual would spend billions of yen for the public good and expect nothing in return, and pick up all losses to boot. It is perhaps understandable that they drew the conclusion, however mistakenly, that Sasakawa was abusing his access to JSIF funds.

VII

A question remains. Why, despite the broad range of contributions he made to society and the great gratitude expressed to him by those who benefited from his actions do so few people know of his life and achievements? The mass media and intellectuals in this country are extremely critical of him to this day. Why is this so? This hostility is an undeniable fact. I have attempted to elucidate its causes. It is perhaps worth pursuing the issue further.

Sasakawa was an idealist who believed in a world where "human beings are all brothers and sisters," but he was at the same time a realist who saw that there are very few people who can be trusted in life.[98] Or, as his son Yohei put it, human beings are a mixture of good and bad after all, life is a tapestry of anomalies. As an example, Sasakawa felt not the slightest compunction about using the proceeds from public gambling for philanthropic ventures.

Sasakawa observed human foibles with amusement. Take, for example, something that he wrote apropos Yasuoka Masahiro, a scholar of the Wang Yang-ming school of Confucianism, who served as an adviser to successive prime ministers in Japan. Yasuoka fell in love in his latter years with a much younger woman. The media picked up on his scandalous passion, and his followers grieved that their teacher suffered from senility — how could a prudent person, such as he, have suddenly become so irresponsible? Sasakawa took a different position: a man who had led a quiet and exemplary life for decades should be congratulated on finding a person to love! When asked to contribute to a posthumous publication devoted to Yasuoka, Sasakawa wrote:

> Yasuoka made news by getting married at an advanced age, but why make a fuss about it? Unlike me, he was an impeccable person of good conduct — it is silly to denounce him for falling in love. Without this love affair to end it, his life would have lacked something.[99]

Transformed by the war

Sasakawa lived it up in his youth, but the war transformed him. From 1945 on he gave all his time, energy, and money to good causes.

> I do not waste my time playing golf or going to parties, because that would mean stealing my precious time and energy. I mean time and energy that I should be using for my mission to better the world. I do not smoke. I drink a little at dinner for health reasons. I work nonstop. I never ease up, unless heaven sends me

repose and I am sick, and that seldom occurs.

Nowadays, I have an annual medical examination, and that is about the only time I pause for breath. At the same time, I make it a point to offer myself as a guinea pig for medical science. I ask my physician, Dr. Hinohara Shigeaki [chair of the International Society of Internal Medicine], to use my old body in any way for research. So, in the course of my examination, my cardiogram is taken and kept at the health center.[100]

Saving money on an actor

He relished a disciplined way of life. To most people he came in contact with it was far too austere. Yet there was another side to him. Sasakawa was not one to apologize for his existence. He enjoyed himself making his notorious TV commercials, appearing with crowds of African children to portray the Green Revolution in action. His critics might shake their heads, but what did he care?

A recent work of literature may serve to illustrate Sasakawa's life. Hoshi Shinichi wrote a masterly short story with the title of "God of Fortune." It is the story of an ambitious man bent on becoming very rich, who signs a contract with a "god of fortune" who promises to bring him longevity and an unimaginable wealth. He sells his soul. He allows himself to be possessed by the god who takes control of him, forcing him to work day in, day out without rest or recreation, neither drinking nor smoking, nor watching TV, nor listening to the radio. If he enjoys himself this may hinder his drive to riches. In the end, the hero of the tale can bear it no longer. He breaks down and begs the god to allow him to eat well occasionally, if only for his health. The god, however, will not listen to him except for keeping his promise to let him live out his natural span of life in good health. "What have I done?" he laments.[100]

The life of the hero of the tale and that of Sasakawa are remarkably similar. The difference is that while the man in "God of Fortune" was forced to live an austere life, as dictated by the deity, in the case of Sasakawa, this was a life of his choosing. An austere lifestyle was right for him. He himself was a God of Fortune.

Sasakawa extended his thinking to everyone. He regarded it as ideal to live an austere life, and he made it a point to rebuff any criticism. "I have no fear of being exposed," he said.

> I do nothing against my conscience.... We must all become world citizens who live for great causes and have the bigness of heart to support good deeds regardless of who initiates or sponsors them.

He challenged his opponents to be better caretakers of the planet.[102]

Sasakawa asked an audacious question: "Who created Shakyamuni or Christ?" According to him these founders of religion were "created by their jealous opponents." He took pity on those who slandered him, he said, because he knew that those who despised the saints and men of virtue went down in history as nobodies. "Saints and men of virtue are not made by themselves," he said.

> I was once arrested and thrown into prison for three years in Osaka before the war, after jealous men wrote anonymous letters to the authorities denouncing me. I am what I am today because I met misfortune with a firm resolve... Those who have the spirit to survive adversity — and serve their fellow human beings — may become today's saints, by leaving behind them memories that remain long after they die.[103]

On missing martyrdom

Did Sasakawa set himself on a pedestal with the founders of Buddhism and of the Christian religion? There is no doubt he saw himself as a man of virtue, which is attested to by his numerous remarks along the lines above. Perhaps his biggest setback, one may say, was his failure to die a martyr's death in Sugamo. After all, he had volunteered to be arrested with the aim of being indicted as a Class A war criminal, and he had prepared his own tomb in advance. Consciously or not he does seem to have had something of a martyrdom complex.

Sasakawa's life after his release in 1948 may have seemed a bit of a letdown in his own eyes. Week after week, in the 1970s and 1980s, television viewers saw Sasakawa repeat the slogans, "One good deed a day," "Respect your mother and father," "The world is one family, and human beings are all brothers and sisters. Let's all be friends," "Do a big cleanup once a week" and "Lock your door and watch out for fire." They are fine principles but may well have given the impression of somehow lacking punch after years of repetition. He was saved, largely because he remained a private citizen. But had he decided to reenter politics or to occupy a high government post, he could have incurred far crueler criticism than he experienced. Understandably, all too often his words were received with skepticism, as so much high-sounding hypocrisy.

In fact, Sasakawa led an ascetic life and was preoccupied with serving the peoples of the world as best he could. At the same time, he made a great success of his secular life. Especially in the postwar years, he was spiritually aloof from worldly matters such as building a fortune. Such a person is usually not successful in business. In other words, anyone who is a success soils his hands and cannot transcend secularity. People respect ascetics for this reason. It is only human for intellectuals to sus-pect anyone who proclaims, as did Sasakawa, that he had "not told a sin-gle lie" since he was scolded by his parents during his first year at school.

Given that Sasakawa was using proceeds from public gambling on motorboat racing to fund his huge philanthropic initiatives even he could not have been completely free from the burden of living in both the secular and ascetic worlds. Living daily with this dilemma Sasakawa still managed to keep his hands clean. His resolve may have been rein-forced by his decision not to return to politics after the war. As Max Weber put it, one who enters politics signs a contract with the devil. No wonder then that observers had mixed feelings about Sasakawa.

A novelist wonders

Endo Shusaku (1923-96), a well-known Catholic novelist with a world-wide reputation, once suggested that Sasakawa's fine deeds were not known about despite his frequent appearances on television commer-cials, sometimes wearing a naval captain's uniform or waving the na-tional flag. He thought that clowning of that type easily backfired in Japan. Sasakawa agreed with him, and in a recorded dialogue he told Endo that he realized people were perhaps jealous of him. Shrewdly, Endo said he did not think the problem was jealousy but something else. "People think there must be more to you than meets the eye. Some even suspect your whole life is an exercise in self-advertisement. Surely there must be a better way for you to communicate your goodwill."[104]

Sasakawa seemed to invoke a sense of self-induced guilt in people around him. That he was selfless and uncompromisingly virtuous was almost a fault. Wise as he was in many ways, Sasakawa failed to under-stand this. Even the most humble prophet is unwelcome in his home-town and rejected in his time, Jesus had said. In the end Jesus died on the cross, betrayed by one of the twelve disciples. It took some time for his teachings to be widely followed.

In worldly terms Jesus was a failure, his short life a defeat. But his death made his transcendent spirit manifest. Sasakawa died at the ripe age of ninety-six crowned with worldly success (though he may have thought it premature having publicly declared he would live to be two hundred). It will probably take time for Sasakawa to be given fitting rec-ognition in Japan.

Tsurumaki Yasuo who had conducted interviews with fourteen fa-mous personalities including Sasakawa, wrote, "It is probable that few know the real Sasakawa."[105] While this judgment is correct the funda-mental cause of this failure lies not in Sasakawa's negligence nor in the bias of the people (though this exists). For ordinary folk, and intellectuals in particular, seeking to understand Sasakawa leaves them feeling confused and uncomfortable.

Lastly, let us see what grounds there are for the many slanders Sasakawa suffered. To start with, that he was a Class A war criminal. Certainly, he was suspected of war crimes but was freed without ever having been formerly indicted. It is simply inconsistent for liberal intellecturals to accuse him while preaching that no one should be presumed guilty or punished on the grounds of mere suspicion.

Again, there is no substance to the belief that Sasakawa was a mastermind of the right wing. As I have written, he appeared a somewhat flamboyant figure in the prewar right wing movement but his People's Patriotic Party had never been in the mainstream. There is little evidence that he engaged in right-wing activities after the war. A certain political critic once asked Sasakawa to support an anticommunist campaign radio program. Sasakawa declined. "You know," he said, "some of our motorboat racing customers are members of the Communist Party."[106] Sasakawa was not one to support something just because it bore an anticommunist label.

The author of *Dai Uyoku Shi* [the Great History of the Right Wing], the most systematic catalogue of the right-wing movement from the Meiji Restoration to the postwar period, lists in his acknowledgments the names of many right-wing leaders. Fuji Yoshio's name appears but no where is Sasakawa's to be found. Ino Kenji, a biographer of Kodama Yoshio, cites from Nago Urataro's *Nihon no Uyoku* [Japan's Rightwing], published by Sanichi Shobo, a passage stating that no one would object to naming Yasuoka Masahiro, Miura Yoshikazu, and Kodama Yoshio as three main leaders of the postwar right-wing movement.[107] The only exception may have been Sasakawa's brief involvement with the International Anti-communist League (Kokusai Shokyo Rengo) until unconvinced, he parted from Sun Myung Moon.

It is not clear what is meant by Japan's kuromaku (masterminds) and dons, or what they actually do. It is even difficult to know to what extent such activities apply to Sasakawa. By custom kuromaku is someone powerful who stays behind the scenes, and a don a person who exercises dominant influence in a certain field. Both kuromaku and dons are shadowy figures with suspicious characters. No matter how powerful a prime minister or president, he would not be regarded as a don if legitimately elected in a democratic country. Documents, even if they existed, recording clandestine activities of dons are usually not available to the outsiders. So there is no way of knowing if a person is a don. Uemae Junichiro called Sasakawa a chatterbox mastermind. This is an oxymoron of a kind as the hallmark of a mastermind is to be incognito. In most cases kuromaku or dons are created much the same way as conspiracy theories to satisfy suspicious minds by simplifying complex realities.

Where the public activites of Sasakawa are concerned there are plenty of materials that show him to be most unlike a kuromaku. In studying Sasakawa the most difficult question is to know how he came to amass such a great private fortune. It is said that he did it through successful dealings in stocks and commodities trading. That probably is true, but given the untransparent nature of these markets in Japan it is not possible to shed light on the details. It is a fact, however, that not once has Sasakawa's name been cited in all political scandals of his time. It is safe to say that he did not make his fortune in collusion with powerful politicians.

Given Sasakawa's intense sense of mission and self-confidence and extreme loyalty shown by those around him, it is understandable that he gave the impression of being full of himself and given to self-aggrandisment. However, in the course of my research, there is no evidence that Sasakawa sought honor or status. It is a mean-spirited and suspicious person who sneers at Sasakawa for giving away his money in order to earn a Nobel Peace Prize. Having once given up his life by submitting himself to imprisonment in Sugamo he has ceased to crave honor and distinction, as he tirelessly stressed, at least after the war.

How long will it take this unselfish man burdened by his image of wealth and worldly success to be recognized in his own country for what he was?

Notes

1.   Abe Shinnosuke, ed., *Gendai Nihon Jinbutsuron* [Contemporary Japanese personality portraits] (Tokyo: Kawadeshobo, 1952), 260-61.

2.   Paula Daventry, ed., 2d ed., *Sasakawa: The Warrior for Peace, the Global Philanthropist* (New York: Pergamon Press, 1987), 68.

3.   Ibid., 66.

4.   Zenkoku Motaboto Kyosokai Rengokai, ed., *Motaboto 30 Nenshi: Sosoki hen* [History of thirty years of motorboat racing: The beginnings] (Fukuoka: Zenkoku Motaboto Kyosokai, The Federation of Motorboat Racing Associations, Bulletin, 1981), 5.

5.   Ibid., 4.

6.   *Nihon Senpaku Shinkokai 30 nen no Ayumi* [History of thirty years of Japan Shipbuilding Industry Foundation], 1.

7.   Zenkoku Motaboto Kyosokai Rengokai, *Topikkusu hen* [History of thirty years of motorboat racing: Topics], 2.

8.   Zenkoku Motaboto Kyosokai Kyogikai [Japan Motorboat Racing Operators' Council], ed., *Motaboto Kyosoho Kokkai Gijiroku* [Motorboat Racing Law Parliamentary minutes], Zenkoku Motaboto Kyososekokai Kyogikai, 1979, 5.

9.   Ibid., 75.

10.   Ibid., 97, 20.

11.   Ibid., 40.

12.   Ibid., 47.
13.   Ibid., 25.
14.   Ibid., 47.
15.   Daventry, *Sasakawa: Warrior for Peace*, 68.
16.   Motorboat Racing Law Parliamentary Minutes, 1979, 245ff.
17.   Ibid., 328.
18.   Zenkoku Motaboto Kyosokai Rengokai, ed., *Motaboto 30 Nenshi: Topikkusu hen*, 22.
19.   Ibid., 75-76.
20.   Ibid., 53-54.
21.   Zenkoku Motaboto Kyosokai Rengokai, ed., *Motaboto 30 Nenshi: Sosoki hen*, 21, quoting Marui Kan'ichi, assistant, administrative section, Ships Bureau, Ministry of Transport.
22.   Ibid. 21, quoting Tsuboi Kurotake, Maritime Coordinating Director General, Maritime Bureau, Ministry of Transport.
23.   Sasakawa Yohei, *Chie Aru Mono wa Chie de Tsumazuku: Doro wo Kabutte koso* [A little knowledge can ruin a man: Be prepared to take the blame] (Tokyo: Crest, 1996), 84, 88.
24.   Ibid., 89.
25.   Tsurumaki Yasuo, *Zaidan no Keizaigaku: Shirarezaru Nihon Senpaku Shinkokai no 30 Nen wo Kensho Suru* [Economics of the JSI Foundation: Verifying unknown aspects of the Foundation's thirty years] (Tokyo: IN Press, 1993), 109-10.
26.   Ibid., 112-13, 114-15.
27.   *History of thirty years of motorboat racing: The beginnings*, 15ff.
28.   Ibid., 17-19.
29.   *History of thirty years of motorboat racing: Topics*, 5.
30.   Kageyama Yukio interviewed by the author, 13 August 1997.
31.   *History of thirty years of motorboat racing: Topics*, 7.
32.   *History of thirty years of motorboat racing: The beginnings*, 25.
33.   Zenkoku Motaboto Kyosokai Rengokai, ed. *1981-90 Motaboto Kyoso Nenshi: Kyotei Gannen karano Ayumi* [History of motorboat racing, 1981-90] (Fukuoka: Zenkoku Motaboto Kyosokai Rengokai, 1991), 5.
34.   Daventry, *Sasakawa: Warrior for Peace*, 68-69; and Takei Buhei, interviewed by the author, 3 May 1997.
35.   Zenkoku Motaboto Kyosokai Rengokai, ed. *1981-90, Motaboto Kyoso Nenshi*, 5.
36.   Sasakawa Yohei, *Chie Aru Mono wa Chie de Tsumazuku*, 88-89.
37.   Sasakawa Ryoichi, "Watashi no Teigen: Minshushugi no Mokuteki wa 'Kokuri Minpuku'" [My proposal: The object of democracy is to "Promote national interests and the welfare of the people"] *Zenkoku Motaboto Kyosokai Rengokai Kaiho* [Bulletin of the Federation of All-Japan Motorboat Racing Associations], 1 January 1976 Issue.
38.   Sasakawa Ryoichi, ""Watashi no Teigen: 'Jinmei' Atteno 'Jinken Soncho'" [My proposal: "Human life comes before human rights"], *Zenkoku Motaboto Kyosokai Rengokai Kaiho*, 1 April 1978.

39.   Aki Yoshiharu, interviewed by the author, 20 June 1997.
40.   *Motorboat Racing: Topics,* 8.
41.   Ibid., 8.
42.   Ibid., 12.
43.   Ibid., 25.
44.   Ibid., 32.
45.   Ibid.
46   Ibid., 29.
47.   Sasakawa Yohei, *Chie Aru Mono wa Chie de Tsumazuku,* 88.
48.   Aki Yoshiharu, interviewed by the author, 20 June 1997.
49.   *Thirty Years of Motorboat Racing: The Beginnings,* 23.
50.   Ibid., 13.
51.   Parliamentary Minutes on Motorboat Racing Law, 339, 497ff.
52.   Ibid., 617.
53.   Ibid., 717ff.
54.   Nihon Senpaku Shinkokai [Japan Shipbuilding Industry Foundation], ed. *Nihon Senpaku Shinkokai 30 Nen no Ayumi* [Japan Shipbuilding Industry Foundation Thirty-year history] (Tokyo: Nihon Senpaku Shinkokai, 1992), 9.
55.   Parliamentary Minutes on Federation of Motorboat Racing Law, 845ff.
56.   Ibid., 769ff.
57.   *History of Motorboat Racing, 1981-90..* See opening dialog between Hayashi Junji (administrative vice minister of transportation from 1989) and Sasakawa Yohei, and specifically remarks by Hayashi Junji.
58.   Ibid.
59.   Sasakawa Ryoichi, *Jinrui Mina Kyodai* [Human beings are all brothers and sisters] (Tokyo: Kodansha, 1985), 125-26.
60.   Ino Kenji, "Ichinichi Ichizen to Sasakawa Jimmyaku" [Doing one good deed a day, a JSIF slogan, and Sasakawa connection], *Shimpyo,* December 1977, 23-24.
61.   Sasakawa Ryoichi, *Jinrui Mina Kyodai,* 123-24.
62.   Takayama Masayuki, "Takayama Masayuki no Ikenjizai" [Takayama Masayuki has a freehand dissent," *Sankei Shimbun,* 25 April 1998.
63.   Jimmy Carter, in an interview by the author, 13 March 1998.
64.   Sasakawa Ryoichi, *Kono Keisho wa Nariyamazu* [The alarm bell never stops] (Tokyo: Shirakawashoin, 1981), 35.
65.   Sasakawa Ryoichi, *Jinrui Mina Kyodai,* 141-42.
66.   Nishibe Tsutomu Susumu, "Gyoseikaikaku no Genri: Kokyosei, Kokueki, and Gyoseigaku" [Principles of administrative reform: Its public nature, national interest and public administration," *Seiron,* April 1997.
67.   Sasakawa Yohei, *Chie Aru Mono wa Chie de Tsumazuku,* 183-84.
68.   Ibid., 184.
69.   Sasakawa Ryoichi, "Watashi no Teigen: Koeikyogi wa 'Hitsuyoaku': Sansho wa Shiso Toitsu wo" [My proposal: Public sports are "a necessary evil."

Three ministries should standardize their policies], *Zenkoku Motaboto Kyosokai Rengokai Kaiho,* 1 April 1973 Issue.

70.   Shigemitsu Mamoru, "Shigemitsu Mamoru Kankei Bunsho" [Shigemitsu papers]. Unpublished documents kept at Kensei Kinen-kan, nos. 3A-115, dates unknown.

71.   *History of Thirty Years of Motorboat Racing: Topics,* 40.

72.   Sasakawa Yohei, *Chie Aru Mono wa Chie de Tsumazuku,* 89.

73.   *History of Motorboat Racing, 1981-90,* 94.

74.   Sasakawa Yohei, *Gaimusho no Shiranai Sekai no "Sugao"* ["Real world" unknown to the Ministry of Foreign Affairs], Sankei Shimbun News Service, 1998), 58-59.

75.   Jimmy Carter, interviewed by the author, 13 March 1998.

76.   Sasakawa Ryoichi, *Jinrui Mina Kyodai,* 230-31.

77.   *Thirty-Year History of Japan Shipbuilding Industry Foundation* (Tokyo: JSIF, 1992), 188.

78.   Sasakawa Yohei, *Chie Aru Mono wa Chie de Tsumazuku,* 189.

79.   Ibid., 189-90.

80.   Ibid., 192.

81.   Ibid., 193.

82.   Ibid., 193-94.

83.   Yamamoto Eiichi, *Yomigaere Afurika no Daichi: Sasakawa Global 2000 no Kisekii* [Rise Africa: Sasakawa global 2000] (Tokyo: Daiamondosha, 1997), 46.

84.   Nihon Senpaku Shinkokai, *Nihon Senpaku Shinkokai 30 Nen no Ayumi,* 231-32.

85.   Yamamoto, *Yomigaere Afurika no Daichi,* 126-28.

86.   Ibid., 133.

87.   Ibid., 135.

88.   Ibid., 219-20.

89.   Nihon Senpaku Shinkokai, *Nihon Senpaku Shinkokai 30 Nen no Ayumi,* 136-37.

90.   Kamiyama Eiichi, interviewed by the author, 8 August 1997.

91.   Tamayama Kazuo and John Nunneley, *Tales by Japanese Soldiers of the Burma Campaign, 1942-1945* (London: Cassell, 2000), 6.

92.   Ibid., 9.

93.   Tsurumaki, *Kaikaku no Jidai,* 26.

94.   Sasakawa, *Kono Keisho wa Nariyamazu,* 30.

95.   Ibid., 31.

96.   Sasakawa, *Jinrui Mina Kyodai,* 19-20.

97.   Kageyama Yukio, Sanjo Nobuhiro, Hashizume Tokuomi, Okitsu Yoshiaki, and Morimoto Kazuo, interviewed by the author, 13 August 1997.

98.   Sasakawa Yohei, *Chie Aru Mono wa Chie de Tsumazuku,* 78-80.

99.   Ibid., 170.

100.   Sasakawa, *Jinrui Mina Kyodai,* 202-3.

101.   Hoshi Shinichi, *Yosei Haikyu Gaisha* [Fairy distribution enterprise] (Tokyo: Hayakawa Bunko, 1973), 9-15.

102.   Sasakawa, *Kono Keisho wa Nariyamazu,* 74-76.

103.   Ibid., 242.

104.   Tsurumaki, *Kaikaku no Jidai,* 51.

105.   Ibid., 321.

106.   Sasakawa Yohei, *Chie arumono wa chie de tsumazuku,* 147-48.

107. Ino Kenji, *Gendai no Kuromaku: Kodama Yoshio no Kyozou to Jitsuzou* [Contemporary mastermind: Kodama Yoshio's false and true images] (Tokyo: Soukon Shuppan, 1970), 7.

Postscript

I SHALL NOT BE SURPRISED if not a few readers find me excessively lenient toward Sasakawa Ryoichi. After all, three years after his death the media in Japan continues to put him down.

Not long ago, *Shukan Shincho*, a weekly magazine, published a special issue on one hundred Japanese of the twentieth century — including among them Sasakawa Ryoichi, Kodama Yoshio, and Osano Kenji. These three appeared on the same page. The magazine noted that, late in life, Sasakawa had the habit of appearing in TV ads that called for viewers to perform "one good deed a day." However, he had been an outright right-wing nationalist prior to World War Two and then had been incarcerated in jail after the war ended as a Class A war criminal suspect, along with Kodama and Kishi Nobusuke. After the war, the magazine continued, he took on the chairmanship of the newly created Japan Shipbuilding Industry Foundation, and he built up his position in politics behind the scenes, using huge funds he obtained from organizing motorboat racing. Furthermore, he helped the Unification Church's Rev. Sun Myung Moon make inroads into Japan, serving as an advisor to him. In 1978 he was awarded a First Class Order of Sacred Treasure, thereby provoking protest.[1]

Why succumb to bias? I prefer to consider Sasakawa's actual words and deeds, as I found them in the course of research. I warmed to him — his words rang out, as I read them day after day. I never met him, but some who did and who may be regarded as completely independent in their attitudes — Endo Shusaku, the Catholic novelist, and Oshima Nagisa, the film director — quite simply liked him.[2]

I received help from many people in preparing this volume. I would like to thank the Nippon Foundation and its president, Sasakawa Yohei. He gave me free access to papers in the possession of the family and the foundation. I thank also managing director Utagawa Reizo and the foundation's advisor Torii Keiichi, as well as Funagoshi Makoto, the head of the secretariat. They gave me access to the materials I needed and arranged interviews. I received help from Muto Michiko, subchief of general affairs, in making copies of documents and other matters.

Let me express my sincere gratitude to these people and to all those who generously shared what they knew of Sasakawa (please refer to the list of interviews). *Chuo Koron*'s chief managing director, Hirabayashi Takashi, and magazine editor-in-chief, Yukawa Yukiko, and also librarian, Hasegawa Hiroshi, were unfailingly patient, when I let slip my deadlines; they encouraged me and gave me the benefit of their comments. Without their cooperation and that of many others I have not named here I would have been unable to complete my work, given my limited time and physical strength.

My eldest son, Takeshi, a writer, helped me with the book — and with the typing. I make the traditional disclaimer. I alone am responsible for this work.

May 1998
Sato Seizaburo

Notes

1. See *Shukan Shincho*, 30 April 1998.
2. See the work by Tsurumaki Yasuo, *Kaikaku no Jidai* [An era of reform] (Tokyo: IN Press, 1989), 304, for meetings between Sasakawa and thirteen people from various walks of life.

Bibliography

Title Unknown. *Asahi Shimbun,* 14 May 1943.

Abe Shinnosuke, ed. *Gendai Nihon Jinbutsuron* [Contemporary Japanese personality portraits]. Tokyo: Kawadeshobo, 1952.

Arahara Bokusui. *Dai Uyoku Shi* [Great history of the Right Wing]. Tokyo: Dai Nihon Kokumin To [Great Japan National Party], 1966.

Awaya Kentaro. "Tokyo Saiban eno Michi" [The road to the Tokyo Trials]. *Asahi Journal,* 5 April 1985.

Awaya Kentaro and Yutaka Yoshida, eds. *Kokusai Kensatsukyoku (IPS) Jinmon Chosho* [Official records of interrogations by examining prosecutors]. Vols. 24 and 25. Tokyo: Nihon Tosho Center, 1993.

Counter Intelligence Corps, "90th Army Post Office 660." Unpublished document no. 4, declassified by Occupation Authority on 26 November, 1990. 10 December 1945.

Daventry, Paula, ed. *Sasakawa: The Warrior for Peace, the Global Philanthropist.* 2d ed. New York: Pergamon Press, 1987.

Eigasekaisha. *Eiga no Tomo* [Friends of the film]. Tokyo: Eigasekaisha, 1942.

Endo Minoru. *Shiawase no Genryu* [The source of happiness]. Tokyo: Kodansha, 1997.

"Fairu Dai 185" [File no. 185]. Unpublished document, dated 21 July 1947.

Fukuda Tsuneari. "Geijutu to wa Nani ka" [What is art?]. Vol. 2. *Fukuda Tsuneari Zenshu* [Collection of Fukuda Tsuneari's works]. Tokyo: Bungei Shunju 1987.

Gekkan Animeju [Monthly Animation]. Tokuma Shoten Publishers, August 1981.

Healey, Samuel. "Fairu Dai 185" [File no. 185]. Unpublished memorandum, dated 13 April 1946.

Hoshi Shin'ichi. *Yosei Haikyu Gaisha* [Fairy distribution enterprise]. Tokyo: Hayakawa Bunko, 1973.

Hoshi Shin'ichi. "Kusurinado" [Drugs and the like], in *Dekisokonai Hakubutsukan* [A washout of a museum]. Tokyo: Tokuma Bunko Publishers, 1981.

Ino Kenji. "Ichinichi Ichizen to Sasakawa Jimmyaku" [Doing one good deed a day, a JSIF slogan, and Sasakawa connection]. *Shimpyo,* December 1977, 23-24.

Ishihara Hiroichiro, Shiro Akazawa, and Kentaro Awaya, eds. *Ishihara Hiro-ichiro Kankei Bunsho* [Ishihara Hiroichiro and related papers]. Tokyo: Kashiwa Shobo, 1994.

Kaga Takahide. "'Nahimofu' ni Mushibamareru Teikoku" [An empire eaten up by Nahimov]. *Bungei Shunju,* September 1993.

Kishi Nobusuke et al. *Kishi Nobusuke no Kaiso* [Memoirs of Kishi Nobusuke]. Tokyo: Bungeishunju, 1981.

Kiyosawa Kiyoshi. *Ankoku Nikki: 1942-1945* [The dark diary: 1942-1945]. Ed. Yamamoto Yoshihiko. Tokyo: Iwanamishoten, 1990.

Kodama Yoshio. *Fu-un: Kodama Fujio Chosaku Senshu* [Winds and clouds: The collected works of Yoshio Kodama]. 3 vols. Ed. Kazuo Kurihara. Tokyo: Nihon Oyobi Nihonjinsha, 1972.

"Kodama Yoshio Jinmon Chosho" [Records of Yoshio Kodama's interrogation]. Unpublished document, 20 June 1947.

Kokushidaijiten Henshu Iinkai [The Editorial Committee of the Encylopaedia of National History], ed. Vol. 2. *Kokushi Daijiten* [Encyclopedia of national history]. Tokyo: Yoshikawa Kobunkan, 1980.

Kurose Shojiro. *Sasakawa Ryoichi Den Yonotame Hitonotameni* [Sasakawa Ryoichi, a biography: For the world, for mankind]. Tokyo: Chichishuppan-sha, 2001.

Maruyama Masao. *Sengo Nihon no Nashonarizumu no Ippanteki Kosatsu* [Na-tionalism and the Right Wing in Japan: A study of postwar trends]. Vol. 6 of *Maruyama Masao Shu* [The collected works of Maruyama Masao]. Tokyo: Iwanamishoten, 1995.

Nihon Gin Ken Shibu Shinkokai [The Japan Recitation, Dancing, and Fencing Association]. *Sasakawa Ryoichi Kaicho to Zaidan 25 Nen no Eiko no Kiseki* [Chairman Sasakawa Ryoichi and twenty-five years of the glorious history of our association]. Tokyo: Nihon Gin Ken Shibu Shinkokai, 1993.

Nihon Senpaku Shinkokai [Japan Shipbuilding Industry Foundation], ed. *Nihon Senpaku Shinkokai 30 Nen no Ayumi* [Japan Shipbuilding Industry Foun-dation thirty-year history]. Tokyo: Nihon Senpaku Shinkokai, 1992.

Nishibe Susumu. "Gyoseikaikaku no Genri: Kokyosei, Kokueki, Soshite Gyosei-gaku" [Principles of administrative reform: Its public nature, national inter-est and public administration]. *Seiron,* April 1997.

Ochiai Nobuhiko. "Futarino Shuryo, Sasakawa Ryoichi to Kodama Fujio" [Two dons: Sasakawa Ryoichi and Kodama Fujio]. *Shukanbunshun,* 11 April 1977.

Ochiai Nobuhiko. "Sasakawa Ryoichi Kenkyu: Sono Kimmyaku" [Study of Sasa-kawa Ryoichi: His money pipeline]. *Shukanbunshun,* 21 April 1977.

Okitsu Yoshiaki. "Kaicho Goroku" [Chairman's quotation]. Unpublished docu-ment, date unknown.

Okitsu Yoshiaki. "Ko Sasakawa Ryoichi Shi wo Omou" [Remembering the late Sasakawa Ryoichi]. Unpublished document, date unknown.

Onishi Hajime. "Sugamo no Oya" [Parents of Sugamo], *Sakuraboshi* [Cherry blossoms and stars], 1 June 1956, 11.

Ozaki Yukio. "Kobe Joriku no Omoide" [Reminiscence of landing at Kobe]. Vol. 8 in *Ozaki Gakudo Zenshu* [Collected works of Ozaki Gakudo]. Ed. Ozaki Gakudo Zenshu Hensan Iinkai. Tokyo: Koronsha, 1955, 483-84.

Pacific US Army GHQ Intelligence Section. "Fairu Dai 19" [File no. 19]. Unpublished document, dated 8 January 1946.

Sasakawa Ryoichi. *Sasakawa Ryoichi Kankei Bunsho* [Sasakawa papers]. Unpublished documents kept at Nippon Foundation, date unknown.

Sasakawa Ryoichi. Unpublished documents, submitted to International Prosecution Section (IPS), nos. 6, 9, and 10, date unknown.

Sasakawa Ryoichi. "Kokumin no Giwaku wo Isso no Gen'an" [proposed ways to dispel the misgivings of the people]. Unpublished document, submitted to Occupation authorities, no. 10, dated 8 January 1946.

"Sasakawa Ryoichi Jinmon Chosho" [Records of Sasakawa Ryoichi's interrogation]. Unpublished document, dated 18 January 1946.

"Sasakawa Ryoichi Jinmon Chosho" [Records of Sasakawa Ryoichi's interrogation]. Unpublished document, dated 10 April 1946.

Sasakawa Ryoichi. "Watashi no Teigen: Ningen no Meisuu towa" [My proposal: On a natural span of life]. *Zenkoku Motaboto Kyosokai Rengokai Kaiho* [Bulletin of the Federation of All-Japan Motorboat Racing Associations]. 1 February 1969.

Sasakawa Ryoichi. "Watashi no Teigen: Goku wo Tanoshimu" [My proposal: Enjoying prison]. *Zenkoku Motaboto Kyosokai Rengokai Kaiho* [Bulletin of the Federation of All-Japan Motorboat Racing Associations]. 1 March 1969.

Sasakawa Ryoichi. "Watashi no Teigen: Heta na Anma" [My proposal: A bad masseur]. *Zenkoku Motaboto Kyosokai Rengokai Kaiho* [Bulletin of the Federation of All-Japan Motorboat Racing Associations]. 1 July 1969.

Sasakawa Ryoichi. "Watashi no Teigen: Koeikyogi wa 'Hitsuyoaku': Sansho wa Shiso Toitsu wo" [My proposal: Public sports are a necessary evil. Three ministries should standardize their policies]. *Zenkoku Motaboto Kyosokai Rengokai Kaiho* [Bulletin of the Federation of All-Japan Motorboat Racing Associations]. 1 April 1973.

Sasakawa Ryoichi. "Watashi no Teigen: Hiiki no Hikidaoshi wa Yameyo" [My proposal: Stop showing too much partiality, it can be a disservice]. *Zenkoku Motaboto Kyosokai Rengokai Kaiho* [Bulletin of the Federation of All-Japan Motorboat Racing Associations]. 1 April 1974.

Sasakawa Ryoichi. "Watashi no Teigen: Mitsuketai Tenka no Meii wo" [My proposal: Looking for the best doctor in the land]. *Zenkoku Motaboto Kyosokai Rengokai Kaiho* [Bulletin of the Federation of All-Japan Motorboat Racing Associations]. 1 July 1974.

Sasakawa Ryoichi. "Watashi no Teigen: Satori wo Hirake" [My proposal: Be enlightened]. *Zenkoku Motaboto Kyosokai Rengokai Kaiho* [Bulletin of the Federation of All-Japan Motorboat Racing Associations]. 1 October 1974.

Sasakawa Ryoichi. "Watashi no Teigen: Kuwazu Girai wa Shippai no Moto" [My proposal: Disliking something without even tasting it is a stepping stone to failure]. *Zenkoku Motaboto Kyosokai Rengokai Kaiho* [Bulletin of the Federation of All-Japan Motorboat Racing Associations]. 1 April 1975.

Sasakawa Ryoichi. "Watashi no Teigen: Chuken Muku no Shi wo Itamu" [My proposal: I mourn the death of Muku, my faithful dog]. *Zenkoku Motaboto*

Kyosokai Rengokai Kaiho [Bulletin of the Federation of All-Japan Motorboat Racing Associations]. 1 July 1975.

Sasakawa Ryoichi. "Watashi no Teigen: Minshushugi no Mokuteki wa 'Kokuri Minpuku'" [My proposal: The object of democracy is to promote national interests and the welfare of the people]. *Zenkoku Motaboto Kyosokai Rengokai Kaiho* [Bulletin of the Federation of All-Japan Motorboat Racing Associations]. 1 January 1976.

Sasakawa Ryoichi. "Watashi no Teigen: Chi, Jo, I wo Fumaeta Kyoiku wo" [My proposal: Education should stimulate intellect, emotion and mind]. *Zenkoku Motaboto Kyosokai Rengokai Kaiho* [Bulletin of the Federation of All-Japan Motorboat Racing Associations]. 1 August 1976.

Sasakawa Ryoichi. "Watashi no Teigen: Nikutai Nenrei 77 sai, Seishin Nenrei Jiyu Jizai" [My proposal: Biological age 77; Spiritual age, free]. *Zenkoku Motaboto Kyosokai Rengokai Kaiho* [Bulletin of the Federation of All-Japan Motorboat Racing Associations]. 1 September 1976.

Sasakawa Ryoichi. "Watashi no Teigen: Heiwa de Subarashii Toshi ni" [My proposal: For this year to be peaceful and wonderful]. *Zenkoku Motaboto Kyosokai Rengokai Kaiho* [Bulletin of the Federation of All-Japan Motorboat Racing Associations]. 1 January 1977.

Sasakawa Ryoichi. "Watashi no Teigen: Shimbun wa Koki wo Shibutsuka" [My proposal: Newspaper abuses its role as a public organ for private ends]. *Zenkoku Motaboto Kyosokai Rengokai Kaiho* [Bulletin of the Federation of All-Japan Motorboat Racing Associations]. 1 February 1977.

Sasakawa Ryoichi. "Watashi no Teigen: Happuu ni Dojinu Toku wa Tsumu" [My proposal: build up your virtues so that you will not be swayed by winds from all directions]. *Zenkoku Motaboto Kyosokai Rengokai Kaiho* [Bulletin of the Federation of All-Japan Motorboat Racing Associations]. 1 September 1977.

Sasakawa Ryoichi. "Watashi no Teigen: Tayorubeki wa Onore Hitori" [My proposal: None but myself to trust]. *Zenkoku Motaboto Kyosokai Rengokai Kaiho* [Bulletin of the Federation of All-Japan Motorboat Racing Associations]. 1 February 1978.

Sasakawa Ryoichi. "Watashi no Teigen: 'Jinmei' Atteno 'Jinken Soncho'" [My proposal: Human life comes before human rights]. *Zenkoku Motaboto Kyosokai Rengokai Kaiho* [Bulletin of the Federation of All-Japan Motorboat Racing Associations]. Unpublished document, 1 April 1978.

Sasakawa Ryoichi. "Watashi no Teigen: Nanigotomo Hayameni Te wo Ute" [My proposal: Be sure to always act ahead of time]. *Zenkoku Motaboto Kyosokai Rengokai Kaiho* [Bulletin of the Federation of All-Japan Motorboat Racing Associations]. 1 July 1978.

Sasakawa Ryoichi. "Watashi no Teigen: Toku wo Suru Higaisha tare" [My proposal: Learn to profit from your losses]. *Zenkoku Motaboto Kyosokai Rengokai Kaiho* [Bulletin of the Federation of All-Japan Motorboat Racing Associations]. 1 August 1978.

Sasakawa Ryoichi. "Watashi no Teigen, Meiwaku Shigoku na Yumeizei" [My proposal: The nuisance of being famous]. *Zenkoku Motaboto Kyosokai Rengokai Kaiho* [Bulletin of the Federation of All-Japan Motorboat Racing Associations]. 1 April 1980.

Sasakawa Ryoichi. "Watashi no Teigen; Zeikin wo Torarenai 'Toku' wo Tsume" [My proposal: Build your virtues and untaxable assets]. *Zenkoku Motaboto Kyosokai Rengokai Kaiho* [Bulletin of the Federation of All-Japan Motorboat Racing Associations]. 1 December 1983.

Sasakawa Ryoichi. "Watashi no Teigen; Kassatsu Jizai no Shita wo Katsuyo seyo" [My proposal: Use your tongue well. It has the power to kill or to console]. *Zenkoku Motaboto Kyosokai Rengokai Kaiho* [Bulletin of the Federation of All-Japan Motorboat Racing Associations]. 1 July 1980.

Sasakawa Ryoichi. *Kono Keisho wa Nariyamazu* [The Alarm Bell Never stops]. Tokyo: Shirakawashoin, 1981.

Sasakawa Ryoichi. "Watashi no Teigen; Mukon no Nikutai wa Sanmon no Kachi mo Nai" [My proposal: A body which lacks a soul is worth less than three cents]. *Zenkoku Motaboto Kyosokai Rengokai Kaiho* [Bulletin of the Federation of All-Japan Motorboat Racing Associations]. 1 February 1988.

Sasakawa Ryoichi. "Watashi no Teigen: Kin'yu Oshoku Boshi ni Tsuite" [My proposal: Regarding prevention of financial corruption]. *Zenkoku Motaboto Kyosokai Rengokai Kaiho* [Bulletin of the Federation of All-Japan Motorboat Racing Associations]. 1 January 1990.

Sasakawa Ryoichi. "Watashi no Teigen: Tokuni Koshitsu wo Taisetsu ni Suru Riyu" [My proposal: My particular reasons for cherishing the imperial family]. *Zenkoku Motaboto Kyosokai Rengokai Kaiho* [Bulletin of the Federation of All-Japan Motorboat Racing Associations]. 1 February 1991.

Sasakawa Ryoichi. *Sasakawa Ryoichi no Mita Sugamo no Hyojo* [Expressions of Sugamo, as seen by Sasakawa Ryoichi: Secret records of a "war criminal suspect"]. Osaka: Bunkajinshobo, 1947.

Sasakawa Ryoichi. *Jinrui Mina Kyodai* [Human beings are all brothers and sisters]. Tokyo: Kodansha, 1985.

Sasakawa Ryoichi. *Sugamo Nikki* [Sugamo diary]. Tokyo: Chuokoronsha, 1997.

Sasakawa Takashi. *Nihon no Don wo Norikoero* [Go beyond "the Don of Japan"]. Tokyo: Kiriharashoten, 1986.

Sasakawa Yohei. Interview records, kept at the Nippon Foundation. Unpublished document, date unknown.

Sasakawa Yohei. *Chie Aru Mono wa Chie de Tsumazuku: Doro wo Kabutte koso* [A little knowledge can ruin a man: be prepared to take the blame]. Tokyo: Crest, 1996.

Sasakawa Yohei. *Gaimusho no Shiranai Sekai no "Sugao"* [Real world unknown to the ministry of foreign affairs]. Tokyo: Sankei Shimbun News Service, 1998.

Sato Seizaburo. *Sasakawa Ryoichi Kenkyu* [Study of Sasakawa Ryoichi]. Tokyo: Chuokoronsha, 1998.

"Shigemitsu Mamoru Kankei Bunsho" [Shigemitsu papers]. Unpublished documents kept at Kensei Kinen-kan, no. 3A-115, date unknown.

Shihosho Keijikyoku [Justice Ministry Criminal Bureau]. *Showa 15 Nen ni Okeru "Kokkashugi" Undojosei no Gaiyo* [1940 outline of nationalist movements]. Tokyo: Government Publication, December 1940.

Shioda Michio. *Tenno to Tojo Hideki no Kuno* [Anguish of the emperor and Tojo Hideki]. Tokyo: Nihon Bungeisha, 1988.

Shugiin [House of Representatives], *Shugiin Yosan Iinkai Giroku* [The Budget Committee]. Tokyo: Government Publication, February 6th, 1943.

Shugiin [House of Representatives]. *Shugiin Yosan Iinkai Dai-ichi Bunka Kai Giroku* [First Subcommittee of the Budget Committee]. Tokyo: Government Publication, 9 February 1943.

Shugiin [House of Representatives]. *Shugiin Yosan Iinkai Dai-ni Bunka Kai Giroku* [Second Subcommittee of the Budget Committee]. Tokyo: Government Publication, 10 February 1943.

Shugiin [House of Representatives]. *Shugiin Yosan Iinkai Dai-yon Bunka Kai Giroku* [Fourth Subcommittee of the Budget Committee]. Tokyo: Government Publication, 10 February 1943.

Tachibana Takashi. "Bunshun Toshokan" [Bunshun Library]. *Shukan Bunshun,* April 10 1997.

Takahashi Shin'ichi ed. *Waga Kaigun to Takahashi Sankichi* [The Navy and Takahashi Sankichi]. Publication site unknown: Shin'ichi Takahashi, 1970.

Takayama Masayuki. "Takayama Masayuki no Ikenjizai" [Freehand dissent]. *Sankei Shimbun,* 25 April 1998.

Tamayama Kazuo and John Nunneley. *Tales by Japanese Soldiers of the Burma Campaign 1942-1945.* London: Cassell, 2000.

"Tenseijingo" [Vox Populi front page column]. *Asahi Shimbun,* 12 March 1976, 1.

The International Prosecution Section (IPS). Supreme Command of the Allied Forces. Unpublished document, dated 4 August 1947.

Tokyo Broadcasting Service. *The Death of the Last Don.* TV program, broadcast on 6 August 1995.

Tokyo Saiban Handobukku Henshu Iinkai [Tokyo Trial Handbook Editorial Committee], ed. *Tokyo Saiban Handobukku* [Tokyo Trial handbook]. Tokyo: Aokishoten, 1989.

Tsurumaki Yasuo. *Daremo Kakenakatta Nihon Senapku Shinkokai no Jitsuzo* [The truth about the Japan Shipbuilding Industry Foundation that no one cared to write]. Tokyo: IN Press, 1987.

Tsurumaki Yasuo. *Kaikaku no Jidai* [An era of reform]. Tokyo: IN Press, 1989.

Tsurumaki Yasuo. *Zaidan no Keizaigaku: Shirarezaru Nihon Senpaku Shinkokai no 30 Nen wo Kensho Suru* [Economics of the JSI Foundation: Verifying unknown aspects of the Foundation's thirty years]. Tokyo: IN Press, 1993.

Uemae Jun'ichiro. "Oshaberi na Kuromaku Sasakawa Ryoichi Ron" [Sasakawa Ryoichi: A chatterbox wirepuller]. *Shukan Bunshun,* 29 January 1976.

Yamamoto Eiichi. *Yomigaere Afurika no Daichi: Sasakawa Global 2000 no Kiseki* [Rise Africa: Sasakawa Global 2000]. Tokyo: Daiamondosha, 1997.

Yamaoka Sohachi. *Hatenko Ningen Sasakawa Ryoichi* [Sasakawa Ryoichi: Record Breaking Man]. Tokyo: Yuhosha, 1978.

Yamaura Kan'ichi. "Senpan Shakuho" [Releasing war criminals]. *Tokyo Shimbun,* 21 June 1952.

Yui Masaomi, ed. *Kokkashugi Undo* [Nationalistic movements], Vol. 6 of *Shiryo Nihon Gendai Shi* [Documentary material, contemporary history of Japan]. Tokyo: Otsukishoten, 1981.

224   Sasakawa Ryoichi

Zenkoku Motaboto Kyosokai Rengokai, ed. *Motaboto 30 Nenshi: Sosoki hen* [History of thirty years of motorboat racing: The beginnings]. Publication site unknown: Zenkoku Motaboto Kyosokai, 1981.

Zenkoku Motaboto Kyosokai Rengokai, ed. *Motaboto 30 Nenshi: Topikkusu hen* [History of thirty years of motorboat racing: Topics]. Publication site unknown: Zenkoku Motaboto Kyosokai, 1981.

Zenkoku Motaboto Kyosokai Rengokai, ed. *1981-90 Motaboto Kyoso Nenshi: Kyotei Gannen karano Ayumi* [History of motorboat racing, 1981-90]. Publication site unknown: Zenkoku Motaboto Kyosokai, 1991.

Zenkoku Motaboto Kyososekosha Kyogikai [Japan Motorboat Racing Operators' Council], ed. *Motaboto Kyosoho Kokkai Gijiroku* [Motorboat racing law Parliamentary minutes]. Zenkoku Motaboto Kyososekosha Kyogikai, 1979.

List of Interviews

Date	Interviewee	Location
3 May 1997	Nagata Shina, a relative of Sasakawa Ryoichi on his mother's side	at home in Mikuni
	Sasakawa Shizuko, wife of brother Shunji	at home in Kosaka
	Hiroko, second daughter	same place
	Michiko, third daughter	same place
	Nakai Takebei, former mayor of Minoo	at home in Minoo
	Morimoto Kazuo, general affairs manager, Osaka Motorboat Racing Association	in the car in Osaka City
4 May 1997	Sasakawa Kazue, family member	at home in Ibaragi
	Sasakawa Yoshiko, Ryoichi's younger sister	at home in Onohara
	Okitsu Yoshiaki, Sasakawa Yoshiko's son-in-law	same as above
	Kisee, Sasakawa Yoshiko's daughter	same as above
	Uojima Kosaku, Ryoichi's childhood friend	at home in Onohara
	Sasakawa Teruyo, oldest daughter of Ryohei, Ryoichi's younger brother	at home in Minoo
	Morimoto Kazuo, general affairs manager, Osaka Motorboat Racing Association	in the car in Osaka City

16 June 1997	Hinohara Shigeaki, president, St. Luke's International Hospital	in his office at the hospital
20 June 1997	Aki Yoshiharu, chairman, Japan Motorboat Racers Federation	at the Federation office
8 August 1997	Kamiyama Shoichi, president, Japan Maritime Science Promotion Foundation	reception room, Maritime Museum
13 August 1997	Kageyama Yukio, chairman, Osaka Motorboat Racing Association	Chinzan-so, Toranomon
	Sanjo Nobuhiro, former executive manager, Federation of All Japan Motorboat Associations, president, Motorboat Racing Modernization Center	Chinzan-so, Toranomon
	Hashizume Tokuomi, managing director, Motorboat Racing Modernization Center	Chinzan-so, Toranomon
	Okitsu Yoshiaki, Sasakawa Yoshiko's son-in-law	Chinzan-so, Toranomon
	Morimoto Kazuo, general affairs manager, Osaka Motorboat Racing Association	Chinzan-so, Toranomon
14 August 1997	Sasakawa Katsumasa, Ryoichi's oldest son	executive meeting room, the Nippon Foundation
	Sasakawa Shizue, wife	at home in Sengoku
21 August 1997	Sasakawa Yohei, Ryoichi's third son	president's room, the Nippon Foundation
19 September 1997	Sasakawa Takashi, Ryoichi's second son	Takashi's office in Ginza
14 November 1997	Sasakawa Shizue, wife	at home in Sengoku
12 December 1997	Azumazeki Daigoro, former Sumo champion Takamiyama	reception room at his stable
??	Mrs. Kazue	??
22 January 1998	Yoshida Hironobu, chief Buddhist priest, Ninwaji, the head temple of Buddhist sect	reception room, the Nippon Foundation
	Kuranobu Ryugen, executive officer, Ninwaji temple	same place as above

	Horikawa Wakai, officer, Ninna-ji temple	same place
21 February 1998	Nakayama Tatsuo, former director, general affairs, Federation of All Japan Motorboat Racing Associations	executive meeting room, the Nippon Foundation
??	Former executive director, former Japan Motorboat Association	??
5 February 1998	Shibuichi Mitsuo, former staff, Federation of All Japan Motorboat Associations	same place
	Sohma Yukika, daughter, Ozaki Yukio, vice chairman, Ozaki Yukio Memorial Foundation	conference room, Ozaki Yukio Memorial Foundation
9 February 1998	Endo Minoru, composer	Endo Minoru office, Shinjuku
	Ide Hiromasa, former staff, Federation of All Japan Motorboat Associations, composer, same as above	
13 March 1998	Jimmy Carter, former US president	guest room, the Nippon Foundation
22 April 1998	Robin Chandra Duke, chairperson, Population Action International, director, US-Japan Foundation	Hotel Okura
	Sengoku Setsuko, former staff, the Nippon Foundation; director, Tokyo Office, Great Britain Sasakawa Foundation	Hotel Okura

Life of Sasakawa Ryoichi
in Chronological Order

Year	Age	Events	National and World Events
1899	0	Born, Toyokawa Village, Mishima County, Osaka Prefecture, 4 May	Boxer Rebellion in China
1901	2	Brother Shunji born, 20 February	
1904	5		Russo-Japanese War starts, 10 February
1906	7	Enrolled at Toyokawa Ordinary Primary School, April	
1910	11		Annexation of Korea by Japan, 22 August
1911	12	Sister Yoshiko born, 30 March	
	13	Graduates Ordinary Primary School Enrolls in Advanced Primary School	
1914	15	Graduates Advanced Primary School Enrolls in Auxiliary Agricultural School	World War One starts, 28 July

1915	16	Brother Ryohei born, 2 January Graduates from Auxiliary Agri- cultural School. Trains under Abbot Harada at Shonenji temple near home	
1916	17	Studies flying and maintenance of aircraft under pilot Nishide Kiyoshi for two years	
1917	18		October Revolution in Russia, 7 November
1918	19	Passes conscription examination	World War One ends, 11 November
1919	20	Serves as a private army combat engineer, attached to Second Air Battalion based at Kagamihara	Independence movement in Korea Antigovernment struggle in China
1921	22	Discharged on account of right shoulder broken by propeller	Prime Minister Hara Takashi assassinated, 4 November
1922	23	Father, Tsurukichi, dies, 18 January	Washington Naval Treaty signed, 6 February Anglo-Japanese Alliance abrogated
1923	24		Great Kanto Earthquake, 1 September
1925	26	Elected Toyokawa Village As- semblyman, serves one four-year term	*Security Maintenance Law*, 19 March
		Starts commodity trading at Dojima, Osaka, makes a fortune	*Male Suffrage Law* passed, 29 March
1926	27	President of National Defense Co. on request Pays for the publication of its monthly organ, *Kokubo*	

1927	28	Establishes Ichikawa Udaemon Productions, becomes its president	Financial crash in Japan, 15 March
1929	30		Wall Street crash, 24 October
1930	31		London Naval Treaty signed, 22 April Prime Minister Hamaguchi injured in assassination plot, 14 November
1931	32	Establishes National People's Party; president, 10 March Warns Mitsui Zaibatsu against purchasing US dollars, 5 November Advises Prime Minister Inukai on Manchurian policies, 17 December	Manchurian Incident erupts, 18 September

1932	33	Visits Manchuria to comfort soldiers, 21 March-9 April, from Osaka Visits Shanghai to comfort officers badly injured by terrorist attack, as well as Minister Shigemitu, 13 May Establishes National Volunteer Flying Unit; commander, 20 May Sasakawa brings a charge against Takahashi in Tokyo District Court for breach of trust over Meiji Sugar Co. tax evasion, 22 August First son, Katsumasa born, 23 August Establishes National People's Transportation Union; president, 6 November Establishes National People's Aviation Union; president, November Establishes National People's Party (NPP) Kanto Headquarters, November	Assassinations of former finance minister, Inoue, 9 February, and Mitsui and Co. president, Dan Takuma, 5 March Manchurian State established, 1 March Prime Minister Inukai assassinated May 15 Incident Lytton Commission issues its report, October
1933	34	National Rally against arms reduction; chairman, 11 November Offers the Army an airfield to be completed in Nakakochi County, Osaka, the following year, November	Hitler assumes government, 30 January Japan withdraws from the League of Nations, 27 March
1934	35	Opening of Osaka Air-Defense Field, 19 June Presents the airfield to the Army, 7 September Operates mining businesses around the country	

1935	36	NPP Kanto HQs Voluntary Unit commander Fuji attacks home of Ichiki, chair of the Privy Council for his support of the theory of the emperor being an organ of the state, March Sasakawa and 9 NPP leasers arrested for extortion, 7-8 August Second son, Takashi, born, 5 October	Movement denouncing "organ theory" rises, 18 February Italy attacks Ethiopia, 3 October
1938		Acquitted by the court of first instance, December	*National Mobilization Law* proclaimed, 1 April
1939	40	Third son, Yohei, born, 8 January Found guilty by an appellate court, 11 December Flies to Italy in *Yamato,* meets Mussolini, January	Nomonhan Incident between USSR and Japan, 12 May Second World War starts, 1 September
1941	42	Supreme Court returns the case, appellate court acquits, 9 August	"The Pacific War" begins, 8 December
1942	43	Elected to the House of Representatives as a non-government-sponsored candidate in Imperial Rule Assistance Election, April	Battle of Midway, 5 June
1945	46	Enters Sugamo Prison as a Class A war criminal suspect, 11 December	Great air raid over Tokyo, 9 March US troops land on mainland Okinawa, 1 April Germany surrenders, 7 May Potsdam Declaration against Japan, 26 July Atom bomb dropped over Hiroshima, 6 August USSR declares war against Japan, 8 August Japanese government accepts Potsdam Declaration, 14 August World War Two ends, 15 August

1946	47	A bill of indictment against twenty-eight suspected Class A war criminals, 28 April Promulgation of the Constitution of Japan, 3 November	
1948	49	Released from Sugamo Prison, 24 December Engages in organizing motorboat racing	Soviet Union blockades Berlin, 1 April
1949	50		NATO established, 4 April People's Republic of China (PRC) established, 1 October
1950	51		Korean War begins, 25 June Police Reserve Forces established, 10 August
1951	52	*Motorboat Racing Law,* June	General Douglas MacArthur fired, 1 April Peace Treaty, Japan-US Security Treaty, 8 September, promulgated 1952, 28 April
1952	53	Successfully petitions General Chiang Kaishek to pardon war criminals related to Republic of China (ROC) Inaugurates mortorboat race in Omura, 6-8 April	
1953	54	Osaka Motorboat Racing Association established, February Federation of All Japan Motorboat Racing Associations established, April	Stalin dies, 5 March Korean War ceasefire agreement, 27 July
1954	55		Defense Agency, *Self-Defense Forces Law,* 9 June Time-limited *Law on Bicycle Race,* 9 June
1955	56	Tokyo Motorboat Racing Association established, April	Integration of Right and Left Wing Socialists, 13 October Liberal Democratic Party founded, 15 November

1956	57		Japan joins the United Nations, 18 December
1957	58		USSR successfully launches a satellite, 4 October
1958	59	Mother, Sasakawa Teru, dies, 17 January	
1959	60		Cuban revolution, 1 January
1960	61		Japan-US Security Treaty effective, 23 June
1961	62		Korean military coup d'état, 16 May
1962	63	Japan Shipbuilding Industry Foundation established, October	Cuban crisis, 22 October-20 November
1963	64	Made an honorary citizen of Minoo City, Osaka, January	John F. Kennedy assassinated, 22 November
1964	65	International War Memorial erected in Ibaragi City, Osaka, with his own money, April Association of War Memorial for All Victims established, August	Japan becomes a member of the International Monetary Fund (IMF), Art. 8, 1 April Japan joins the Organisation for Economic Co-operation and Development (OECD), 28 April Tokyo Olympic Games, 10-24 October
1965	66		United States bombs North Vietnam, 7 February Japan-Korea Basic Treaty, 22 June Government bond issued, 19 November
1966	67	Uses own money to support building Philippines Culture Center and Philippines Veterans Center	Cultural Revolution in China begins, 16 May

1967	68	Establishes Japan Maritime Science Foundation, April Establishes Aviation Industry Association, June	European Community (EC) established, 1 July ASEAN established, 8 August
1968	69	Establishes Aviation Pollution Prevention Association, August (name changes to Airport Environment Association in April 1993) Japan Poetry, Swordplay, Dancing Association established, October	University campus riots begin from Tokyo University, 29 January Ogasawara Islands returned to Japan, 26 June
1969	70	Establishes All Japan Karate Federation, January Chairman, Japan Veterans Association	US Spaceship *Apollo* lands on the moon, 20 July
1970	71	Establishes World Karate Federation	JAL *Yodo* hijacked, 31 March
1971	72	Uses own money to head a delegation to collect remains of the war dead in New Guinea, January Japan Award Association established, May Establishes Aviation Safety Association, October	Gold Standard discontinued, 15 August PRC replaces ROC in the United Nations, 25 October
1972	73	Chinese Academy of Science bestows honorary doctorate of philosophy	President Nixon visits China, 21-27 March, Okinawa reversion, 15 May, Japan-China relations resumed, 29 September
1973	74	Establishes Blue Sea and Green Land Foundation, March Sasakawa Shunji dies, 30 June	Vietnam Peace Accord, 27 January Fourth Middle East War, 6 October First oil crisis, 17 October

1974	75	Kingdom of Tonga, honorary counsel general, January Manila honorary citizen, March Establishes Life Planning Center, March Establishes Japan National Music Foundation (renamed to Japan Musical Foundation, 1994), March Central African Republic, honorary counsel general, May Establishes Sasakawa Memorial Health Foundation, May Establishes Federation of All Japan Kendo Dojo, October	Nixon resigns over Watergate, 8 August Tanaka Kakuei resigns over money scandals, 26 November
1975	76	Establishes Japan Hotel Education Center, March Draper World Population Fund, honorary founder, May Managua City, Nicaragua, special citizen, July Establishes Japan Shipbuilding Promotion Foundation (renamed Ship and Ocean Foundation in December)	Vietnam War ends, 30 April
1976	77		Lockheed scandal exposed, 6 February Tanaka Kakuei arrested, 27 July Mao Zedong dies, 9 September
1977	78		Two maritime laws promulgated: 12-mile territorial waters and 200-mile fishing zone, 2 May

1978	79	Receives the First Class Order of the Sacred Treasure, May 9 Chairman of Japan Firefighters Association, May	New Tokyo International Airport (Narita) opens, 20 May Japan-China Peace and Friendship Treaty signed, 1 2 August OPEC decides to boost crude oil prices, second oil crisis, 16 December Vietnamese Army invades Cambodia, 25 December
1979	80	Appointed admiral of the State of Georgia, January Establishes UNESCO Peace Education Party, November	US-China relations normalized, 1 January Chinese Army invades Vietnam, 17 February Israel and Egypt sign peace accord, 26 March Pak Chunghee assassinated, 26 October
1980	81	Made honorary citizen of the City of Los Angeles, May	Iran-Iraq War starts, 9 September Second Ad Hoc Administrative Reform Council established, 5 December
1982	83	Sasakawa Ryohei dies, 15 April Receives UN Peace Award, 30 April Establishes UN Sasakawa Environment Award, May Receives honorary doctor of philosophy from ROK Yenko University, June Establishes World Volunteer Firefighters Federation, December	Tokyo Gold Exchange established, 23 March 500 yen coin issued, 1 April
1983	84	Made honorary citizen of the State of Oklahoma, February Receives Linus Pauling Humanitarian Award, February Receives honorary doctor of law degree from Long Island University, Southampton College, May	Yasuoka Seitoku dies, 13 December

1983 (cont'd)	84	Receives Helen Keller International Award, May Made honorary citizen of the State of Washington, September ade first class honorary citizen of the City of Seattle, September Made general of the State of Washington honor guard, September State of Washington names 24 September, "Sasakawa Ryoichi Day" City of Seattle names 30 September, "Sasakawa Ryoichi Day"	
1984	85	Establishes UN Sasakawa Health Award, May Establishes US-Japan Foundation, May	Kodama Yoshio dies, 17 January Establishes Ad Hoc Education Council, 21 August
1985	86	Establishes Federation of Japan Gate Ball, January Sasakawa Memorial Health Establishes Scandinavia Japan Sasakawa Foundation, March Establishes Great Britain Sasakawa Foundation, May Made honorary citizen of Nice, France, July Establishes World Federation of Gate Ball, September	Gorbachev becomes general secretary of USSR Communist Party, 11 March Privatization of Telephone and Telegraph Co., Japan Tobacco, 1 April
1986	87	Made honorary citizen of Sydney, Australia, May Receives Martin Luther King Jr. Nonviolent Humanitarian Award, May Establishes UNDRO Sasakawa UN Disaster Prevention Award, June	Marcos regime collapses and Corazon Aquino is made president of the Philippines, 22-25 February Chernobyl nuclear power plant accident, 26 April Diet passes eight laws to split up the National Railways, 28 October

1987	88	Made honorary ambassador by mayor of Cairns, Australia, March Made honorary citizen of the state of Queensland, Australia, March Made honorary mayor of Honolulu, March Establishes Motorboat Safety Association, April Receives First Class Order of the Rising Sun, 8 May Made honorary citizen of Haifa, Israel, November	President Roh Taewoo declares democratization of the Republic of Korea, 29 June
1988	89	Made honorary professor, Houston University Space Architecture, September Houston sets 6 September as "Sasakawa Ryoichi Day" Made honorary mayor of New Orleans, Louisiana, September New Orleans sets 7 September as "Sasakawa Ryoichi Day"	Recruit scandal exposed, 5 July Diet passes law to introduce consumption tax, 24 December
1989	90	Appointed WHO Goodwill Ambassador, May Bestowed honorary doctorate from Sussex University, U.K., 3 June	Demise of Emperor Showa, 7 January Tiananmen Incident Anticommunist Solidarity wins overwhelming victory in Poland's first free election, 4 June Collapse of the Berlin Wall, 9 November Collapse of the communist regime follows in East Europe
1990	91	Establishes Japan-France Sasakawa Foundation, March Establishes Motorboat Racing Modernization Center, July Made honorary counsel of the {something missing}	Iraqi Army begins offensive in Kuwait, 2 August Unification of East and West Germany, 3 October

1991	92	Made honorary citizen of São Paulo, Brazil, May Establishes Sasakawa Sports Foundation, June	US and multinational military force attacks Iraqi Army in Kuwait, 17 January Civil war in Yugoslavia, 6 May Soviet Conservatives coup d'état fails against Gorbachev, 19-21 August Soviet Communist Party dissolved, 24 August Three Baltic states declare independence, 26 August Collapse of the Soviet Union, 21 December Gorbachev resigns, 25 December
1992	93	Establishes International Sumo Federation, September	Diet passes PKO Cooperation Law, 15 June Self Defense Forces dispatched to Cambodia, 17 September
1993	94	Shiragiku Survivors' Association dissolved and memorial services discontinued	Liberal Democratic Party splits on the eve of general election, 21-23 June Non-LDP coalition government established with Japan New Party representative Hosokawa Morihiro as prime minister, 9 August
1994	95		Diet passes *Electoral System Revision Law,* 28 January LDP, Japan Socialist Party, and Sakigake form a coalition government under Murayama Tomiichi, JSP chairman, 30 June

| 1995 | 96 | Sasakawa Ryoichi succumbs, 18 July
Private wake, 19 July
Wake, 20 July
Private funeral, 21 July
Third rank bestowed, 15 August
Public funeral and farewell, 14 September | Great Hanshin Earthquake, 17 January
Sarin gas attack in the Metro, eleven dead, 20 March
Aum religious sect investigated, 22 March |

1996   First anniversary Buddhist memorial service held, 3 July

1997   Chuo Koron Sha publishes *Sugamo Diary*, 10 February

1998   Third anniversary Buddhist memorial service held, 18 July

SATO SEIZABURO was born in Tokyo in 1932. After receiving degrees in Literature and Law from Tokyo University, he taught in the Faculty of Law at Rikkyo University and then at his alma mater. He also taught at Keio and Saitama universities and was a vice rector of the National Graduate Institute for Policy Studies. Professor Sato was chief researcher at the World Peace Research Institute and served as adviser to prime ministers Ohira Masayoshi and Nakasone Yasuhiro. His published works included "Shi no choyaku wo koete: Seiyo no Shogeki to Nihon" (About the impact of the West on Japan) and "Sasakawa Ryoichi kenkyu: ijigen kara no shisha" (A study of Sasakawa Ryoichi). Professor Sato died in 1999.

HARA FUJIKO holds a master's degree in the history of international relations from Sophia University in Tokyo. She was raised in both Japanese and British cultures and has given her life to international understanding. She has interpreted for many of the world's leaders and heads a interpreting and translation company, Diplomatt Inc. Among her published works is a translation of the memoirs of her statesman grandfather, Ozaki Yukio.